KU-262-972

Nelson's Women

By the Same Author

Nelson and His World
Chelsea Reach
Fighting General
Remember Nelson
The Young Nelson in the Americas
1945: The Dawn Came Up Like Thunder
East and West of Suez
Horatio Nelson
Alan Moorehead
Sailor King
Rider Haggard and the Lost Empire
Norfolk
A Thirst for Glory
Travels of a London Schoolboy, 1826–1830 (ed.)
Battle for Empire

TRAVEL

London Walks
Essential Venice

Nelson's Women

Tom Pocock

André Deutsch

First published in 1999 by
André Deutsch Limited
76 Dean Street
London WIV 5HA
www.vci.co.uk

A catalogue record for this book is available from the British Library

ISBN 0 233 99479 3

Typeset by Derek Doyle & Associates
Mold, Flintshire.
Printed and bound in Great Britain by
MPG Books, Bodmin, Cornwall.

For Diana Devlin

Contents

Illustrations		ix
Introduction and Acknowledgements		1
A Note on Style		5
1	Catherine	7
2	Mary	23
3	Fanny	46
4	Mrs Nelson	60
5	Lady Nelson	77
6	Emma	99
7	Dearest Emma	119
8	Fanny Meets Emma	145
9	Charlotte	174
10	Horatia	198
11	Mrs Nelson Ward	225
Notes		248
Bibliography		269
Index		272

Illustrations

1 Horatio Nelson: hero and charmer. The long-lost smiling portrait in marble of 1797 by Lawrence Gahagan; discovered in Norfolk and presented to the Royal Naval Museum, Portsmouth, by Mr Bryan Hall in 1996.

2 The Mothers
(left) Catherine Nelson (née Suckling) as a young woman. (*National Maritime Museum*)
(right) Mary Cadogan (formerly Lyon), mother of Emma Hamilton. (*Royal Naval Museum*)
(bottom) The parsonage, birthplace and home of Horatio Nelson in Burnham Thorpe, Norfolk, painted by Francis Pocock. (*National Maritime Museum*)

3 (left) Susannah ('Sukey') Bolton (née Nelson). (*Private collection*)
(right) Catherine ('Kate') Matcham (née Nelson), Horatio's youngest and favourite sister. (*Private collection*)
(bottom)'The Hat Shop', a milliners such as that at Bath where both sisters worked as sales assistants; attributed to John Nixon. (*Private collection*)

4 (top) Susannah's home: the farmhouse at Cranwich in south-west Norfolk as it was in 1998.
(bottom) Kate's home: Barton Hall in eastern Norfolk – one of the elegant houses rented by her and her husband, George Matcham – as it is now.

5 (top) Elizabeth Andrews, the clergyman's daughter, whom Nelson met in Saint-Omer. (*Private collection*)
(bottom) Mary Moutray, the young wife of an elderly official, whom Nelson met in Antigua; by John Downman. (*Private collection*)

6 Frances Nelson (née Woolward; formerly Nisbet), the young widow Nelson met and married in Nevis. (*Royal Naval Museum*)
(top) Women as idealised in Nelson's time: a loving daughter cares for her elderly father, a naval officer and possibly Nelson's friend Captain William Locker; painted by Sir David Wilkie. (*Private collection*)

7 (bottom) Sympathetic womenfolk give alms to a crippled sailor in 'Affliction of Providence Relieved by Attention', painted by Lawrence Cosse in 1804. (*Private collection*)

8 Nelson afloat: painted after the Battle of the Nile and attributed to Leonardo Guzzardi. (*Private collection*)

9 Lady Hamilton: one of Emma's favourite portraits of herself by George Romney, which was to hang at Merton Place. (*Southside House, Wimbledon*)

10 (top) Powerful friends: King Ferdinand IV and Queen Maria Carolina of the Kingdom of the Two Sicilies. (*National Gallery of Scotland*)
(bottom) Emma in Naples: a portrait by an unknown Neapolitan artist circa 1798. (*Private collection*)

11 Nelson's Homes: (top) Merton Place in Surrey painted by Thomas Baxter. (*National Maritime Museum*)
(bottom) The Castello di Maniace: Nelson's house near Bronte in Sicily, which he was never to visit, as it is now.

12 (top) Seen fondly, as by her father: Horatia, daughter of Nelson and Emma Hamilton.
(bottom) Seen cruelly by the caricaturist James Gillray: Emma Hamilton bewails the departure of her lover to sea. (*National Maritime Museum*)

13 (top) Seen in retrospect through the sentimental eye of an artist a century later: Nelson dances with Emma in Naples. (*Private collection*)
(bottom) Seen by an imaginative Edwardian artist: Nelson in church at Merton. (*Private collection*)

14 Charlotte Nelson, the admiral's niece, as she was when staying at Merton Place and before her marriage to Samuel Hood; painted by Isaac Pocock. (*Private collection/ National Portrait Gallery*)

15 Lady Hamilton and Charlotte caricatured by James Gillray in 'Attitudes Faithfully Copied from Nature and Humbly Dedicated to All Admirers of the Grand and Sublime'. (*Private collection*)

16 (top) Horatia mourns at the memorial to her father, painted by Isaac Pocock. (*Private collection*)
(bottom left) As a young woman after returning to her father's family from Calais. (*National Portrait Gallery*)
(bottom right) Photographed as a widow following the death of the Rev Simon Ward in 1859. (*National Maritime Museum*)

Introduction

In the life of Horatio Nelson, the significance of women, long recognized as a vital component of his enduring legend, went beyond that of his wife and his mistress. Fanny Nisbet gave him tranquillity and confidence in the early years of their marriage and Emma Hamilton inspired dreams of glory during their love affair. In a sense, each complemented the other and each occupied his life for about the same length of time.

But other women exerted influence, several of them for much longer. Although his mother died when he was nine, he thought of her for the rest of his life, and two of his three sisters remained in as close touch as was possible. Others shot through his youth, burning brightly but briefly, and one could wonder what course his career might have taken if Mary Simpson or Elizabeth Andrews had reacted differently, or if Mary Moutray had been widowed in Antigua rather than in Bath.

Nelson's company was equally important to women: as one friend was to write to a mutual female acquaintance, he knew that she had always regarded Nelson '*con amore*'. It has been said that there was a feminine streak in the strongly heterosexual man himself: he discussed people as individuals rather than as factors in his own prospects; he was sympathetic to human problems, however uncomfortably they might lie with the demands of naval discipline; he enjoyed gossip.

When biographers have emphasized the influence of women in his life – notably that of Fanny and Emma – they have risked distorting the image of the man whose greatness lay, of course, in his activities away from female company. The heart of any portrait of Lord Nelson must be his achievement in giving his country a century of maritime dominance, during which Britain became the most powerful nation in the world, the ruler of a global empire. A naval commander of intuitive genius in fighting and leadership, Nelson also revealed his humanity and his human weaknesses. Here was a man with qualities the British might share, and this made him the first national hero to be recognized as such, but also one subject to the common run of human problems and emotions.

There are no descriptions of naval battles in this book. It presents a gallery of women who shared Horatio Nelson as a common factor in their lives, each influencing and being influenced in varying degrees. Those unfamiliar with the full cast of characters will meet women such as Cornelia Knight, the intelligent but class-conscious spinster on whom the pressures of polite society were to bear so heavily; Couba Cornwallis, the Jamaican who saved sick officers from almost certain death in hospital with her herbal remedies; Adelaide Correglia, the blowsy 'dolly' with whom Nelson dallied in Leghorn; and the pretty, if ingenuous, Charlotte Nelson, whose dewy charm Emma exploited with such social success. It is not always an edifying story: weaknesses and jealousies came to the surface, there was self-seeking and jockeying for position; loyalties shifted, sometimes full circle. But there were also moments of altruism, constancy, generosity and courage.

Much of the story is told in the words of the main players taken from letters relating to Nelson. These are to be found notably in the great archives in the British Library, the National Maritime Museum and the Monmouth Museum, and many of them have been printed in the three principal collections edited by Sir Harris Nicolas, Alfred Morrison and George Naish. There are other archives, public and private, as well as printed collections, of course, and large numbers of unpublished letters pass through the salerooms and the manuscripts market every year and can sometimes be caught on the wing. Even when particular letters are well known, biographers may have quoted only passages relevant to Nelson and his naval achievements, while the same letter may also include illuminating references to personal relationships and domestic detail, which can come fresh to most readers.

Among those who have helped with this book, I must particularly thank John and Cynthia Thompson for suggesting the idea of writing it. The great-great-great-granddaughter of Nelson and Emma Hamilton, Anna Tribe, who radiates qualities of both, offered advice and hitherto unpublished letters between Nelson's sister-in-law and Emma. At Newhouse, the Matchams' house in Wiltshire, their descendants, George Jeffreys and his family, were unfailingly welcoming and helpful. Sir Nicholas Bonsor kindly allowed access to his collection of family manuscripts. For visits to Norfolk houses relevant to the story I am grateful to the late Colonel Richard Allhusen and his wife Jane of Bradenham Hall, and to Group Captain Anthony Barwood and his wife Norah of Bolton House. Also in Norfolk, Judge Adrian Head talked about his ancestors, the Boltons; Bryan Hall showed me Suckling documents in his collection; and I was encouraged by Michael Tapper and Les Winter of Burnham Thorpe, helped by Paul Cattermole of Wymondham and shown the remains of the Sucklings' great house at Woodton by Elaine Hill of Woodton Park.

In my search for obscure sources I was expertly steered by two Nelsonian bibliophiles, Michael Nash and Ronald Fiske, who also read and commented upon my typescript. Lady Gunning explained the part played by her ancestor Robert Fagan, the painter, in Nelson's Italian entanglements; Elizabeth Drury offered fascinating information on the portable ship's bed in which Horatia might have been conceived; Carol Evans reported on the fate of Horatia's twin sister; and John Sugden for his work on the Andrews family. In Naples Dr Carlo Knight and Fernando Savarese, proved as shrewd historical advisers as they are good company.

The staffs of the London Library, the National Maritime Museum, Greenwich, and the Royal Naval Museum at Portsmouth were as helpful as ever; the Deputy Director of the latter, Colin White, again proved himself a valuable consultant in the study of Nelson's world. Ian Hessenberg kindly photographed several paintings. I am grateful to Simon Houfe, Clive Richards, Vincent Lawford, Stephen Courtney, Richard Walker and Messrs Christie's and Sotheby's and the Trustees of Southside House, for their help with illustrations. Andrew Lownie, Jackie Gumpert and my wife Penny played valuable parts in the production of the book.

Tom Pocock
Chelsea, 1999

A Note on Style

Two centuries ago, spelling and punctuation were more haphazard than they are today. Although this may seem to add authenticity and sometimes amuse, it can hinder the progress of the narrative and make the letter-writer seem quaint and archaic. So both have been somewhat modernized, with the intention of making the writers' words more accessible to our eyes and they themselves appear as the intelligent, aware people that they were. Occasionally, the capital letters and italics they loved have been left in place when they seem to have been used for particular emphasis.

1
Catherine

The date of the baptism of Catherine Nelson's sixth child was dictated by the date of the annual harvest fair, 21 October, when the rector and his wife would be prominent in both festivities and devotions. Their child, who had been born on 29 September 1758, was christened at the Parsonage House, where his father had blessed baptismal water in a china bowl; three sons had died in infancy and the utmost care was being taken of their successors. Despite the balmy East Anglian autumn, there were dangers ranging from the malarial fever that plagued the marshy coasts and valleys of Norfolk to the chill of the dank stone church beside the stream running through Burnham Thorpe.

So the formal, public christening ceremony at All Saints' church was delayed until 15 November, when the whole family, including relations from across the county, neighbours from the village and the smarter citizens from nearby Burnham Market gathered round the font of Purbeck marble that stood white against the dark of the box pews.

The child was called after a dead brother who had briefly borne the classical name of Horatio. This had been a favourite name of his mother's grand relations, the Walpoles, although one of them, a witty dilettante, preferred to be called Horace, explaining that this was, 'an English name for an Englishman'.[1] The Nelson family also called their son Horace, his father soon writing to the others about 'your bro. Hor.'.

The family grouped about the font presented a tableau of contentment: the mother, now aged thirty-three, handsome rather than beautiful, with open, confident looks that owed something to an assured position in the upper reaches of rural society; the father, three years older, with his long, lugubrious, scholarly face framed by shoulder-length hair rather than a fashionable wig. Those sensitive to the social nuances of English life would have noted that while Catherine's bearing and manner marked her as a member of the landed gentry, if not the aristocracy, her husband was clearly a cultivated member of what the family called 'the middling class of people'. She was forthright, while he was diffident. Their differences, however, were complementary and they were a happy couple, united now in joy, as they had been earlier in grief for the first Horatio, as their surviving sons, Maurice and William, were joined by his namesake.

When the ceremony ended, the christening party left in a clattering cavalcade for the parsonage, half a mile away at the southern end of the village. It was a modest building with the looks of a small Norfolk farmhouse, its high-pitched, pantiled roof given a touch of sophistication by fashionable Venetian windows. Behind the house, a walled garden and orchard spread up the gentle slope towards a crest commanding a distant view of the sea; in front, beyond the lawn, the little River Burn swirled its way from the chalk uplands of High Norfolk to Overy Creek, which wound through the salt marshes two miles to the north.

The brick-floored house, so chill in winter, differed from the comfortable country houses, sometimes mansions, in which Catherine had been brought up and in which her own family, the Sucklings, lived. She had spent her childhood at Barsham rectory to the south of the River Waveney, which flows between Norfolk and Suffolk. That had been a comfortable country house with an imposing Dutch gable, where her father, a clergyman of high social standing, felt happy to entertain the aristocracy. It was grander than her present home but far less grand than her family's principal residence, north of the river in the village of Woodton, where her father was also rector of the little round-towered church. There Woodton Hall, a fine country house with a new, brick façade crowned by a pediment and 'enclosed by Pleasure Grounds, Shrubberies, Plantations and beautifully shaded Serpentine Walks',[2] stood in its park and farmland.

This house was now owned by her brother Maurice who was a captain in the Royal Navy. He was a brother to be idolized – handsome, debonair and brave – and she had named her first-born son after him. Two years before, war had broken out with France over rivalry on the Continent and in North America and since then he had been away on active service. In going to sea, Maurice had followed one of several family traditions, indeed, he wore the sword he had inherited from his great-uncle, another naval officer, Captain Galfridus Walpole.

In 1757, a year before Horatio was born, Captain Suckling had been commanding the *Dreadnought*, one of three ships of the line to intercept a French convoy lying off Cap François in the Caribbean. As their escort of four sail of the line and three frigates made ready for action, the senior British captain consulted the other two and told them, 'Well, gentlemen, you see they are come out to engage us', to which Suckling replied characteristically, 'I think it would be a pity to disappoint them.'[3] In the sharp action that followed, the French had been worsted but, after two and a half hours, managed to escape. The date of the battle was that of the harvest fair at Burnham Thorpe, giving the Nelson family another reason to remember 21 October.

Catherine's other, younger brother William was also connected with the sea, albeit obliquely. Not for him the dangers of active service, though. His dealings with seaborne trade could be conducted from the Excise Office in London, where he was a commissioner, and a comfortable house in the northern suburb of Kentish Town.

Her most distinguished connection was a great-uncle, Sir Robert Walpole, the country's first prime minister, who had been created Earl of Orford and had built the magnificent, turreted Houghton Hall in the west of the county. His brother had been the first Lord Walpole of Wolterton, who was best known to the

Sucklings, and his son, the writer and wit, was also named Horace. Her relations spread across the county and its great estates and houses included also the lordly, political and military Townshends, whose mansion, Raynham Hall, stood in its park some fifteen miles to the south of the Parsonage. She carried her upbringing lightly, for the life of the great house with its myriad servants, coachmen, grooms, gardeners and gamekeepers was, to her, only to be expected.

What had been unfamiliar had been the modest ways of the Nelsons, the little house she now ruled and its few servants, male and female, including 'Will, indoors', 'Peter, without' and Nurse Blackett, who was to help care for the infant Horace. In place of those gravelled walks decorated with follies and statues, the groves of ornamental trees and broad sweeps of parkland, she now ruled a modest garden and orchard set in the thirty acres of her husband's glebe.

As a girl, Catherine had found the choice of eligible young men limited. The eldest sons of the landowners tended to seek young women who might be similarly endowed and younger sons often left home to make their way as officers in the Navy, or Army, or simply to seek diversion in London. One of the few suitable young bachelors was the curate of the church at Beccles, the market town a mile to the east of Barsham. This was Edmund Nelson, whom she was to marry.

The Nelsons had originally come to Norfolk from Lancashire in the seventeenth century and established themselves through farming and the church; indeed, the infant Horace was related to fifteen clergymen of the past two and the present generations. This ensured education – his paternal grandfather had been schooled at Eton College and his father at Caius College, Cambridge – and a social position. It was not that a country parson ranked highly in the rural hierarchy; usually he was seen as being somewhat above the doctor, who was one grade above the tradesman, but below the squire unless he was himself from the landowning class, in which case he was a regular guest at the mahogany dining tables of the great houses and probably hunted and shot with his hosts. What gave him an underlying significance was the knowledge, in a religious age, that eventually the squire and the landowner, even the monarch, would ask for a clergyman's intercession with the Almighty.

The clergy mingled with farmers and tradesmen in their ancestry. While his wife's family bore names like Walpole, Townshend, Jermyn and Durrant, Edmund's included simpler surnames like Pigg, Alp, Bland and Prettyman. Horace's paternal great-great-grandfather was described by Edmund as 'a Norwich manufacturer'.[4] Another relation was an apothecary; a third, a silk mercer. Indeed commerce had introduced money into the family, via John Bland, a prosperous baker in Cambridge. Like the Nelsons, the Blands had moved to East Anglia from Lancashire after persecution during the Civil War by the Royalists because of their Parliamentary and Presbyterian views. As Edmund put it, 'They began the world with but very little but by industry in trade they acquired considerable fortunes.'[5]

John Bland and his wife, Thomazin, who lived in Petty Cury, were ambitious for their children. Their eldest son was ordained and became chaplain to the Duke of Ancaster, while two daughters were married to newly ordained curates who had attended the university: Alice to Robert Rolfe, a young man of means and fashionable connections, and Mary to Edmund Nelson, Horace's grandfather, who had been educated at Eton and graduated from Emmanuel College. The latter was set up by John Bland as the parson of East Bradenham, to the east of Swaffham, where he had bought the patronage, and subsequently acquired the additional living of Sporle through his old school, Eton, which owned it. John Bland himself retired to Hilborough, a village south of Swaffham in Norfolk, bought the right of patronage and Edmund Nelson moved there as rector.

The Nelsons had eight children, several of whom died in infancy and one of whom, John, 'enlisted as a soldier, after various unlucky circumstances and misconduct, embarked for some foreign service abt. the year 1760; supposed dead as never heard of since.'[6] Another son, also named Edmund, was educated at a country school and then Cambridge University, from which he was ordained. His first appointment was as curate to the Reverend Thomas Page at Beccles, where he met Catherine Suckling. Then, on his father's death at Hilborough at the age of fifty-three in 1747, the young Edmund succeeded him there and at Sporle. At first he lived with his mother in the little red-tiled rectory at Hilborough,* spending his stipend on her while living on his annual £80 from Sporle. In May 1749, he and Catherine Suckling were married by the rector of Beccles, setting up house first at Swaffham, then in a rented house at Sporle.

Happily for Edmund, Catherine was as well connected in the Church of England as she was in the county, for her father was a Prebendary of Westminster as well as rector of Barsham and Woodton. Through her great-uncle Lord Walpole of Wolterton, Edmund was presented with the living of Burnham Thorpe and three small, neighbouring parishes – Ulph, Sutton, and Norton – on the death of the incumbent at the end of 1755. Edmund's brother-in-law, Robert Rolfe, succeeded him at Hilborough and that winter the couple moved with their two surviving children, Maurice, aged two, and Susannah, who had been born on 12 June that year, to the chilly little rectory at the southern end of the straggling village of Burnham Thorpe. Two other children, Edmund and the first Horatio, had died in 1750 and 1751 respectively; another son, William, was to be born in their new house on 20 April 1757.

Life in Burnham Thorpe settled into a contented seasonal pattern. The beginning of each year was likely to be raw, cold and windy, but then the long spring and summer stretched into a benign autumn that could continue well past the October harvest festival until Christmas. Catherine Nelson had scaled down the country-house routine with which she had been so familiar to fit the little parsonage. Social activity was limited to visits to neighbouring farmers living in what Horace would describe as 'homesteads by the stream',[7] the genteel occupants of residences around the green at Burnham Market a mile away, the merchants in the little seaport of Wells some three miles distant,

*It is now known as the Nunnery.

the market town of Fakenham to the south and the far more fashionable town of Swaffham beyond. The county town of Norwich, then the third largest in England, was a world in itself; Catherine's elderly aunt, Sarah Henley, lived with her two daughters in part of the ancient Suckling mansion in its centre.

After William and Horatio, Susannah (known as Sukey in the family) was joined by another daughter, Anne, on 20 September 1760. Daughters were not expected to be educated as were the boys, but Catherine saw to it that Susannah was given what her father called 'a good school education'[8] in Norfolk, while Catherine herself taught both girls music and needlework.

As the boys grew, their characters began to emerge and they were surprisingly different. The eldest, Maurice, was dutiful, conscious of his position amongst the children, taking his responsibilities seriously, but seeming to lack spark and ambition. William, four years younger, was big for his age, greedy, selfish and lacking in initiative. Little Horace, however, began to show remarkable spirit and generosity, always seeming 'game'.

Once, it was said, when the children were visiting their grandmother at Hilborough, the boys went searching for birds' nests in the woods around Hilborough Hall on the far side of the narrow, fast-flowing River Wissey. As dusk began to fall, they became separated and William returned to the house without Horace. When the little boy was eventually found alone and brought to his grandmother, she expressed surprise that hunger and fear had not driven him home. 'I never saw fear,' he is said to have replied. 'What is it?'

The war with France and, latterly, Spain had ended in 1763 and with it the threat of invasion. This had galvanized the Norfolk landowners into raising militia for local defence and often commanding it themselves. Catherine's distant cousins, the Townshends of Raynham, had been particularly active and one of them, the Honourable George Townshend, a professional soldier, had gone to Canada, where he fought at Quebec as one of General Wolfe's brigadiers and, when the latter was killed, had succeeded to the command of the army. Although herself without experience of foreign countries or foreigners – beyond, perhaps, the occasional French dancing master or Dutch sea captain – Catherine, true to type, enjoyed a brisk xenophobia, combined with a zestful patriotism, particularly focused on the heroism of her brother Maurice. Indeed, one of her daughters remembered that 'somehow the Navy must always be interesting to me. I may say I suck'd it with my mother's milk for she was quite a heroine for the sailors,' and Horace's only recorded direct memory of his mother was that 'she hated the French'.[9]

The autumn of 1767 was miserable, with 'high, frosty winds and a great fall of rain',[10] rivers flooding and crops ruined. Catherine Nelson, although only forty-two, was now worn and prematurely aged. She had borne eleven children, three of whom – the first Edmund, the first Horatio and George, born in September 1765 – had died in infancy; the survivors since Horace were Edmund, Suckling, Anne (usually called Nancy or Nanny) and the last, Catherine (called Kate or Kitty), born on 19 March 1767. When Catherine was taken ill in the damp, chilly parsonage, her resistance was low and she is thought to have developed pneumonia. Christmas was stiff with dread and on Boxing Day she died.

Her funeral was conducted by her husband and she was buried before the altar at All Saints', near the coffins of their dead babies. Thereafter, he would remind the children of the anniversary of the 'day your mother was laid in the peaceful grave'.[11] As befitted his wife's social rank, Edmund ordered a tombstone of black marble, cut with a swirling Suckling coat of arms impaling his own and her epitaph in Latin, including the sombre command, in English, 'Let these alone. Let no man move these bones.'

Edmund was resigned to what he saw as the divine will. 'It has fallen to my lot to take upon me the care and affection of a double parent,' he was to write. 'They will hereafter excuse where I have fallen short and the task has been too hard.'[12]

The family continued to live in a hushed parsonage under the care of their Norfolk domestics, but the sadness never wholly lifted. At nine, Horace was particularly vulnerable and, many years later, he was to paraphrase Shakespeare's words from *King*

Henry V and write sadly, 'The thought of former days brings all my Mother to my heart, which shows itself in my eyes.'[13]

The bereaved family settled into a new routine. The eldest girl, Susannah, was now aged twelve and becoming conscious of her position as the senior daughter. Not as attractive and spirited as little Kate promised to be, or as winsome as Nancy, she was jolly and, like her mother, forthright, her practicality showing in her blunt face and determined chin. She would now, in effect, take charge of the household.

Edmund sank into a state of sad acceptance, accentuated by his lack of self-confidence. 'As to the Society in me,' he was to write, 'I never mixed with the world eno' at a proper period of Life to make it entertaining, or valuable on any account, except a willingness to make my family comfortable. . .'[14]

The boys had to be placed in schools, but Maurice, the eldest, was now aged fifteen and eligible for employment. Catherine's younger brother, William Suckling, used his influence to find him work as a junior clerk to the auditors of the Excise Office in London. William would have to go to school, as would Horace, who, in 1769, was told by his father that thereafter he must always be known as Horatio; Edmund himself crossed out his son's signature in the parish register and substituted the classical name.

One of the principal schools for boys in Norfolk was the High School in the cathedral close at Norwich, which mostly taught the sons of the county town's citizens, and the other was the boarding school at North Walsham, which had been more recently established by the landowning Paston family. William and Horatio were to be sent to Norwich, to board and, if necessary, stay with their great-aunt Sarah Henley, who lived with her two middle-aged daughters in part of the rambling Suckling house facing St Andrew's Plain, a few minutes' walk from the school. But, after a year at Norwich, their uncle, Captain Suckling, who had returned to Woodton Hall from sea after the end of the war in 1763, visited Burnham Thorpe and recommended that they should be moved to the Paston School as boarders, while Maurice could move from the Excise Office to the Navy Office in Somerset House, which housed the Admiralty's administration.

The following winter saw Susannah and her sisters with only their father and two younger brothers, Edmund and Suckling, at the parsonage house. Although Edmund liked to romanticize the seasons – 'the pomp and parade of winter, wind and storm and rattling hail; clothed with frosted robes, powdered with snow, all trimmed in glittering icicles; no blooming dowager was ever finer'[15] – he decided to avoid the cold weather after Christmas by visiting the mild, sheltered valley of Bath in the Somerset hills.

The family kept in touch with the outside world through the weekly *Norfolk Chronicle* and there they read of the mobilization of the Navy to meet a threat from Spain to the newly acquired Falklands Islands in the South Atlantic. Captain Suckling had been recalled to duty and given command of a former French prize, the sixty-four-gun ship of the line *Raissonable*. He was not sorry to go, for he was a lonely man. In June 1764, he had married his cousin Mary, a daughter of Lord Walpole of Wolterton, but two years later she had died, leaving him childless.

William Nelson was to prepare for ordination at Cambridge University, but for Horatio the news offered a chance of escape. So he asked his elder brother, 'Do write to my father at Bath and tell him I should like to go with my Uncle Maurice to sea.'[16] The letter reached Bath in a few days and the rector, delighted that his third son had identified a career that might one day bring prosperity through prize money, immediately wrote to his brother-in-law. Amused and happy to treat Edmund's children as his own surrogate family, Captain Suckling replied from Chatham, where his ship was lying, 'What has poor Horace done, who is so weak, that he, above all the rest, should be sent to rough it out at sea? But let him come and the first time we go into action a cannon-ball may knock off his head and provide for him at once.'[17] Captain Suckling at once entered his nephew's name in the ship's muster-book so that the progress of his seniority could begin. But arrangements would take some time, so Horatio returned to North Walsham for the beginning of the first term of 1771 to await instructions.

Orders to join his ship arrived early in March and Edmund took his son by coach to King's Lynn and thence to London. They stayed briefly with William Suckling at his comfortable house in Kentish Town before Horatio was taken back into London and out on the coach for Chatham.

Careers would now have to be found for the other boys. Maurice was already in London and was to move from the Excise Office to the Navy Office, where he would occasionally come under the eye of his other uncle, when he was ashore. William was going up to Christ's College, Cambridge, and there should be no difficulty in finding him a living in rural Norfolk. Edmund and Suckling would probably go into trade when apprenticeships could be arranged.

The three girls presented a more difficult problem since the only career open to middle-class women was marriage and motherhood. There was, however, one type of temporary employment which paid wages and teetered on the edge of respectability and that was as a shop assistant. This would not be in any shop but only in the best class of millinery, where a young lady could presume to offer an opinion on the suitability of a hat to a woman customer who might be of her own social standing outside the shop door. Edmund Nelson had had this in mind when staying in Bath and it was there that he made arrangements for Susannah to be apprenticed to one such milliner. The best he could do for Anne – or Nancy, as she was usually known – was in London, where she was apprenticed for a premium of £100 to a rather less genteel establishment, the Capital Lace Warehouse in Ludgate Street. Little Kate was still too young to be sent into the world to earn a living.

All the family followed Horatio's career with wonderment and worry through their father's letters. Uncle Maurice had been unable to take him to sea himself as his command was a guard ship at the Nore,* so he arranged for him to sail to the West

* The anchorage off Sheerness in the Thames estuary at the mouth of the Medway.

Indies in a merchant ship commanded by an old shipmate. On this first voyage, Horatio was influenced by his own shipmates, who feared the Royal Navy, which was likely to impress them for service in wartime and which had a reputation for brutality towards its own men. Back under naval discipline, he settled down and was soon sailing on a scientific expedition to the Arctic, where, the family heard, he had tried to kill a polar bear in order to provide a rug for the stone-flagged hearth in the parsonage. He had then been appointed to the frigate *Seahorse* and on a voyage to India had contracted malaria, from which he had almost died. It was while making a slow recovery, as his ship sailed homeward from the Cape of Good Hope, that he underwent a mystical experience, albeit in a secular context. Deeply depressed about his prospects in the Navy, he suddenly had a vision of 'a radiant orb' and 'a sudden glow', and with that came the belief that, as he was to put it, 'I will be a hero, and confiding in Providence, will brave every danger.'[18] On his return he took his examination for lieutenant. Although Captain Suckling – now Comptroller of the Navy at the Admiralty and, as such, a powerful influence – sat on the examining board, he did not tell the other members of his relationship with Midshipman Nelson, who passed in any case. Next day, Lieutenant Nelson was appointed to the frigate *Lowestoft*, bound for the Caribbean.

His first task was to command a press gang on the London waterfront, seizing unwary young men and putting them aboard a tender to be taken downriver to the frigate to become reluctant seamen. Even though the officer controlled his gang from his lodgings, it was an unpleasant duty and it threw into relief a little act of courtesy. Nelson was briefly quartered in the house of a hosier, it was said, when his host came in from the street laughing at a scene he had just watched. An apple-woman had set up her cart outside and a young man, pretending to show interest in her apples, had tied one end of a rope to a leg of her stall and another to the wheel of a waiting hackney coach; when the coach lurched forward, the stall collapsed and the apples rolled across the street. Nelson did not join in the laughter but ran out of the house to give the apple-woman a few coins.

Soon afterwards, the frigate sailed for Jamaica. Horatio was on active service because, in 1775, the American colonies had rebelled against the British crown and, three years later, France declared war in their support. There was now the certainty of a major war at sea and the warm, blue water of the Caribbean would become what Horatio himself called 'The Grand Theatre of Actions'.[19] Edmund's anxiety for his safety combined with worry about his two eldest girls, working behind shop counters. Susannah seemed able to look after herself in Bath and there were distant relations of the Sucklings, John and Dorothea Scrivener, from Suffolk, who lived there in style and could be expected to keep a kindly eye upon her; but in the capital, Anne's lace shop was close to the taverns of Fleet Street and its disreputable warrens of courts and alleys, while her uncle William lived four miles away, beyond Holborn and Clerkenwell in Kentish Town. Her other uncle, Maurice, had a smart new house in Park Street, Mayfair, but he had not been well and could do little for his niece.

Then, in July 1778, the Nelson family were shocked to hear that Captain Suckling had died on the 14th of that month. He was only fifty-three but his life at sea had involved risk and, having no direct heirs, he had made careful provision for his nephews and nieces. During his last weeks, when Edmund Nelson had attended him, he had said that he would leave each of his nephews a legacy of £500; then, on reflection, he added that he would send for his lawyer and do something more for Horatio. Soon afterwards, he was dead and that particular legacy was still undefined. However, the bulk of his estate had been left to his brother, William, who made sure that Horatio received not only his £500 but also the sword worn in battle by their ancestor, Captain Galfridus Walpole. Each of the girls he had left £1,000, which would free Sukey and Nancy from their shops and give Kitty, now eleven, an eventual dowry. The eldest returned to Burnham Thorpe well funded to search for a husband; but for Nancy it was too late. In London, she had been seduced and, when she became pregnant, was abandoned by her lover; she too returned to Norfolk.

For Susannah, the immediate catchment area for husbands was limited to Burnham Market, Fakenham and Wells. Through the harbour and dockside warehouses of the latter passed a busy trade: exports of corn and malt, imports of coal from the Tyne, general cargoes from the Thames and, during the herring season, fishing boats ran a secondary trade in Dutch pottery. But Wells was not all dockside pubs and fishermen's cottages; Staithe Street led from the waterfront to the Buttlands, a green surrounded by genteel residences, and near the church stood numbers of comfortable houses fit for merchants and the minor gentry.

There she met Thomas Bolton, the third son of Samuel Bolton of Coddenham in Suffolk, whose bluff looks matched her own. The Boltons, who originally came from Woodbridge, were socially placed between the Nelsons and the Sucklings, with both squires and parsons among their immediate forebears. In Wells, however, they were in trade, exporting corn and malt and importing coal. Tom Bolton was twenty-eight when, in 1780, he and Susannah married in what appeared to be an ideal match.

On Susannah's wedding day, her brother Horatio was close to death. In June of the preceding year, he had been given his first important command in the West Indies. This had been the frigate *Hinchinbroke* and, when Spain declared war in support of France, he was on more active service. The British had conceived a bold strategy to make up for the impending loss of the American colonies and planned to send an expeditionary force up the San Juan river to cross the central American isthmus through Nicaragua to the Pacific. Then, having cut the Spanish American empire in two, they would be able to advance south into Peru and north into Mexico and annex the whole. Nelson was ordered to escort a troop convoy to the mouth of the river but on arrival he realized that the soldiers could not manage an amphibious operation on this scale and decided to accompany them himself. Had his advice to act boldly been accepted by the military commander, the first stage at least of the plan might have succeeded. As it was, the key fortress near the head of the river was finally captured, but the British were already infected with malaria, dysentery and, it was reported, yellow fever. Nelson himself survived the disaster and was lucky to be sent downriver and shipped to Jamaica. There his life was probably saved by a black nurse, Couba Cornwallis, who had a reputation for saving the lives of sick officers and had been named after one of them. Instead of bleeding him, she applied warm bricks to feet chilled by fever and dosed him with herbal brews, her cheerfulness inspiring a will to live. Once out of danger, he was invited to stay at the admiral's residence, although Admiral Parker and his wife were away. As he wrote in a letter, 'Lady P. not here and the servants letting me lie as if a log and take no notice'.[20] Eventually, Lady Parker returned, but Nelson proved a difficult patient until his medicine was brought to him by his hostess's youngest daughter as his 'little nurse'.[21] By the end of the year, he was on his way home.

Captain Nelson was still delicate when he reached Portsmouth in December and, instead of returning to his family in Norfolk, he went to Bath for medical attention and to take the medicinal waters. In April 1881, he was well enough to travel to London and stay with his uncle William Suckling and finally to return to Burnham Thorpe in the company of his brother Maurice. There he found his sister Anne at home with his father and fourteen-year-old Kate. Susannah was now living with her husband in Wells and Captain Nelson was introduced to the pleasures of the town. This was little more than the twice-weekly meetings of the Wells Club, which played cards at the Royal Standard or the Three Tuns taverns.

In early summer a letter arrived from the Admiralty informing Nelson that he had been appointed to command the small frigate *Albemarle* of twenty-eight guns. She was at Woolwich dockyard, where her bottom was being sheathed with copper, which suggested that she might be being prepared for service in the tropics, as this was protection against the wood-boring teredo worm that plagued warm waters. Returning to London with Maurice, he joined his ship at the end of August.

Now that his sisters were freed from the shop counters, there should have been little for him to worry about when at sea. But Kate seemed vulnerable and, remembering what had happened to Anne, he fussed about her prospects. He would miss not only her company but that of his other sisters and, indeed, their mother. He was ready to look for a wife.

2
Mary

In Quebec, the social life of the garrison was that of an occupying force in a hostile country. It was twenty-one years since New France had fallen to the British but France was again at war with Britain, allied to the rebellious American colonies. When the colonists had risen against British rule, they had sent an expeditionary force against Quebec in 1775, but it had proved inadequate, the season too late for fighting, and been repulsed. However, the war continued to the south and the British were well aware that the French majority in the city and the St Lawrence Valley would welcome their defeat and even assist in it. In April 1782, the shock of the surrender of General Cornwallis, besieged by the Americans and blockaded by the French in Yorktown, six months before was still fresh. Quebec was deep in French-speaking territory and the garrison considered itself to be on active service.

Still living there were middle-aged men who had fought on the Plains of Abraham outside the city, when General Wolfe had died at the hour of victory. There had recently been an influx of Loyalists from the American colonies, people who had preferred, or been forced, to leave their homes for British territory. British contractors and merchants, busy supplying the garrisons in Canada and the field forces further south with provisions, ammunition and clothing, had set themselves up in business. British traders had arrived to replace the French in shipping furs – notably beaver – and corn to Europe, while many discharged British solders and sailors had chosen to remain in Canada. So now the population of the city, which had been entirely French twenty years before, was a quarter English-speaking and the *Quebec Gazette* printed its news in English on the left of its pages and in French on the right. The social mix was also reflected in the architecture: grey stone houses that might have stood around the harbours of Brittany and more modern buildings with handsomely proportioned façades and balanced arrangements of doors and sash windows that came from the builders' pattern-books of contemporary England.

The social life of the officers of the garrison was further limited by the shortage of young, nubile, English-speaking women and those that there were could pick and choose their suitors. Predominant among these was Mary, the sixteen-year-old daughter of the provost-marshal, Colonel Saunders Simpson. Like his cousin Miles Prentice, the city's overseer of works and proprietor of the Lion d'Or hotel, 'Sandy' Simpson had fought under Wolfe and, having remained in the city ever since, was well established, with a handsome house near the St Louis Gate.

Mary may not have been as pretty as some of her rivals – notably her first cousin, the daughter of another survivor of Wolfe's army – but she had 'marvellous beauty'.[1] But even 'if Mary Simpson was not the most beautiful girl in Quebec,' said a neighbour, a Mrs Harrower, 'she was, at any rate, the handsomest I have ever beheld.'[2] Her classical looks prompted an admirer to compare her with Diana, the Roman goddess of hunting.

She cut such a dash in the ballroom that the *Quebec Gazette,* published a hymn of praise in her honour:

> Sure you will listen to my call
> Since beauty and Quebec's fair nymphs I sing.
> Henceforth Diana is Miss S—ps–n see,
> As noble and majestic is her air . . .[3]

She was the belle of the garrison assemblies and balls and, it seemed, could take her pick of the young officers of the garrison. Indeed, social assemblies were her field of conquest, because, while her uncle's hotel was frequented by junior officers, those of or above the rank of colonel, or post-captain in the Navy, visited it only when on official business, as it was not thought to be of suitable standing for their private use. Among young officers, the most promising as potential husbands were in the Army, because they could be assumed to have purchased their commissions and therefore to have some private means. In 1782, her most attentive suitor was a Captain Robert Matthews, who had recently arrived in Quebec with an infantry regiment from the American colonies.

Naval officers, on the other hand, could be more exciting and even mysterious, as there was always a chance that some act of heroism and a capture at sea could have made them rich with prize-money. Looking northward from Quebec, the wide basin of the St Lawrence was often crowded with shipping, the port had become not only a depot for military stores destined for the war and the occupation but also an entrepot for luxuries from Europe and sugar and rum from the Caribbean. Occasionally, among the small merchant ships could be seen the tall masts of a frigate that had escorted them upriver and then, for a time, the social life of the garrison would be augmented by naval officers in blue, white-faced uniforms, their faces ruddy or tanned from wind and sun.

In September 1782, another frigate appeared off the Ile d'Orléans to the north of Quebec. She was the *Albemarle*, commanded by Captain Horatio Nelson, which had been escorting a convoy across the Atlantic and then patrolling the coast of Massachusetts in search of French or American shipping. Off Boston, she had been chased by four French ships of the line – fugitives from Admiral Rodney's crushing victory over the French fleet at the Battle of the Saints in the Caribbean – but had managed to escape into shoal water, where they dared not follow. By the end of the summer, the frigate had been at sea since April. Without fresh vegetables and fruit and subsisting on salt beef for two months, the men were beginning to go down with scurvy.

Orders to make for Quebec saved them from disaster. The *Albemarle* glided up the wide river between wooded hills touched with red and gold as the leaves began to assume their autumn colours, and anchored off Quebec on 17 September. At once twenty-two men were sent ashore to hospital and her captain confessed that he himself was 'knocked up with scurvy'. The ship was replenished with fresh vegetables, beef, bread and beer. The clear, crisp air and rest improved the crew's health so fast that, a month later, Captain Nelson was writing to his father, 'Health, that greatest of blessings, is what I never truly enjoyed until I saw Fair Canada. The change it has wrought, I am convinced, is truly wonderful.'[4]

Five days after Nelson's arrival, the twenty-second anniversary of the coronation of King George III was celebrated by the British at Quebec. The *Albemarle* fired a salute of seventeen guns. There was a military parade and, in the evening, a ball. It was probably then that Mary Simpson met Horatio Nelson. 'Captain Nelson . . . appeared to be the merest boy of a captain I ever beheld,' wrote Prince William Henry, the future King William IV, who was to meet him soon afterwards. 'And his dress was worthy of attention. He had on a full-laced uniform: his lank, unpowdered hair was tied in a stiff Hessian tail of an extraordinary length; the old-fashioned flaps on his waistcoat added to the general appearance of quaintness of his figure . . .' But 'there was something irresistibly pleasing in his address and conversation'.[5]

The boyish captain, a few days short of his twenty-fourth birthday, cut a striking figure. He was not only very young but a veteran and, indeed, a hero of the dramatic and disastrous campaign in Nicaragua, which he had been lucky to survive. The contrast between his appearance and youth and his experience attracted immediate attention; some found him 'stern of aspect'[6] and then were surprised by his charm. When Captain Nelson met Mary Simpson there was instant attraction but while for him it was infatuation, for her it was largely delight in flattery, as she did not fall in love. Captains, as he was, did not visit the Lion d'Or and she at once set herself new and socially higher standards in the young men whose attentions she allowed, telling the ardent Captain Matthews, 'I cannot think of accepting anyone belonging to the Army whose rank was below that of colonel after having been sought by a captain of the Royal Navy.'[7] Nelson hoped that continued attention would win her in the end. Soon the river would freeze and he would be ice-bound in Quebec for the winter, allowing time for endeavour to be rewarded by success. Mary seems to have been attracted and intrigued, but not ready for such devotion, let alone marriage.

Then, early in October, orders arrived from London to prepare transports for the reception of troops to be shipped to New York. Soon after, Nelson received the half-expected order to escort the convoy: 'A very *pretty* job at this late season of the year,' he wrote to a friend, 'for our sails are at this moment frozen to the yards.'[8]

The frigate lay at anchor in the roads off the Ile de Bec, down-river from Quebec, and Nelson's new friends in the city assumed that he had gone. Until, on 15 October, one of them happened to be walking by the wharves and warehouses of the Lower Town when he saw Nelson's boat being pulled towards the landing-steps. This was Alexander Davison, a Scottish bachelor of thirty-three, sharp in looks and perception, who had made a success in shipping and trading by becoming a recognized agent for replenishing the Royal Navy and had been elected a member of the city's legislative council. He greeted Nelson and asked why he had returned. 'Walk up to your house,' came the reply, 'and you shall be acquainted with the cause.' Once alone with his friend, he continued, as Davison was to recall, 'I find it utterly impossible to leave this place without again waiting on her whose society has so much added to its charms and laying myself and my fortunes at her feet.'

Davison urged him not to throw away his promising career, remembering that he said, 'Your utter ruin, situated as you are at present, must inevitably follow.' Nelson replied, 'Then let it follow, for I am resolved to do it.' To which Davison declared,

'And I positively declare that you shall not.'[9] The older man was authoritative and persuasive and Nelson could not fail to see the sense of his advice, allowing himself to be led back to his boat. Five days later, the *Albemarle* in company with another frigate and twenty-three troop-transports, sailed for New York. Soon ice began to form in the river and Captain Matthews returned to his courtship of Mary Simpson, confident in his prospect of promotion to major in the coming year.

Nelson sailed down the St Lawrence to the Atlantic, determined to sublimate his distress and concentrate on the winning of glory. 'I think it very likely that we shall go to the Grand Theatre of Actions, the West Indies,'[10] he wrote to his father. Arriving off New York on 13 November, he reported to Rear-Admiral Digby who remarked, 'You are come on a fine station for making prize-money.' Nelson replied, 'Yes, sir, but the West Indies is the station for honour.'[11] Ambition jostled depression and he now wrote to a naval friend, 'My interest [i.e. influence] at home, you know, is next to nothing, the name of Nelson being little known. It may be different one of these days, a good chance only is wanting to make it so.'[12] Nelson was determined to make an impression, particularly when the admiral introduced him to one of his midshipmen, Prince William Henry, the son of King George III. While noting the young captain's old-fashioned appearance, the prince was admiring of his 'enthusiasm when speaking on professional subjects that showed he was no common being'.[13] Still affecting to despise prize-money – 'Money is the great object here; nothing else is attended to'[14] – Nelson was delighted when ordered to the Caribbean.

His months among the islands were not rewarding financially – most of the prize-money for a valuable French ship he captured was claimed by his admiral since it had been taken within sight of his squadron, and he failed to take a small island defended by the French – but were memorable for the development of his friendship with the King's son. The war was now ending, the American colonies having won their independence, and preliminaries for a peace treaty were signed at Versailles on

20 January 1783. The *Albemarle* was ordered home at the end of the month and anchored off Portsmouth on 25 June.

It was a hot summer in London but Nelson did not go to Norfolk, although he had initially planned to do so. News reached him from his brother William, who was staying at Burnham Thorpe, that Nancy had returned home and their father was taking her to Bath in the hope of inspiring a fresh start. Susannah, who had given birth to twins at the end of 1781, had accompanied her husband Tom Bolton to Ostend soon afterwards, staying while he conducted his trading from there and returning early in 1783. Kate, he heard, was not well. He himself was ill – probably with a bout of recurrent malaria – and was confined to his room in Salisbury Street for a fortnight, before visiting his uncle William in Kentish Town 'to breathe a little fresh air'.[15]

Resuming his friendship with Prince William Henry, he was invited to Windsor Castle and was presented to the King at a levée in St James's Palace. Alexander Davison, who had dissuaded him from resigning his commission, was also in London and Nelson spent hours at his rooms in Lincoln's Inn discussing their plans for the future, including, in Davison's case, politics. One handicap of which Nelson was conscious was his inability to speak any foreign language. Now that the war had ended, there was a chance to travel on the Continent, so he decided to learn French, the language of the traditional enemy. His ship having been paid off, he was granted six months' leave and, in October, set out for France.

That summer and autumn, it was the fashion for the English to cross the Channel, whether out of curiosity, or seeking opportunities for trade, or to learn French and acquire some of the cultural polish for which France was celebrated. After several hours of bouncing across to Calais, they usually headed inland, because the port itself had a rough, waterfront reputation for being frequented by English smugglers and exiled debtors. Far more seemly was the substantial town of Saint-Omer-en-Artois, with its fine Gothic churches and streets of stone-fronted houses, some of which let rooms to the visiting English. At one of these there arrived that autumn the Andrews family: the Reverend Robert Andrews from Tiverton in Devon with his son and two daughters.

Travelling with another naval officer, Nelson had landed at Calais, spent an uncomfortable few days stopping at dirty inns along the road and noted the social stratification of France – 'no middling class of people'.[16] On reaching Saint-Omer, he had been pleasantly surprised to find 'instead of a dirty, nasty town . . . a large city, well paved, good streets and well-lighted'. There they had taken rooms at Madame La Mourie's lodging-house, which seemed the more agreeable for the presence of their landlady's vivacious daughters. One girl brought them their breakfast and the other, their tea; after supper, both would sit with them and play cards. However, neither girl spoke English and neither naval officer spoke French so social intercourse was limited to smiles, sign language and girlish giggles.

Despite Nelson's purchase of Chambaud's *Grammar of the French Tongue*, his studies made little progress. This was partly because there was little need to speak French when the town seemed so full of English. It was early in November that they met another, much younger naval officer, Midshipman George Andrews, who had gone to sea in 1778, aged twelve. He had already served in American waters and the Caribbean and fought in three actions, but his career had faltered when in one of those his uncle and patron, Captain John Nott, with whom he had gone to sea, had been killed. He was the son of the Devonshire parson and one of his sisters, Elizabeth, had come to perfect her French and put into practice the accomplishments and social graces expected of her kind. A girl of fresh, open prettiness, with soft, dark hair and large, gentle brown eyes, her ladylike manner was accentuated in this foreign setting. When the two young captains introduced themselves to her father, it was natural that she and her sister should engage them in conversation and, in the evening, sing and play for them on the piano.

There did not seem any reason for Elizabeth to be particularly attentive until, soon after their arrival, a letter reached Nelson. This told him that his sister Anne – poor Nancy – was dead.

Staying at Bath with her father in the hope of rehabilitation, she had died, aged twenty-three, 'after a nine days' illness . . . occasioned by coming out of the ballroom immediately after dancing'.[17] Nelson wrote to his brother William, 'My surprise and grief upon the occasion are, you will suppose, more to be felt than described.' He had, he said, 'been very near coming to England',[18] but there was nothing he could do, since she had died more than a week before he heard the news. Meanwhile, he was comforted by Elizabeth Andrews, whose sympathy engendered a sudden intimacy, made more potent by her artless sincerity.

Nelson was soon in love, even writing to an old naval mentor, Captain William Locker, that although 'my mind is too much taken up with the recent account of my sister's death to partake of any amusements', he had met an English clergyman with 'two very agreeable daughters grown up, about twenty years of age, who play and sing to us whenever we go. I must take care of my heart, I assure you.'[19]

On 4 December, Nelson was writing to his brother William about worries arising from his sister's death. He feared for his father after such a shock: 'Tell me, if he recovers, whether he means to return to Burnham in the summer. I hope most sincerely he does not for the journey alone is enough to destroy him and a Burnham winter must kill him.' Even more, he worried about his youngest sister, his mind filling with dire imaginings: 'What is to become of poor Kate? Although I am very fond of Mrs Bolton [Susannah], yet I own I should not like to see Kate fixed in a Wells' society.' He would, if necessary, return to England immediately 'and most probably fix in some place that might be most for poor Kitty's advantage. My small income shall always be at her service and she shall never want a protector and a sincere friend while I exist.'

He then turned to himself:

> St Omer increases much upon me and I am as happy as I can be . . . My heart is quite secured against the French beauties: I almost wish I could say as much for an English

> young lady, the daughter of a clergyman, with whom I am just going to dine and spend the day. She has such accomplishments that, had I a million of money, I am sure that I should at this moment make her an offer of them: my income is at present by far too small to think of marriage and she has no fortune.[20]

Yet as intimacy increased, he discovered that the Andrews family was socially well connected. Elizabeth's mother, Sarah Andrews, was the daughter of Sir Caesar Hawkins, a surgeon to the King, and the negro's head in their family crest suggested that her father's family had profited from the slave trade; and, Nelson learned, Elizabeth herself possessed 'a small fortune – £1,000, I understand'.[21] However, a proud young man like Nelson would not consider living on his wife's money and would need to offer more than that capital. His own annual income was £130 and what remained of Maurice Suckling's legacy was held in readiness for a family emergency, particularly one affecting Kate.

Elizabeth Andrews was probably no more in love with Nelson than Mary Simpson had been, although she was sympathetic and clearly liked him. Everyone found him good company; he had a lively mind and was a good story-teller (stories of the Nicaraguan jungle must have been exceptionally exciting in Saint-Omer, particularly to her young brother, George). But Nelson was in love with her and imagined that, if only he was a man of means, she would consider a proposal of marriage. One bond might be through George and here the benefit would possibly be mutual. The boy's grandfather, Sir Caesar, was a friend of Admiral Lord Howe, the First Lord of the Admiralty, and might put in a word for Nelson who in turn could, and did, offer to replace John Nott as George's patron and, when he was appointed to another command, take the boy to sea with him and foster his career.

The key to success then, as Nelson saw it, was money. If he could offer Elizabeth the continuation of her standard of living, his courtship would succeed. But promotion and the prospect of prize-money lay in the future; for the present he would need a loan and the only relation of means who could be asked was William Suckling. Nelson wrote a letter to his uncle that bore the signs of having been revised repeatedly and eschewed cajolery and blandishment to the point where it became demanding.

> There comes a time in a man's life (who has friends), that either they place him in life in a situation that makes his application for anything further totally unnecessary, or give him help in a pecuniary way, if they can afford and he deserves it. The critical moment in my life is now arrived that either I am to be happy or miserable – it depends solely on you. You may think I am going to ask too much. I have led myself up with hopes you will not – till this trying moment. There is a lady I have seen, of a good family and connexions, but with a small fortune – £1,000, I understand. The whole of my income does not exceed £130 per annum. Now I must come to the point – will you, if I should marry, allow me yearly £100 until my income is increased to that sum either by employment, or any other way? A very few years I hope would turn something up, if my friends will but exert themselves.

If his uncle could not, or would not, help, Nelson asked him to use his influence with Lord North, who had, in fact, just resigned as Prime Minister, to have him appointed to a sinecure, such as the command of a guardship or some post ashore. Otherwise, he would be happy with the command of the East India Company's small naval force, a job which would be well paid. In conclusion, he wrote:

> You must excuse the freedom with which this letter is dictated. Not to have been plain and explicit in my distress has been cruel to myself. If nothing can be done for me, I know what I have to trust to. Life is not worth preserving without happiness; and I care not where I may linger out a

> miserable existence. I am prepared to hear your refusal and have fixed my resolution if that should happen; but in every situation I shall be a well-wisher to you and your family and pray they, or you, may never know the pangs which at this instant tear my heart.[22]

It says much for William Suckling's generosity of mind, as well as of pocket, that he agreed to comply. But by the time his nephew knew of this he was back in England, his dream of connubial bliss ended. There had been no quarrel and no falling out with Elizabeth, who had gently led him to understand, without hurting his feelings, that she did not wish to marry him.* At first he tried to lose himself in fast-living, writing to his brother William, 'My time has been so much taken up by running at the ring of pleasure that I have almost neglected all my friends – for London has so many charms that a man's time is wholly taken up.'[23] He considered the possibilities of politics, encouraged by Alexander Davison, for the great general election campaign of 1784 was in spate and several naval officers, including Lord Hood, were standing. He then went to visit his father in Bath, intending to travel to Norfolk, where Kate – 'She is a charming young woman and possesses a great share of sense' – was staying with Susannah. He longed for Norfolk, sending his compliments to his friends there and wondering about news he had heard of dangerously high tides along the east coast: 'Is the bank down at Wells? Tell me all your Norfolk news.' Yet the prospect of returning to Burnham Thorpe without the joy of introducing Elizabeth to his family and friends, blighted the prospect. 'I return to many charming women,' he told William, 'but no charming woman will return with me.'[24]

The idea of returning to Saint-Omer for a final effort at persuasion he tried to dismiss with the casual aside, 'I want to be proficient in the language, which is my only reason for returning. I hate

* Elizabeth Andrews (1762–1837) married the Reverend Richard Farrer and, after his death, Lieutenant-Colonel Roger Warne, who died in 1845, aged ninety-one. She had no children.

their country and their manners.'[25] He was saved from this temptation on 18 March by orders from the Admiralty to take command of the frigate *Boreas*, which was 'ready to sail from Woolwich but to what part of the World I know not'.[26] This gave him the added satisfaction of being able to respond to Elizabeth's kindliness with a gentlemanly gesture: he wrote to offer her brother George a berth in his new command.

To be captain of a ship of twenty-eight guns bound for the West Indies to join the small squadron of frigates on the Leeward Islands Station, commanded by Rear-Admiral Sir Richard Hughes, was a stimulating prospect. There might be no war, but there was the task of trade-protection in stopping American ships trading with the British islands while still making use of the privileges they had enjoyed when themselves colonials. The voyage across the Atlantic would be crowded, because he would have thirty midshipmen, bound for other ships, as passengers, one of them a distant cousin, named after his uncle, Maurice Suckling; another, George Andrews, was to follow in another frigate. Also on board would be his own brother William, who had cultivated a romantic ambition of becoming a naval chaplain; now Horatio was giving him his chance.

It did seem that for at least a month he would be away from female company – other than the purser's wife – that might prompt distracting thoughts of Elizabeth and worries about Kate. Then he was ordered to embark two more passengers at Portsmouth: Lady Hughes, the wife of the admiral he was to serve, and her daughter, Rosy. So crowded was the ship on this long passage that one evening he counted on the narrow quarterdeck twenty-seven officers, non-commissioned officers and midshipmen, apart from himself, his brother, the purser and his wife and the two Hughes women. Those two were a trial to Nelson: the mother was voluble and irritated him by calling his ship 'dear *Boreas*'[27] because her husband had once commanded the frigate; and the daughter was as plain as she was excitable. 'What a specimen of English beauty,'[28] he remarked sarcastically. Even worse than Lady Hughes's 'eternal clack'[29] was the realization that she was casting a predatory eye over eligible officers

– himself included – in search of a potential son-in-law. Yet Lady Hughes was a more intelligent and perceptive passenger than Nelson may have thought, particularly in her assessment of himself. As an admiral's wife, she was aware of the qualities necessary for command and she found them in Nelson. She was to say later:

> As a woman, I can only speak of those parts of his professional conduct which I could comprehend, such as his attention to the young gentlemen, who had the happiness of being on his quarter-deck. Among the number of thirty, there must have been timid spirits as well as bold: the timid he never rebuked but always wished to show them he desired nothing that he would not instantly do himself: and I have known him say, 'Well, sir, I am going a race to the mast-head and beg I may meet you there.' No denial could be given to such a request and the poor little fellow instantly began to climb the shrouds. Captain Nelson never took the least notice in what manner it was done: but when they met in the top, spoke in the most cheerful terms to the midshipman and observed how any person was to be pitied, who could fancy there was any danger, or even anything disagreeable in the attempt. After this excellent example, I have seen the same youth, who before was so timid, lead another in the like manner and repeat his commander's words. How wise and attentive was such conduct in Captain Nelson![30]

When the ship arrived off Barbados and anchored in Carlisle Bay on 26 June, Lady Hughes and her daughter were put ashore, having invited Nelson to dine with her husband and General Shirley, the Governor of the Leeward Islands. 'You must permit me, Lady Hughes, to carry one of my aide-de-camps with me,' he replied, asking if he might bring a midshipman with him, explaining later to the Governor, 'Your Excellency must forgive me for bringing one of my midshipmen, as I make it a rule to introduce them to all the good company I can as they have few to look up to, beside myself, during the time they are at sea.'[31]

Despite the irritation of his passengers, Nelson had performed his task to the satisfaction of the admiral, but the approval was not reciprocated. Sir Richard made a poor impression on him – 'The Admiral and all about him are great ninnies'[32] – and he was glad to be away from his womenfolk. It was common gossip that the arrival of Lady Hughes had interrupted a love affair her husband had been enjoying on the island. Meanwhile, Rosy's hunt for a husband succeeded and Nelson reported, 'A bold Major Browne of the 67th. Regiment is the man . . . God help the poor man, has he taken leave of his senses? O, what a taste. The mother will be in a few years the handsomest of the two.'[33] He himself was relieved at being ordered to his own station, which was to command the frigates to the north, based on English Harbour in Antigua, where they were to be laid up for the imminent hurricane season.

The *Boreas* arrived off Antigua on 28 July 1784, in heavy tropical rain that obliterated the view of the hills above English Harbour. The downpour drummed on the wooden shingles roofing the wide-eaved, single-storey houses and warehouses and blotted out the prospect of the dockyard and the deep, almost landlocked basins. It was here in this secluded 'hurricane hole' that British frigates on the Leeward Islands Station sheltered from summer storms and spent the time refitting and preparing for another season at sea. There were wooden houses for officers down by the dockyard; one, Windsor, built on a little hill above it to catch what sea breeze there might be, was the grandest and this was the residence of the Admiralty's Commissioner for the Dockyard and his family.

This was currently Captain John Moutray, his wife Mary and their eleven-year-old twins, James and Kate. From their veranda, they would be able to see, once the rain had cleared, the frigate *Mediator*, which was already lying off the dockyard, and the *Boreas* as she approached the shore batteries at the harbour mouth from the open sea. The Moutrays had already met Captain Cuthbert Collingwood of the *Mediator*, because they had travelled to the West Indies in his ship and had heard from him about his friend Captain Nelson. During the coming hurricane season, the couple would rely heavily on the two officers for company at their house.

Captain and Mrs Moutray were an unlikely pair to meet in such a place. Both belonged to the Lowland Scottish, or Border, gentry: he, related to the Mowbray family, came from a line of lairds in Fife; she, the daughter of Captain Thomas Pemble of the Royal Navy, had been brought up in Berwick on the other side of the Firth of Forth. She had been an attractive, vivacious girl welcomed into aristocratic circles through her friendship with a daughter of the Marquess of Lothian. At twenty, she had married Captain Moutray, then a widower aged forty-nine. They had moved to London, where she had borne the twins, and joined its smart society. She had had her portrait painted by John Downman and this showed her, fashionably dressed, her powdered hair piled high, as an intelligent, sophisticated woman, with laughter-wrinkles around the eyes suggesting wit.

Then, in 1780, Captain Moutray's career collapsed in ignominy. Commanding the escort of a valuable convoy, he had lost the merchant ships to a Franco-Spanish squadron but saved the warships and himself. There was outrage in Britain, where it was expected that the commander of an escort should fight to the last. The Admiralty ordered Moutray to be court-martialled and he was found guilty and dismissed from his ship. Yet Moutray was well connected and generally liked, so two years later he was found alternative employment. Retired from active duty on half-pay, he was appointed Commissioner to the Dockyard at English Harbour. All too aware of his disgrace, he insisted on wearing his post-captain's uniform rather than a commissioner's plain blue uniform coat. Throughout, his wife had stood by him and now set about being not only supportive but also a charming hostess to those naval officers who came their way.

She had begun by welcoming Captain Cuthbert Collingwood. An apparently sombre Northumbrian, lacking Nelson's connections, his promotion had been slower and in his mid-forties he was still commanding only a frigate. When he had been ordered to carry the Moutrays to Antigua, he sniffed, 'Those Moutrays will be an expense to me. I don't mind that if they are pleasant and satisfied: their going to the country I am to be stationed in will give them an opportunity of showing their thankfulness for my attentions.'[34] Despite Collingwood's curmudgeonly manner, though, Mary Moutray saw another side to his character and, at the end of the Atlantic crossing, was able to declare:

> Although the vigour of his mind was soon discovered, there was a degree of reserve in his manner which prevented the playfulness of his imagination and his powers of adding charms to private society from being duly appreciated. But the intimacy of a long passage in his ship gave us the good fortune to know him as he was, so that after our arrival at St John's, or English Harbour, he was as a beloved brother in our house.[35]

Nelson too had discovered the humour and generosity behind the austere presence of the tall, dour Collingwood since they had first met as midshipmen and for the past six years the latter had repeatedly followed the former in sea appointments, despite the fact that, although junior in rank, he was a decade senior in age. So, soon after the *Boreas* berthed at English Harbour, Collingwood took Nelson and his brother William, the frigate's chaplain, up the hill to meet the Moutrays at Windsor. Despite his irritation that Captain Moutray, who was now sixty-one, was wearing an apparently unauthorized naval uniform, Nelson found him an agreeable host and his wife – now thirty-two and so more than five years his senior – delightful.

William Nelson was glad to be out of the cramped, lurching little ship and had decided that the life of a naval chaplain was not for him. At English Harbour it was even worse, for the ship was to be refitted and painted, so the officers lived in a mess ashore, tormented by mosquitoes at night. Not sorry to be rid of his self-centred, loud-voiced brother, Horatio arranged for

William's passage home and meanwhile he and Collingwood were invited to stay at the Moutrays' house, which was less plagued by mosquitoes. Soon he was writing to William:

> I hope you are quite recovered and very near to old England. The weather has been so very hot since you left us that I firmly believe you would hardly have weathered the fever, which has carried off several of the ship's company of the *Boreas* since you left us . . . I have been living here for this past week, whilst my ship has been painting . . . Mrs. Moutray desires her love to you.'[36]

When Mary Moutray first met Horatio Nelson he was not at his best. Since leaving New York, he had had another bout of malaria, which he had first suffered when a midshipman on the coast of India; he had probably been reinfected in Nicaragua. Because of sweating and irritation, he had shaved his head and, since he had been in the habit of powdering his own hair on formal occasions, he did not own a wig. On the Caribbean islands he had visited the only wig he had been able to buy was small, crudely made and yellow. This was now perched on his head and appeared so comical, particularly beside Collingwood, who still wore his hair in a neatly tied queue falling to his shoulders, that Mary Moutray was amused. However, aware that Nelson was sensitive to ridicule, she managed to laugh with him and not at him, and even suggested that he and Collingwood draw portraits of each other and their contrasting hairstyles. Nelson managed a creditable silhouette of Collingwood, who himself painted Nelson, also in profile, looking tense and ill at ease in his yellow wig.

Nelson must have been as surprised as he was delighted to meet such a woman in such a place. There below, in the 'hurricane hole', lay his ship, his cabin hot, stuffy, reeking of paint and tar, noisy by day with hammering and by night with the whine of mosquitoes. Up above on the hill was elegance shaded by louvre'd windows, with silver reflected on polished mahogany and a hostess he might have expected to meet in London. She obviously delighted in the company of these two new friends and Collingwood warmly responded, but in Nelson there was probably something more. Twice disappointed in love, he was hungry for romantic affection and, although out of reach, Mary Moutray represented an ideal. His mentions of her in letters home suggest that his feelings for her went beyond ordinary friendship. 'Was it not for Mrs. Moutray, who is *very*, *very* good to me,' he wrote to his friend Captain Locker, 'I should almost hang myself in this infernal hole.'[37]

Jealousy may have played a part in a confrontation that now arose between Nelson and Captain Moutray. Already Nelson had been irritated by the fact that Moutray wore full naval uniform and angered by receiving letters addressed to himself as 'Second in Command of His Majesty's Ships at English Harbour', which he took to imply that Moutray and not he was the senior naval officer. This came to a head early in 1785, when the weather had improved and the frigates began to cruise again. On 5 February, when the *Boreas* returned to English Harbour, Nelson was astonished to see another frigate, the *Latona*, commanded by a more junior captain, flying the broad pendant of a commodore. The officer was summoned on board and Nelson asked him brusquely, 'Have you any order from Sir Richard Hughes to wear a broad pendant?' On being told 'No', he went on, 'For what reason then do you wear it in the presence of a senior officer?' and received the answer, 'I hoisted it by order of Commissioner Moutray.' When Nelson then enquired, 'Have you seen by what authority Commissioner Moutray was empowered to give you orders?' and was told 'No,' he said, 'Sir, you have acted wrong to obey any man you do not know is authorised to command you.' The captain then replied, 'I feel I have acted wrong but being a young captain did not think proper to interfere in this matter as there were you and other older officers upon this station.'[38]

Nelson was determined to take the matter further. Although Commissioner Moutray had been his attentive host and, as he wrote, 'my only valuable friend in these islands',[39] he did not discuss the misunderstanding with him. Instead, he wrote

Admiral Hughes a letter of complaint, sending a copy of it to Moutray with a covering note saying, 'I cannot obey any order I may receive from you but shall ever be studious to show every respect and attention which your situation as a commissioner of the Navy demands.' He ended by asking that Moutray be 'assured with what personal esteem I am your devoted, faithful, humble servant, Horatio Nelson'.[40]

The admiral's reply was terse, stating not only that he had authorized Commissioner Moutray to hoist a commodore's pendant but that captains of Royal Navy ships would be under his command while they lay in English Harbour. So Nelson, declaring that he recognized no superiors but the Lords Commissioners of the Admiralty and those above him in the active Navy List, wrote a long letter of complaint to Philip Stephens, the Secretary to the Admiralty, and, by so doing, disregarded the formal courtesies of naval communication, for only Admiral Hughes should have referred the case to London. That he did so suggests that he wished to assert himself by getting the better of Moutray, whom he saw, albeit subconsciously, as a rival. The outcome was that Nelson, in due course, was reprimanded by the Admiralty for not having passed his complaint through the admiral, with whom he had, as a result, soured his relations. However, his point was made and thereafter naval commissioners were always serving officers on full pay.

Surprisingly, the incident did not spoil his friendship with the Moutrays. The commissioner was magnanimous and his wife may have understood the underlying tensions that had provoked it. She recognized Nelson as a driven man, sometimes under-confident and over-zealous, while she was able to maintain a happy, relaxed friendship with Collingwood. It was he, not Nelson, with whom she would share confidences; it was he who was allowed such intimacies as helping her prepare for a dance – as he recalled it in a letter to her, 'frizzing your head for a ball at Antigua'.[41]

Yet the joys of Windsor were about to end. 'Commissioner Moutray has but ill health,' wrote Collingwood. 'I am afraid we shall lose them: they are very desirous to get home and if he is not recalled I think he will resign. I shall miss them grievously; she is quite a delight and makes many an hour cheerful that without her would be dead weight.'[42] A few days afterwards, Nelson was writing to his brother William:

> My dear sweet friend is going home. I am really an April day; happy on her account but truly grieved were I only to consider myself. Her equal I never saw in any country, or in any situation. She always talks of you and hopes, if she comes within your reach, you will not fail visiting her. If my dear Kate goes to Bath next winter, she will be known to her; for my dear friend has promised to make herself known. What an acquisition to any female to be acquainted with: what an example to take pattern from. Moutray has been very ill: it would have been necessary he should have quitted this country had he not been recalled.

He added in a postscript, 'My sweet, amiable friend sails the 20th. for England. I took my leave of her with a heavy heart three days ago. What a *treasure* of a woman. God bless her.'[43]

When Collingwood made his farewell, she gave him a purse of netting that she had made for him and he thanked her with a verse he had written for her:

> Your net shall be my care, my dear,
> For length of time to come,
> While I am faint and scorching here
> And you rejoice at home.
> To you belongs the wondrous art
> To shed around you pleasure;
> New worth to best of things impart,
> And make of trifles – treasure.[44]

Again life in English Harbour became an ordeal. As Nelson wrote:

> This country appears now intolerable, my dear friend being absent. It is barren indeed; not all the Rosys can give

> a spark of joy to me. English Harbour I hate the sight of and 'Windsor' I detest. I went once up the hill to look at the spot where I spent more happy days than in any one spot in the world. E'en the trees dropped their heads and the tamarind tree died: all was melancholy. The road is covered with thistles: let them grow; I shall never pull one of them up. By this time I hope she is safe in old England. Heaven's choicest blessings go with her.'[45]

At once, both men wrote to her, and she replied from Bath. Again Nelson's jealousy – or, perhaps, suspicion of what he imagined might be a jealous husband – returned when it seemed that the sealing-wafer on her letter to him had been opened, as, she told him, had that on his letter to her. 'My first letter from her came to me with the wafer open but it is very odd that both our letters should be in the same situation. They were welcome to read mine; it was all goodness, like the dear writer.'[46] Collingwood's letters to her were written with a light touch and did not forget her children: 'I wish you had one of those fairy telescopes that can look into the hearts and souls of people a thousand leagues off, then you might see how much you possess my mind and how sincere an interest I take in whatever relates to your happiness and that of dear Kate.'[47]

It seemed probable that John Moutray would not live long. Although both captains wrote regularly to Mary Moutray in Bath, there was, after her initial replies, a long silence and Nelson took this as a personal slight. After six months he wrote with a touch of sarcasm, 'Mrs. Moutray is still there [Bath] but I have not had a line from her, it is wonderful and I can't account for it. I know myself to be so steady in my friendships that I can't bear the least coolness or inattention in others.'[48] Then a stricken letter did arrive from her to say that her husband had died in November 1785.

If Commissioner Moutray had died before departing English Harbour, leaving his widow and children under the protection of their two friends until future plans could be made, both men might have entertained thoughts of an eventual marriage. Under such circumstances, would Mary Moutray have considered either of them? If so, it is tempting to think that Nelson would have been her choice, but the truth is it was more likely to have been Collingwood.

3
Fanny

Twenty-five miles across the sea from Antigua rose the volcanic cone of Mount Nevis, often flying from the summit a streamer of cloud, white as the image of snow that gave the island its name. The mountain stood some 3,000 feet above the thirty-six square miles of green slopes falling away from tropical scrub through evergreen trees to groves of tall palms, white surf and blue or peacock sea. Soil compounded of ancient lava had left it vibrantly fertile so that the lower slopes rippled with the leaves of sugar cane. Against the greenery shone the white walls of the plantation houses and sugar factories. For its size, this island, settled by the British, was the richest and most fashionable in the Caribbean.

Among the most charming of some seventy great houses of the sugar plantations was Montpelier, lying more than 600 feet up the southern flank of the mountain and so commanding a serene prospect of sea and sky. Here, the ocean breeze could blow through the open-slatted shutters that shielded the rooms from the sun. On the lawns around the house stood tall trees, while the carriage-drive ran between handsome piers topped with stone globes to the lane that led to the estate's sugar mill and boiling-house worked by African slaves.

The lady of this house was a poised young woman of twenty-seven, Frances Nisbet, known as Fanny to her family and friends and regarded by them as the epitome of sophistication. She had been brought up on Nevis, where her father, William Woolward, had been the senior judge. When just past twenty she had married Josiah Nisbet, the young doctor who had attended her father's last illness, and she had borne him a son, also named Josiah, who was now aged five. Her husband was not suited to the tropics, being over-sensitive to strong sun, and suffering from other ailments arising from the climate. For this reason they had returned to England, but Josiah had sickened and died at Salisbury in 1781, leaving his widow to return in sorrow to her family in the West Indies.

As it happened, Fanny's maternal uncle, John Herbert, the President of the Council of Nevis, was a widower and had quarrelled with his daughter, Martha, over her choice of husband, so suggested that his niece take over her duties as chatelaine of Montpelier. Herbert was a rich and demanding man, but Fanny was able to perform her undemanding tasks as hostess, arranging her uncle's social calendar, organizing hospitality and overseeing the servants with confidence, lack of apparent effort and to his satisfaction. Fanny was an ornament to his house, competent in such ladylike accomplishments as playing the piano, sewing, conversation and speaking drawing-room French; her refined good looks – an English complexion, shielded from the sun, dark eyes and brown curls, a delicately bridged nose with arching nostrils – gave her an air of gentility.

For Fanny and the other young women of the plantation houses and the little town of Charlestown, one of their few problems was finding suitable husbands among so small a community. Such young bachelors as there were often left to find wives in England, or had taken a black mistress, while others had succumbed to the temptations of drink and gambling. One of the occasional chances to meet eligible young men was when a British warship put in to Charlestown, usually to fill her water casks at the nearby spring, which was noted for its purity. So when a ship anchored off the island, the names of the captain and his lieutenants, and, if possible, their social eligibility and professional prospects, were quickly circulated among the young women.

This occurred again in the spring of 1785, when the *Boreas* anchored off Charlestown and Captain Horatio Nelson came ashore. The interlude at English Harbour in the company of Mary Moutray had been a sunlit moment in an otherwise lowering scene. Some of his worries were those occupying to any senior officer, particularly in the tropics: drunkenness, indiscipline and venereal disease among the ship's company. As to the officers, the combination of the climate and abundant alcohol often meant outbreaks of quarrelling, sometimes leading to serious trouble. The worst such problem for Nelson involved young George Andrews, the brother of his once-beloved Elizabeth, who had joined the ship in the Caribbean. In February, Nelson had written to his brother William, who, of course, knew those concerned:

> All my children are well except one, young Andrews. He came out in the *Unicorn*: do you remember him? On 11 November last, he was forced by Mr. Stainsbury to fight a duel, which terminated fatally for the poor lad: the ball is lodged in his back and whether he will ever get the better of it God knows. He has kept his bed ever since. His antagonist, and Mr. Oliver, his second are in irons since the duel. They will stand a good chance of hanging if the youth should unfortunately die.'[1]

In the event, George Andrews survived and Stainsbury and Oliver were discharged from the *Boreas*.

A far more pressing problem was political. Nelson had returned to the West Indies avid to make as much of a mark in peace as he had in war. But with the end of the American war and the independence of the former colonies there, the Royal Navy had only one apparent task. That was to enforce the Navigation Act, which precluded the Americans from trading with British colonies in the Caribbean on the favourable terms they had formerly enjoyed. That they were continuing to assume their lost privileges was immediately apparent and what Nelson soon came to realize was that this was with the connivance of the British merchants with whom they had long been trading to mutual advantage and most of the officials and officers whose duty was to prohibit this.

With the agreement of Collingwood, Nelson had set about enforcing the law, declaring, 'The residents of these islands are American by connexion and interest and inimical to Great Britain. They are as great rebels as ever were in America.'[2] As he stopped and searched ships, seized cargoes and prevented the Americans from trading, he aroused the anger of not only the ship-owners and traders but also the senior officers, including the admiral and the Governor of the Leeward Islands. He reacted strongly, telling the latter, who alluded to his youth, that he belonged to the same generation as William Pitt: 'I have the honour, sir, of being as old as the Prime Minister of England and think myself as capable of commanding one of His Majesty's ships as that Minister is of governing the State.'[3] He even wrote memoranda to the Admiralty and a memorial to the King, but before replies could cross the Atlantic he had been served with a writ charging him with assault and wrongful arrest by American sea-captains, supported by the residents of the island of Nevis.

Nelson knew he had the government and the law on his side and he remained a commanding officer of a king's ship, so those in authority were bound to receive him and he made sure that they did. One of these was the President of the Council of Nevis. 'Herbert is very rich and very proud,'[4] Nelson wrote. 'Although his income is immense yet his expenses must be great as his house is open to all strangers and he entertains most hospitably.'[5] Twice at the beginning of 1785, Nelson took the road from Charlestown, past the newly built Bath House Hotel, which had sulphur baths in its basement, past the little parish church at Fig Tree, to Montpelier. On both occasions, Herbert's principal hostess, his niece Fanny, was away visiting friends on the neighbouring island of St Kitts.

After the second occasion, when he had dined at Monpelier, another of Herbert's nieces had written to Fanny:

> We have at last seen the little captain of the *Boreas*, of whom so much has been said. He came up just before

> dinner, much heated and was very silent yet seemed, according to the old adage, to think the more. He declined drinking any wine: but after dinner when the President, as usual, has the three following toasts, the King, the Queen and the Royal Family and Lord Hood [the naval commander-in-chief], this strange man regularly filled his glass and observed that those were always bumper toasts with him; which, having drank, he uniformly passed the bottle and relapsed into his former taciturnity.
>
> It was impossible during this visit for any of us to make out his real character; there was such a reserve and sternness in his behaviour, with occasional sallies, though very transient, of a superior mind. Being placed by him, I endeavoured to rouse his attention by showing him all the civilities in my power; but I drew out little more than yes and no. If you, Fanny, had been there, we think you would have made something of him for you have been in the habit of attending to these odd sort of people.[6]

No letter could have aroused Fanny's interest more than this. She had not long to wait. On his third visit to Montpelier, the lonely Captain Nelson – barred from most European houses in the Leeward Islands for his uncompromising stand on American trade – arrived early. A negro servant showed him into the drawing-room, where a little boy of five was crawling on the floor. After a few moments Herbert himself entered and later reported, 'Great God! If I did not find that great little man, of whom everyone is so afraid, playing in the next room under the dining-table with Mrs. Nisbet's child.'[7] Soon Fanny herself arrived and the two were introduced. She had been well prepared by curiosity and attraction was sharpened by finding that this notoriously difficult and taciturn officer had been playing with her little son.

Although not handsome, the captain had an intelligent face and, of course, the uniform enhanced any man's appearance. To him, Fanny was not only a charming young woman who presented him with a prospect of idyllic domesticity but was also available. This was no Mary Moutray, committed to her marriage, or a beautiful young woman hunting for a rich and socially eligible husband of rank and title, but a widow, a few months older than himself, who was clearly in need of a second husband and a father-figure for her child. She noted his gentlemanly manners and he, her ladylike poise. Soon he would be writing to his brother William, 'Her manners are Mrs. Moutray's.'[8] The attraction was mutual. Both seemed to have found what they sought.

The *Boreas* was 'always on the wing'[9] but now returned to anchor off Charlestown whenever possible. Up at Montpelier, the relationship developed happily and Fanny met Cuthbert Collingwood, who told her 'of the conquest she had made'.[10] The courtship was conducted discreetly in the seclusion of the plantation house and its spreading gardens. Quite soon, it seems, Nelson proposed marriage and was accepted, but no announcement could be made until Fanny's uncle had granted his assent. Before that could be sought, the *Boreas* was ordered back to English Harbour, so the couple had to rely on letter-writing.

Nelson wrote to Herbert, asking for his niece's hand in marriage, and in August, while awaiting his reply, sent a long, verbose letter to Fanny, beginning:

> To say how anxious I have been and am to receive a line from Mr. Herbert would be far beyond the descriptive powers of my pen. Most fervently do I hope his answer will be of such a tendency as to convey real pleasure not only to myself but also to you for most sincerely do I love you and I trust that my affection is not only founded upon the principles of reason but also upon the basis of mutual attachment, indeed, my charming Fanny, did I possess a million my greatest pride and pleasure would be to share it with you; and, as I am, to live in a cottage with you I should esteem superior to living in a palace with any other I have yet met with.[11]

He was still slightly in awe of her, as his circumlocution seemed to show. And he went on:

> My age is enough to make me seriously reflect upon what I have offered and common sense tells me what a good choice I have made. The more I weigh you in my mind, the more reason I find to admire both your head and heart. But come, don't say, 'What a vain young man is this, 'tis a modest way of telling me I have given proof of my sense by accepting him.' No, to your heart do I own myself most indebted yet I trust you approved of me for this obvious reason. 'He esteems me, therefore he is the person I ought to expect most happiness from by return of affection . . .' My temper you know as well as myself for by longer acquaintance you will find I possess not the art of concealing it. My situation and family I have not endeavoured to conceal. Don't think me rude for this entering into a correspondence with you . . .

Then, relaxing, he showed that they shared a taste for social gossip, beginning a mildly scandalous catalogue of such with, 'The Admiral is in high spirits at having left her Ladyship at Barbados.' Chatter about which young officer was in pursuit of which young lady – discreetly identifying them only by initials – gave way to a wistful reference to his own past attachment: 'I had a long letter from my good Mrs. Moutray, who is well, thank God. A more amiable woman can hardly exist. I wish you knew her.'[12]

When Nelson eventually did hear from Fanny's uncle he was disappointed. Mr Herbert was friendly but circumspect, wanting to discuss matters further before taking decisions and this, he assumed, was because of money and prospects. Nelson knew that Herbert was rich: 'The stock of negroes upon his estate and cattle are valued at £60,000 sterling and he sends to England . . . 500 casks of sugar . . . as he says, and told me at first, that he looked upon his niece as his child, I can have no reason to suppose that he will not provide handsomely for her.' Fearing that Herbert might suspect him of being a fortune-hunter and, in any case, would not want to see her reduced to sharing a captain's pay, or half-pay when unemployed, he cast about for means of increasing his income.

When the two men did meet again, Nelson's apprehensions proved well founded. He decided upon a humble approach to Herbert and lightly declared himself to be 'as poor as Job'.[13] Herbert told him that Fanny stood to inherit £20,000 from him and possibly more. Meanwhile, his own expenses were so high that he could not settle an annual income of more than £300 upon her, and in any case he would require her to stay on Nevis, acting as his hostess until he retired and returned to England in two years' time. He liked Nelson and gave him to understand that if the couple waited two years and he was satisfied with his prospects, he would not stand in their way.

A two-year betrothal and money were the keys to future happiness, it appeared; otherwise there was a problem. As he told Collingwood, 'My dear boy, I want some prize-money.'[14] There was only one other possibility: the uncle who had agreed to help him when he had wanted to marry Elizabeth Andrews. So he wrote another begging letter to William Suckling, beginning, 'I open a business which, perhaps, you will smile at in the first instance and say, "This Horatio is for ever in love." ' He went on to describe Fanny: 'Her personal accomplishments you will suppose *I think* equal to any person's I ever saw: but, without vanity, her mental accomplishments are superior to most people's of either sex.'[15]

He told him about Herbert and his attitude to their engagement, concluding:

> I know the way to get him to give me most is not to appear to want it: thus circumstanced, who can I apply to but you? . . . My future happiness, I give you my honour, is now in your power . . . If you will either *give me*, I will call it – I think you will do it – either one hundred a year, for a few years, or a thousand pounds, how happy you will make a

> couple, who will pray for you for ever. Don't disappointment me, or my heart will break . . .[16]

Suckling responded generously, while showing that he found his nephew's demands a touch presumptuous. In his letter of gratitude, Nelson bridled and he wrote:

> Had it not been for one sentence in your letter, viz., 'Your application has in a great degree deprived me of my free agency', I should have been supremely happy; but my feelings are too quick and I feel sharply what perhaps others would not . . . That sentence would make me suppose that you thought I conceived I had a right to ask pecuniary assistance: if you did think so, you did me a great injustice . . . Oh, my dear uncle, you can't tell what I feel – indeed, I can hardly write, or know what I am writing: you would pity me if you knew what I suffer by that sentence – for, although it does not make your act less generous, yet it embitters my happiness.'[17]

Yet despite the personal and professional worries and the couple's enforced separation, their relationship became increasingly intimate. Secure in their future, each felt more at ease with the other, although she was at the plantation house on Nevis and he at sea, anchored off Barbados, or moored in English Harbour, and this was reflected in their letters. He even shared his little complaints of discomfort at English Harbour such as being 'most woefully pinched by mosquitoes', which got inside his mosquito net and bit him through his clothes, and that he was becoming 'like an Egyptian mummy, for the heat is intolerable'.[18]

Occasionally there seemed to be a shiver of sexual excitement, as when he told her that:

> every morning since my arrival I have had six pails of salt water at day-light poured upon my head and, instead of finding what the seamen say to be true, I perceive the contrary effect and, if it goes on so contrary to the

> prescription, you must see me before my fixed time. At first I bore absence tolerably but now it is almost insupportable . . .[19]

He was trying to improve his physical condition, concluding one letter, 'A pint of goat's milk every morning and beef tea will make me what I wish to be for your sake, for indeed I am with the most ardent affection, ever your Horatio Nelson.'[20]

While Fanny awaited the outcome at Montpelier and Nelson worried about his financial prospects and the Navigation Act, his life took a sudden and unexpected turn. Prince William Henry, who had taken a liking to him when they had met in New York, was in the Caribbean to carry out official visits to British islands and asked Nelson to accompany him as his aide-de-camp. This was a command that could not be refused; indeed, it might lead to social, if not naval, advancement and would certainly enhance his prestige in the eyes of Mr Herbert.

When they met again in December 1786, the prince, although, at twenty-one, eight years younger than Nelson, was now also a post-captain on the permanent list for automatic promotion. A florid, overweight young man with a taste for alcohol and an eye for pretty young women, he was in command of a frigate, the *Pegasus*, with an experienced first lieutenant to ensure the proper working of the ship. In the naval hierarchy, Nelson might be his senior officer, but he was bound to obey royal commands and these, as he soon discovered, were that he was to accompany the prince on a continuous round of parties ashore on a succession of islands. As he told Fanny after their first social expedition:

> Our young Prince is a gallant man. Some ladies at Dominica seemed very much charmed by him. He is volatile but always with great good nature. There were two balls during his stay and some of the old ladies were mortified that His Royal Highness would not dance with them, but he says he is determined to enjoy the privilege of all other men, that of asking any lady he pleases.[21]

Knowing Fanny's delicacy, he did not say that he was also liable to tell coarse jokes in the presence of ladies, simply writing, 'Mrs. Parry dined the first day at the Government House but never afterwards appeared at dinner, nor were any ladies at Governor Orde's dinner.'[22]

From Dominica, they sailed to Antigua, landing at St John's, the capital, for another round of parties. When the frigates returned to English Harbour on the far side of the island on Christmas Eve – with the prospect of spending Christmas Day there, although Nevis would be in sight from the summit of Shirley Heights above them – Nelson wrote to Fanny:

> We returned last night from St John's and I fancy many people were as happy to see His Royal Highness quit as they were to see him enter St John's, for another day or two's racquet would have knocked up some of the fair sex. Three nights' dancing was too much and never broke up until near day. Miss Athill is the belle of the island and, of course, attracted His Royal Highness's attention. I will tell you much when we meet for you know the danger of putting too much upon paper. I could not have supposed there had been near the number of females on his island as appeared at the balls, and all being in their best clothes made them look tolerably well.
>
> You will wonder I have been able to get through all this fatigue. I have not more than twice, or thrice, been in bed till morning . . .

Yet, he remained attached to the Prince, or, perhaps, in awe of his royalty: 'as an individual I love him, as a Prince, I honour and revere him'.[23] Yet the honour was to wear thin and, less than three weeks later, he was writing, 'What is it to attend on Princes, let me attend on you and I am satisfied. Some are born for attendants on great men, I rather think that is not my particular province.'[24]

He was much happier revelling in social gossip and the domestic detail, albeit at long-range, arising from shopping on

Fanny's behalf. He had been asked to find a songbird for Fanny's cousin and wrote from Barbados, 'Tell Miss Herbert my endeavours for a red bird have hitherto been fruitless but I shall always remain on the look-out till I get one' – he finally found her a grey bird – and he made an expedition to a milliner's: 'The strings I have got but the hat and ribbon is not at present in this town.'[25] There was the shipping of a piano to Nevis and having it tuned for her. 'A man is cracking my head with tuning your pianoforte,' he told her. 'However ... he assured me there is nothing in this world I would not bear with to please my dearest Fanny.'[26]

Prince William, who did not share such interests, looked on with amusement, remarking on his friend's premature domesticity, which was in such marked contrast to the round of routs and balls with which they continued. This led Nelson to make one of his most tactless observations to Fanny:

> His Royal Highness often tells me he believes I am married for he says he never saw a lover so easy, or say so little of the object he has regard for. When I tell him I certainly am not, he says then he is sure I must have a great esteem for you and that is not what is (vulgarly), no I won't make use of that word, commonly called love.[27]

Yet if such words jarred when read, Fanny was confident of his constancy, which seemed to be reinforced by his regular enquiries after little Josiah.

It was now the year in which Mr Herbert had said the couple should be able to marry. Fanny was somewhat in awe of her uncle and Nelson was careful not to offend him, so it was Prince William who brought matters to a head. Early in March, Nelson wrote to Fanny:

> I am now feeling most awkward. His Royal Highness has ... told me that ... if I am not married this time we go to Nevis it is hardly probable he should see me there again, that I had promised him not to be married unless he was

> present and that he did it to show his esteem for me and should be much mortified if any impediments were thrown in the way to hinder his being present. He intends it as a mark of honour to me, as such I wish to receive it. Indeed, his behaviour to me has ever been that of a friend instead of a person so elevated above me.[28]

This was, in effect, a royal command.

The wedding of Captain Horatio Nelson to Mrs Frances Nisbet was celebrated on the island of Nevis on 11 March 1787. The ceremony was conducted by the Reverend William Thomas, the rector of the parishes of St John and St Thomas in the garden of Montpelier rather than in his hot and stuffy little church at Fig Tree. Prince William Henry, resplendent in his post-captain's uniform, insisted on assuming what would have been Mr Herbert's duty of escorting the bride and giving her away, while Lieutenant Digby Dent of the *Boreas* attended the groom as best man. The *bon ton* of the island's great houses gathered on the lawn beneath the wide boughs of a huge silk cotton tree, having dressed themselves with exceptional style and care in honour of the only wedding to be held there under royal patronage. After the words of the vows had been exchanged, the prince proposed the toast to Fanny as 'the principal favourite of the island'.[29] But next day an old naval friend of Nelson's, Captain Pringle, muttered, 'The Navy, sir, yesterday lost one of its greatest ornaments by Nelson's marriage. It is a national loss that such an officer should marry; had it not been for that circumstance, I foresaw Nelson would become the greatest man in the Service.'[30]

It was now a matter of awaiting orders from the Admiralty to return home. Meanwhile, there was no escaping the realities of naval life and less than a month after his wedding Nelson was, as president of a court martial, having to condemn a seaman to death by hanging for desertion. Having done so, he asked Prince William Henry to grant an immediate reprieve, which he did, and Nelson gave the man an immediate discharge from the Navy. When the Admiralty eventually censured him because he had the power only to suspend but not to quash the sentence,

Nelson maintained, 'I was near, if not cutting the thread of life, at least shortening a fellow-creature's days. The law might not have supposed me guilty of murder but my feelings would have been nearly the same.' When the Admiralty specifically objected to his discharging, and so freeing, the prisoner, he continued, 'I had always understood that when a man was condemned to suffer death, he was from that moment dead in Law; and, if he was pardoned, he became as a new man; and there being no impress [press gang], he had the choice of entering, or not, His Majesty's service.'[31]

At last, orders to sail for home arrived and plans could be made. Fanny and Josiah were to return with her uncle and, as the *Boreas* would be too cramped and uncomfortable, they booked passages in the large and comfortable West Indiaman *Roehampton*. The frigate, after calling at several Caribbean islands, crossed a stormy Atlantic in a month and, on arrival at Spithead off Portsmouth, was ordered to the Nore because of renewed tension with France. While she lay there, used as a receiving ship for men rounded up by the press gangs, Fanny arrived in London and moved into the luxurious house Herbert had rented in Cavendish Square. Both the captain and his wife were miserable, he complaining that he was 'as much separated from my wife as if I were in the East Indies'.[32]

Fanny wrote unhappily to her new father-in-law in Norfolk to introduce herself, striking a complaining, self-pitying note that was expanded by his apprehension of the recruit to the Nelson family circle. Writing to his daughter, Kate, he spoke of the imminence of another war, continuing, 'so portends my daughter F.N., whom I have just now heard of. She has been unwell and in poor spirits. Hard, she says, is the lot of a sailor's wife.'[33]

4
Mrs Nelson

No sooner had Fanny and her husband settled into 5 Cavendish Square with her uncle and begun to enjoy the pleasures of London, than Nelson was called to unexpected duty. On 17 December, a member of the former ship's company of the *Boreas* – James Carse, the cooper – appeared in the dock at the Old Bailey. He was accused of murdering a prostitute in the riverside district of Shadwell and there seemed to be no doubt of his guilt. His only hope – and it was a slender one – was to be found insane, although he was not obviously so. As his former captain, Nelson felt it his duty to attempt to show that Carse's mental stability had been impaired by sunstroke. He gave evidence for the defence and, to general surprise, was successful and the man's life was spared.

Instead of looking forward to a comfortable Christmas in Cavendish Square, Fanny was already hating London. Opulent as the rented house might be, it was in the new suburb of Marylebone, where terraces of large houses were pouring smoke from ranks of chimneys into the winter sky. 'I fear we must at present give up all hope of living in London,' declared Nelson, 'for Mrs. Nelson's lungs are so affected by the smoke.'[1] So, in January 1788, they took the coach for Bath, where Fanny stayed in lodgings while her husband continued to Plymouth for the celebrations arranged to greet Prince William Henry's return from the West Indies. He then returned to collect Fanny and together they stayed with an aunt of hers near Bristol before travelling to the small but genteel seaside town of Exmouth, known for its benign climate, for a holiday. At last, she could relax in the love and companionship of her husband.

He, however, was less content. Litigation arising from his seizure of American cargoes had followed him to England and he did not find himself popular at the Admiralty. He had twice called there in the hope of seeing Admiral Lord Howe, the First Lord, but had failed to do so and there was no hint of a new command. Another worry was that Mr Herbert had not been as generous to his niece as he had hinted. He had been reconciled with his estranged daughter, Martha, and there was to be no financial settlement but only an annual allowance of £100, which, added to a similar amount given to Nelson by his own uncle and his naval half-pay of £146, would give them only a modest income.

So, in the hope that Prince William Henry and his connections might be helpful, Fanny made what was, for her, a bold suggestion and this prompted her husband to write a carefully worded letter to his friend. 'There may be a thing, perhaps, within reach of your Royal Highness; therefore, trusting to your goodness, I shall mention it,' he began. 'The Princess Royal must very soon have a Household appointed her. I believe a word from your Royal Highness would obtain a promise of a situation in her Royal Highness's Establishment not unbecoming the wife of a Captain in the Navy . . .'[2] Nothing came of it and Fanny never became a lady-in-waiting.

Oddly, the couple had neither visited Burnham Thorpe nor seen Edmund Nelson, but it was not for want of trying. The rector had long taken refuge from the worrying world in premature old age, but now he was sixty-six and reality was catching up with affectation. He was suffering not only from asthma, which necessitated his escapes from the damp of the valley of the River Burn to the hills of Bath, but from the ague, the mild malarial fever endemic in East Anglia. To counter the latter, he dosed himself with quinine, just as Horatio had in the tropics, telling Kate that he feared the effect of damp. He wrote:

> The shaking Fiend is driven off his station and batteries of Peruvian Bark [quinine] raised to prevent another lodgement . . . If otherwise, some other auxiliary must be hired, but not the effluvia of Barton Broad. Do you think the charming, open lawns and pure air collected from the large fields of Thorpe, mixed with the fine parts of a clear, purling stream, bordered with cresses, thyme and vervain yield the palm to small, low enclosures, bogs and morasses bounded by sedge and reed? No, it must not be![3]

His daughter-in-law had, on arrival in London, written to introduce herself, but the old parson flinched at the thought of what he imagined to be a lady of fashion from the West Indies with expectations he could not begin to meet:

> Nothing has this week been dropt into my Lion's mouth [Venetian letter-boxes for secret messages], except a letter from Cavendish Square. My very polite correspondent from thence seems to think it will not be many weeks before she visits these Arcadian Scenes: rivers represented by a puddle, mountains by ant-hills, woods by bramble bushes; yet all in taste, if not hid by snow. Forbid it Fate.[4]

His son had written to suggest he meet them at Bath, but he had excused himself on grounds of cost. In March, he wrote to Kate for her birthday: 'Remember, Kate, Time has stolen away your one and twentieth year. A subtle, nimble thief . . .' Then he added bluntly:

> From Captain Nelson I have heard nothing a long time. When they come into Norfolk I shall like it as well if every visit is made before mine begins and, to say truth, I am not now anxious to see them. Him for a day or two I should be glad of, but to introduce a stranger to an infirm and whimsical old man, who can neither eat nor drink, nor talk, nor see, is as well let alone.'[5]

He was, of course, excellent company, if somewhat fey, but was terrified of the prospect of Fanny, whom he imagined increasingly as a grand, demanding gorgon who would unsettle his simple life. In May, he again wrote to Kate about Horatio and his bride:

> I have requested him not to think of bringing his Lady and Suite to Burnham till his other visits are at an end. Indeed, I am in no haste to see and receive a stranger; perhaps you may introduce her by and by. I believe she will form a valuable part of our family connections and certain it is that he has a claim to all my affection, having never transgressed. But every power of mine is in decay. Insipid, whimsical and very unfit for society in truth and not likely to revive by practice . . .[6]

Edmund's own family was enough to occupy his concern. Maurice, working at the Navy Office in London, had got into debt. William had, two years before, married Sarah Yonge, the daughter of another parson, and had followed his forebears as rector of Hilborough; a daughter, Charlotte, had been born in 1787. Edmund had been given employment by Susannah's husband, Tom Bolton, in his office at Ostend, but had fallen ill and returned to Norfolk. Suckling had spent his inheritance from his uncle Maurice on buying the village store at North Elmham, where he was not proving successful as a shopkeeper. The Bolton family, having returned from Ostend in 1783, had moved to Norwich a year later; soon after their return, Susannah had given birth to a daughter, Ann, who had died within a few months. Kate – the favourite; pretty, poised and curly-haired – had met a charming, eligible man of thirty-three, George Matcham, who, on returning from profitable service with the East India Company had written an account of his travels. They became engaged in early 1787, married and went to live in a fine house, Barton Hall, on the Norfolk Broads, the inland lagoons in the east of the county.

George Matcham was the ideal husband for Kate and proved

the perfect son-in-law for Edmund. The old man was invited to stay at Barton and they visited him at Burnham Thorpe, where George's activity made up for the inactivity there of his sons Edmund and Suckling and the absence of Horatio. A strong, enthusiastic man, he gave a lead to the parson's gardener, Peter Black, and proved so imaginative in his plans for digging a small lake, diverting the River Burn and planting flowerbeds that Edmund called him 'Capability' M., after 'Capability' Brown, who had laid out the great park at Holkham over the brow of the hill to the east of the village. 'Myself and Peter as Under Artists in Improvements must have another lesson from "Capability M.",'[7] he wrote, keeping up a series of horticultural reports to Barton Hall, full of detail and whimsy. 'Planted the laylocks and dug the ha! ha!'[8] noted the rector triumphantly.

In March 1788, he wrote to George:

> Nature, undisturbed, only begins to rear her head and, as the Sleeping Venus, shows an inclination to get up. But where she has been so roughly handled by the indelicate hand of a Peter; breaking in upon her retirements at the moment she was undressing for a winter night; tearing away her cloathing; carrying her like an unfeeling assassin to a cold and inhospitable clime; no kind friend at hand to afford shelter, or nourishment, the worst is to be expected. She is ashamed to come forth. Half naked, in tattered clothes, exposed to the ridicule of every dirty boy and therefore much, I fear, will die in obscurity. However, as yet, do not despair. The beech seems to make slow efforts and may perhaps be tempted to come forward. The Scotch are too sullen, silent and obstinate to afford their aid where every pert Englishman shall call them. The aquatics will, I believe, emerge. The primrose, violets, etc., are forward lasses and regard not who pluck them . . .[9]

Grudgingly, Edmund realized that Horatio and the wife who frightened him so would have to visit him. This was brought about with tact. First, little Josiah was sent in the company of his stepfather's servant to William Nelson's rectory at Hilborough and from there would be sent to boarding-school. Then, the couple would themselves stay with Susannah and Tom Bolton in Norwich and visit William and his wife. From there, Nelson rode over to see his father at Burnham Thorpe and discussed family affairs, telling him that when he returned to London he would help release Maurice from the 'galling chain'[10] of his debts. Then, as Edmund told Kate, 'he means to visit you and that you and Mr. M. shall conduct him and his wife to Thorpe, where probably they will cast their anchor for a time'.[11]

First, Nelson visited London in the hope of hearing of active employment from the Admiralty. There he saw Admiral Lord Hood, who was friendly and told him that, although no peacetime command was available, in the event of war he would be recalled to duty. So, encouraged by this assurance, he returned to Norfolk and, in December 1788, at last took his wife to meet his father at Burnham Thorpe. All Edmund's fears and fancies evaporated when he met Fanny and they at once delighted in each other's company: he in her ladylike manners and thoughtfulness; she in his diffidence and sense of humour. Horatio and Fanny had been thinking of going on holiday to France, where he might continue the study of French that had been interrupted by his infatuation with Elizabeth Andrews; but they decided to stay in Norfolk and embark on a round of family visits before settling at Burnham Thorpe.

The rector was now happy not only that the couple should share the house with him but also that Fanny should take control of the household. While they were staying at Barton Hall, the rector wrote to Kate, 'Mrs. N. will, I fear, be disagreeably sensible of the change from the cheerful gaiety of your family to the solitude of Thorpe. Here, indeed, all shall be her own and even that may prove an encumbrance as to servants, not the pleasantest part of government . . .'[12] By the summer of 1789, they were installed and Edmund told Kate, 'The arrangement which has lately taken place here promises to be productive of those comforts, which are adapted to my powers of enjoyment.

Gentleness, quietude and good humour, neither impetuous, nor insensible . . .'[13]

In summer and autumn, the weather was benign and the social round pleasant if not exciting. A mile to the west was the hospitable Sir Mordaunt Martin, who had moved into Westgate Hall, and a mile to the south, Canon Charles Poyntz, the brother of the Countess Spencer, who was adding a library wing to his rectory at North Creake. But, although Captain Nelson rode over to Holkham Hall to ask the great landowner and farmer Thomas Coke, who was also a magistrate, to sign his papers for the authorization of naval half-pay, the two were not close. Coke was a leading Whig and supported the growing revolutionary movement in France, while the Nelsons inclined towards the Tories and did not. In November, Kate gave birth to a baby, George, in Norwich, where she had gone for the delivery, and the rector's happiness was complete.

But, as the year ended, the scene darkened. In December, the younger Edmund, who had been in a decline since his return from Ostend and had moved to Burnham Thorpe, died and was buried near his mother in All Saints' church. The weather deteriorated and the rector wrote to Kate, who was recuperating from childbirth in London, warning her to delay her return, keeping

> at a distance from the cold of an easterly wind . . . and Newmarket Heath is not a spot famous for soft zephyrs . . . The sun is now at its farthest distance and we must wait his return for spring entertainment of the rose and hyacinth and in hopes of these your brother is often amused in the garden, which Mr. M. has engaged to beautify with some Barton roses.[14]

Then winter struck and proved to be the coldest in living memory. Edmund was, of course, used to it and could even greet the ordeal with a verbal flourish: 'December has visited us in all the pomp and parade of winter, wind and storm and rattling hail; clothed with frosted robes, powdered with snow, all trimmed in glittering icicles; no blooming dowager was ever finer . . . all his hush at high noon as at midnight.'[15] Fanny stayed indoors and her father-in-law worried that she was bored, wishing she had 'a little society and an instrument with which she could pass away an hour. Her musical powers I fancy are beyond the common sort.'[16] To Kate, he wrote, 'Your very good sister-in-law finds it not so temperate as Nevis and the very robust Capt. begins to feel a rheumatic twinge now and then.'[17]

The weather worsened and, even indoors, milk froze in the jug. 'Our present cold, dreary, I had almost said uncomfortable state,' the rector told Kate, had 'affected both your brother and his lady. They are moving just out of the bedchamber but both are brought to acknowledge they never felt so cold a place.'[18] Then, as it grew colder still, he reported, 'Horace has been very unwell for some days . . . Mrs. N. takes large doses of the bed and finds herself only comfortable when enclosed in moreen [woollen bedclothes]. Myself, more accustomed to the climate, give no heed to small illconveniences.'[19]

In January 1790, he was writing, 'Whether solitude and exclusion from all the world can be comfortable to a young woman I know not. She does not openly complain. Her attention to me demands my esteem and to her good husband she is all he can expect.'[20] He himself found the couple agreeable company, 'I have . . . no reason to suspect that my ways and whimseys are thought troublesome.' He was suffering from 'that Daemon the toothache', but, as was his way, maintained that although 'the wind is very cold . . . I repel its influence with a pudding battery.'[21]

They survived the winter, but Fanny determined to avoid it in future by visiting her sisters-in-law. There was still no news of an appointment for Horatio, his father noting, 'He is restless, as are thousands more in such a state of uncertainty, and tho' his merit is great, still without interest [influence], I fear it may be overlooked.'[22] If he was recalled to duty, he added, 'Swaffham is the place Mrs. N. has determined to make her residence.'[23] This was a market town with fine houses and its own assembly rooms, the focal point for fashionable society in western Norfolk, and was close to the William Nelsons at Hilborough.

The anger aroused among those West Indian traders by Nelson's professional zeal in enforcing the Navigation Act followed him into his remote Norfolk valley. One spring morning in 1790, when he was away at market hoping to buy a Galway pony, a bailiff from the court at Walsingham arrived at the parsonage and, finding him out, presented Fanny with a writ for damages amounting to £20,000. On his return, Nelson was outraged, not so much by the writ itself, because he had been assured that the Government would take full responsibility, but by the involvement of Fanny. 'This affront I did not deserve!'[24] he complained to the Admiralty, and talked bitterly of resigning his commission and becoming a mercenary in the Russian service.

In his frustration, he worked furiously 'as it were for the purpose of being wearied'[25] in the garden, on his father's glebe and diverting a channel from the river Burn into a pond. Each spring he had to supervise the herding of his father's sheep on the marshes to graze the fresh grass and then higher ground when flooding began. Unlike his neighbours, he did not enjoy field sports, tending to carry his gun at full-cock and fire from the hip, inaccurately too, for, as his father put it, 'An enemy floating game is a better mark',[26] but he did occasionally watch hare-coursing over the fields above the village towards Holkham. Underlying all other frustrations and worries was personal unhappiness. Fanny was still not pregnant. She had once been fertile so the obvious conclusion was the Nelson must be infertile, and with that thought came depression and loss of confidence. He became a difficult husband, since his 'mind was irritable in the extreme and often displayed sudden paroxysms'.[27]

While he dug in the garden, she would sometimes sit nearby painting watercolours of 'Burgundy rose plants, a cluster rose, a hundred-leaf rose and rose *de Meaux*'.[28] Household management was of no interest to her, as her experience of it had been limited to giving orders to cooks and servants in the great house on

Nevis. So when decisions had to be made and orders placed, whether for food or furnishings, she left it to her more practical husband. From Norwich market, he ordered, 'Three very fine, large turkeys, also sausages sufficient to eat with them. Let the turkeys be ready for the spit . . . If sausage meat is more convenient, let it be put in a jar and sent with them . . . You will also choose me a good Gloucester cheese and send it by the carrier.'[29] From the upholsterer, he ordered, 'A sofa cover of blue and white striped Manchester of the pattern sent, or nearly like it . . . A cover is sent, which fits very well except length; let the other be three inches deeper to hang over the legs. Mrs. Nelson desires a handsome, rich blue, but not dark.'[30] He even went shopping for an order placed by his brother William at his other brother Suckling's shop at North Elmham, which was overdue: 'I was at Elmham yesterday and your cloth was packed up but my brother waited till he got down the blue for the turn-ups and lining.'[31]

Social events were few, the most exciting being the annual visit to stay with Nelson's cousin Lord Walpole at Wolterton Hall. The rector wrote to Kate, 'Be so good as to buy for Mrs. Nelson a plain, handsome bonnet, such as she may wear at Wolterton if need be, or what you would for yourself buy for dining, visits, etc. Send it down and if any covering for the neck by way of a cloak is needful, add that also. Place them to my account.'[32] Other entertainments were the Aylsham Assembly and the Lynn Feast in October, but when Thomas Coke gave a magnificent Whig fête at Holkham and invited the Nelsons, Horatio, as a Tory, refused, writing tersely, that it was 'not in his power to accept'.[33]

Always thoughtful, the rector decided that the couple might be more content without his presence, so, towards the end of 1790, he rented a small house close to his church at Burnham Ulph and moved there by himself. '*My town residence*,' he told Kate, 'promises all that could be looked for. It is near my Chapel of Ease, warm and in the vicinity of what is useful in food, clothing and physic and most likely, by and by, a little social chat may take place.' He felt that Fanny would be happier at the parsonage without him, continuing, 'Your bro. is . . . I hope fixed at Thorpe, a place he delights in; but I wish it was a little better accommodated to Mrs. N. as a woman who would sometimes choose a little variety.'[34]

There was some relief in having the parsonage to themselves. Nelson and his wife were fond of old Edmund, but his constant whimsicality would grate on frayed nerves. For example, he was reluctant to wear his spectacles on the grounds that poor eyesight was God's will, so would ask for the newspapers to be read to him.

The newspapers – particularly the weekly *Norfolk Chronicle* – were full of news from France. During the previous summer, Paris had exploded in revolution, the Bastille had been stormed and King Louis brought back from Versailles to his capital by the mob. Throughout 1790, the revolutionaries had become more extreme and in June the following year the King had tried to escape from France but been intercepted and returned to Paris. In 1792, Prussia and Austria invaded France to extinguish the revolution, but in Paris the revolutionaries reacted by storming the Tuileries palace and imprisoning the royal family. A month later they routed the Prussian army at Valmy. By the end of the year King Louis XVI was on trial for his life.

The *Chronicle* was published in Norwich on Saturday and that afternoon, Nelson would ride over to the inn at Burnham Market to await its arrival. Then, rather than take it home, where Fanny would want to hear the social news, or to his father's house, where he would have to read it aloud to the old man, he rode over the low hill to the little seaport of Burnham Overy Staithe. There he would find a sheltered angle in the long embankment beside the creek, from where he liked to watch the coastal trade, and, alone, concentrate on the news of impending war, mobilization and the possibilities of a new command. Ships were being brought forward from reserve and friends were being appointed to them, but it seemed that he was being excluded; his letters to the Admiralty and even to the Duke of Clarence – as Prince William Henry had become – were fruitless. His depression deepened.

Among the almost routine trials of family life at this time was the loss of children in infancy and, in October, 1792, Kate suffered such a bereavement.

'The loss of children is certainly to be expected,' wrote Horatio to her at Ringwood, where they were now living, 'and we are surprised that from so many complaints, which the poor little things are subject to, that so many are spared to a maturer age.'[35]

From France, the hunger for social and economic reform and, indeed, revolution spread to the British Isles thanks to the activities of both liberal idealists and travelling agitators. The fever spread even to Norfolk villages, where there had been a tradition of rebelliousness stretching back to Kett's revolt in the sixteenth century and even beyond, to the revolt of the Iceni against the Romans; now it was being articulated internationally by a Norfolkman, Thomas Paine, author of *The Rights of Man*. In reaction, this was denounced by patriotic worthies in the towns, while the rural gentry raised and joined militia as they had during the Seven Years War four decades earlier.

But Captain Nelson did not just react; he sought the causes. Of some he was already aware, through his talks with the near-destitute farm workers who were his neighbours. While others tried to defend their property, he was interested in eliminating the roots of the trouble. Having completed his research, he wrote a brave memorandum to the Duke of Clarence in which he spoke for those without a public voice with a clarity that could not only have aroused suspicions but have even led to his denunciation as a revolutionary himself.

While stressing his loyalty to the monarchy and calling for the repression of agitators, he explained:

> That the poor labourers should have been seduced by promises and hopes of better times, your Royal Highness will not wonder at when I assure you that they are really in want of everything that makes life comfortable . . . Much has arose from the neglect of the Country gentlemen

> in not making their farmers raise their wages in some small proportion as the price of necessities increased.

He then added a table of earnings and expenditure, concluding, 'Not quite twopence a day for each person; and nothing to drink but water, for beer our poor labourers never taste unless they are tempted, which is too often the case, to go to the ale-house.'[36] It was in the ale-houses that they heard the hot words of the agitators.

For weeks, the *Norfolk Chronicle* had been publishing reports of mounting violence in Paris and what turned out to be premature reports of the violent deaths of the royal family. It also printed news of naval mobilization and, unable to bear the frustration any longer, Nelson took the coach to London in the first week of 1793 and yet again presented himself at the Admiralty. A few days later Fanny, waiting at the parsonage, received a letter from him dated 7 January. '*Post Nubila Phoebus* – after clouds comes sunshine,' he had written. 'The Admiralty so smile upon me, that really I am as much surprised as when they frowned.' He had been offered command of a sixty-four-gun ship which could be seen as either a small ship of the line or an exceptionally powerful frigate able to fight in a line of battle. Nelson naturally chose the latter definition. 'Everything indicates war,' he continued. 'One of our ships, looking into Brest, has been fired into: the shot is now at the Admiralty.'[37]

There was much to be done before he could leave home after five years and he at once returned to Norfolk. Fanny had, of course, always known that this moment would probably come, but there was shock in its imminence and the fact that her husband was euphoric; not only would his life at sea have nothing to do with her, but it would involve long separations. He still awaited the name and location of his new command, but whatever these were much packing and forwarding were to be planned. He would be able to take only one or two trunks with him on the coach, so the bulk of his gear and the provisions he would take to sea would have to be shipped, if possible, from Wells. The latter would need to be fresh, so he would have to leave the buying, packing and sending to

Fanny when he had left.

More important to her was the future of Josiah, who was now aged twelve and whose course in life must be decided. News had just arrived that her uncle, John Herbert, had died on 18 January, but, since he and his only daughter, Martha, were now reconciled, the promised legacy of £20,000 was not for Fanny. However, he did leave her £4,000, with £500 to Josiah on his coming of age. From experience, Nelson thought that the Navy offered a satisfactory career only in wartime and he was averse to a civilian profession ashore for Josiah, while Fanny was reluctant to lose both husband and son to the perils of the sea and war. She hoped Josiah might become a lawyer, but they decided to postpone a decision until her husband had had a chance to consult his worldly-wise uncle, William Suckling.

During the third week in January, a letter arrived from Lord Hood, telling him that his ship was to be the *Agamemnon*, which was lying at Chatham; he was to join her on 7 February. 'This event, though wished for, puts us in a little hurry,' wrote the rector to Kate. 'Poor Mrs. Nelson will, I hope, bear up with a degree of cheerfulness at the separation from so kind a husband . . . However, he himself is in good spirits . . .'[38] There was now more than packing to occupy him, and in particular recruiting. Now that he was back on the active list, he was empowered to send junior officers to find recruits in the seaports, not only in Norfolk but north to Whitby and Newcastle. In the Burnham villages men who knew and liked him were volunteering, among them a tough, stubborn young man, Tom Allen, who would become his servant. Norfolk clergymen and squires were asking him to take younger sons to sea to be trained as midshipmen. Among the latter would be William Hoste, the son of the rector of Tittleshall, John Weatherhead and his young brother from Sedgeford, and William Bolton, Susannah's nephew by marriage. A week before his departure he gave a farewell party at the village inn, the Plough.*

* Now the Lord Nelson.

Then the newspapers reported that on 21 January 1793 King Louis XVI had been executed in Paris. On 1 February, France declared war on Britain. Four days later, Captain Nelson left Burnham Thorpe for London and Chatham. That afternoon, the rector wrote to his youngest daughter that Horatio had left the parsonage 'in health and great spirits'.[39] The future for the others seemed bleak:

> Poor Mrs. Nelson has indeed a severe trial. She will be with me here in the Parsonage a week or two, then makes a visit to Hilborough and look out for a comfortable lodging at Swaffham, where she means to reside. The Thorpe house will be in some measure forsaken; I will not let it, shall put in a labourer and keep myself in this cottage [at Burnham Ulph]. This at present is all I know of our domestic arrangements. If the warlike storm blows over, then most likely the course of matters will return to their old channel.[40]

But it was to the English Channel and beyond that Captain Nelson would be steering.

The letters that now began reflected a simple joy in which Fanny had no share. On 4 March, he wrote as he travelled to Chatham to see his ship for the first time, 'Never a finer night was seen than last night and I am not in the least tired.'[41] A week later he was back in London, having enjoyed a happy meeting with Kate and her husband, who were staying in Kentish Town with William Suckling, who had also invited Fanny to stay for as long as she liked while her husband was away. Then he reported that he had discussed Josiah's future with his uncle and they had decided that legal training would be too expensive: 'It would take our whole income to keep him at the Temple and I suppose we must think of some other walk of life for him.' The modest legacy from John Herbert of Nevis had eased the pressure but, even so, Nelson continued, 'My objection to the Navy, now he will be certain of a small fortune, is in some measure done away. You must think of this. Would you like to bring him up with you? For, if he is to go, he must go with me.' In a postscript, he added, 'Think about Josiah.'[42]

Two days later, writing from his ship at Chatham, he was taken up with professional zeal. 'If the wind is to the northward of west, we go down the river tomorrow and are ordered to proceed to Spithead with all possible dispatch as we are wanted, Lord Hood writes me, for immediate service and hints that we are to go a cruise and join his fleet at Gibraltar.' He complained that his baggage had not arrived and had probably not yet sailed from Wells; if that was the case it should be sent overland to Portsmouth urgently. 'Have not heard from Josiah, which I am sorry for,'[43] he added.

So now she had to take the decision to part with her son too. There seemed no alternative and, accepting William Suckling's invitation, she travelled with the boy to Kentish Town. The *Agamemnon* had been held in the Medway by contrary winds and, on 4 April, Nelson and Josiah boarded the coach for Chatham. The next day, the former wrote to her from the ship, 'Josiah and myself came down very comfortable yesterday morning and he seems quite settled, we slept on board last night and are now at home.'[44] The final words of that sentence were as hurtful as they were telling and prophetic.

Just as hurtful was a complaint that followed four days later:

> You forgot to send my things . . . by the Sheerness boat . . . I have got a keg of tongues, which I suppose you ordered and a hamper of 3 hams, a breast of bacon and a face, not very well packed, there being no straw between them and the motion of the waggon has rubbed them very much. However, they will do.[45]

A few days later came another complaint: 'All my things from Norfolk are safe arrived but the key of my drawers to the bureau is not come.'[46] Fanny, accustomed to leaving such matters to servants, could not begin to emulate the seamanlike efficiency which was now pervading her husband's letters. Nor could she draw any comfort from the assurance in the same letter that,

'Josiah is in high glee that we are going to sail and says he has not time to write to you just yet.'[47]

Fanny left Kentish Town for Ringwood in the New Forest and within easy reach of Portsmouth to stay with her sister-in-law, Kate Matcham, at the house they had rented, Shepherd's Spring. The *Agamemnon* sailed from the Nore and arrived at Spithead off Portsmouth on the evening of the 28th. Two days later, Nelson's brother Maurice and his brother-in-law George Matcham arrived on board to make their farewells. George returned to shore but Maurice lingered on board so that, when a gale suddenly blew up, he could not be landed and had to sail with his brother in a dash across the Channel to Cherbourg and a chase of two French frigates, which ran for safety behind inshore shoals.

On their return to Spithead, Nelson half expected Fanny to be waiting in Portsmouth to meet him. She was not there and he wrote to her at Ringwood, 'I . . . rather expected to have seen you here but Mr. Matcham's said true, there is no certainty in winds and waves. We had some blowing weather, but nothing for *Agamemnon* to mind. Your son was a little seasick for a day or two but soon got over it.'[48] However, it is probable that, spurred by this letter, Fanny and the Matchams did travel to Portsmouth to make their farewells and celebrate Josiah's thirteenth birthday because on 11 May Nelson was writing to her at Ringwood, 'I hope you all got home safe, you had a fine day.'[49] If she did see her husband before he sailed, he would have told her that he now knew for certain that he was bound for the Mediterranean, the enemy coast and the vortex of the struggle with France. The curtain was about to rise on scenes and acts for which he had longed but which she could never have imagined.

5
Lady Nelson

Bereft of husband and son, Fanny Nelson continued her round of social visits, avoiding her own home; the rector wrote to Kate, 'Mrs. N. has no wish to return to Thorpe.'[1] He was relieved that she was staying with the active and optimistic Matchams, writing to his daughter, 'I am glad Mrs. N. is with you . . . I have Mrs. Nelson's very acceptable present of almonds, etc., and thank her . . . Shall be glad to hear a little chat from the ladies. Let them be of good cheer. Mrs. N.'s good sense will tell her to view everything on its fairest side.'[2]

The rector himself had gone to Bath, while his son Suckling, having failed as a village shopkeeper, was reading for ordination at Cambridge University in the hope of becoming his father's curate. William Nelson was at Hilborough, so it was there that Fanny now moved while she sought lodgings in Swaffham. By August, she was settled in the fashionable little town, where the wide marketplace was overlooked by fine houses,* the assembly rooms and, in its centre, a round classical temple surmounted by a statue of the Roman goddess of plenty, Ceres.

Then the letters began to arrive: sheets of paper folded, sealed with wax and addressed in her husband's sloping italics; handed from the *Agamemnon* to homeward-bound ships, landed at Plymouth or Portsmouth and carried onward by the mail-

* Tradition has it that she stayed in a large house facing the market-place named Montpelier House, perhaps after her home on Nevis.

coaches. Mostly they were about naval events – their progress through the Bay of Biscay to join Admiral Jervis's fleet off Cadiz – written with such enthusiasm that little thought seemed to have been given to their appeal to anybody outside his profession. Usually, they ended with an affectionate paragraph, including a line or two about Josiah having overcome seasickness and being a good boy, sending good wishes to family and friends. Occasionally the letters described something entirely different, as when Nelson and his officers went ashore at Cadiz, watched a bullfight and were disgusted by what they saw: 'We felt for the bulls and horses and I own it would not have displeased me to have had some of the Dons tossed by the enraged animal. How women can even sit, much more applaud, such sights is astonishing. It even turned us sick and we could hardly sit it out.'[3]

Nelson was ordered to Gibraltar and thence into the Mediterranean, where he was to join Lord Hood's fleet off Toulon. The great naval base had been seized by the royalists, who had asked the British and their allies for urgent reinforcement before the revolutionary armies could counterattack. Now that he was hearing first-hand accounts of the horrors of civil war within France, Nelson spared Fanny the details and, perhaps in reaction to this, the tone of his letters became more affectionate. 'How I long to have a letter from you,' he wrote on 4 August off Toulon:

> Next to being with you, it is the greatest pleasure I can receive. I shall rejoice to be with you again. Indeed, I look back as to the happiest period of my life being united to such a good woman and, as I cannot show here my affection to you, I do it doubly to Josiah, who deserves it as well on his own account as on yours for he is a real good boy and most affectionately loves me.[4]

Fanny read in the newspapers that Toulon was invested by a revolutionary army and that the French royalist defenders were being reinforced by British, Spanish and Sardinian troops. She was not to know that they would not be nearly enough to hold the twenty-mile perimeter that ran around the crests of the mountains that formed the natural defences of the harbour. She knew only that Nelson had been sent on an urgent diplomatic mission to plead for more reinforcements from Naples, the capital of the Kingdom of the Two Sicilies, covering the whole of southern Italy and Sicily itself. In a letter dated 14 September he reported his success with King Ferdinand IV, the Bourbon monarch, who had promised to send six thousand troops immediately: 'This I have got done through Sir William Hamilton [the British minister, or ambassador] and the Prime Minister, who is an Englishman [Sir John Acton, an expatriate] . . . Lady Hamilton has been wonderfully good and kind to Josiah. She is a young woman of amiable manners, who does honour to the station to which she is raised.'[5]

Fanny would have known exactly who Lady Hamilton was because she was as much the gossip of Swaffham drawing-rooms as she was of London. She was the beautiful *demi-mondaine* who had once, it seemed, been painted by every fashionable artist in London, who had been the mistress of several aristocratic rakes and who had finally married her last lover, Sir William, although he was twice her age. Nelson's next letter explained that he had had to leave Naples even sooner than expected to chase French ships reported off the coast, before steering for Toulon. There was an element of braggadocio in the *Agamemnon*'s precipitate departure because, as he confided to his brother William, Nelson had been entertaining the Hamiltons and other British visitors to breakfast and the King himself had come on board when news of the French ships arrived. 'Unfit as my ship was, I had nothing left for the honour of our Country but to sail,' he wrote. 'It was necessary to show them what an English man-of-war would do.'[6]

The reinforcements duly reached Toulon, but they were of little help. The revolutionaries had surrounded the defences, attacked and driven back the weaker allies, so outflanking the steadier British. Finally, a young Corsican artillery officer,

Napoleon Bonaparte, had managed to mount guns on a promontory that commanded both inner and outer anchorages and the British fleet had had to withdraw. While attempts were made to burn the French warships in the dockyard, as many royalists as possible were evacuated; the remainder were left to face the massacre that would inevitably follow.

Nelson himself was not involved but he was horrified by what he heard from refugees. 'Everything which domestic wars produce usually are multiplied at Toulon,' he wrote to Fanny from Leghorn. 'Fathers are here without families, families without fathers. In short, all is horror which we hear . . . Each teller makes the scene more horrible.'[7] He addressed the letter to her at Wolterton Hall, Lord Walpole's remote mansion in Norfolk, and he was irritated by the chatter about whether or not she should now go to Bath. 'As you desire my opinion about Bath, etc., I have only to *order* that you do what you like and give you full power to give me assent to your own wishes, that is settled.'[8]

In the first week of 1794, the *Agamemnon* sailed from Leghorn for Corsica where, now that Toulon was lost, Lord Hood was determined to establish an alternative base from which to command the western basin of the Mediterranean. This would involve putting troops ashore to besiege and take the two coastal fortress-cities of Bastia and Calvi in the north of the island and the anchorage under the shelter of Cap Corse. Nelson was not optimistic after the débâcle at Toulon, writing to Hamilton, 'The Allies are a rope of sand.'[9] The letters that began to reach Fanny after her arrival in Bath at the end of January were catalogues of hardship and violence, doubly shocking in such genteel surroundings. Even when he sent messages to friends, relations and the parents of the Norfolk boys he had taken with him, he could not resist a callous aside; when he asked her to tell the Hostes that their son, William, was 'an exceeding good boy and will shine in our service', he added, 'He will tell them there is a wide difference between shooting Frenchmen and shooting partridges but we shall talk these matters over again in a winter's evening.'[10]

Although he was usually careful to devote a line to Josiah – most often as 'a good boy' – Nelson was aware that Fanny wished her son safe ashore and he was not averse to the idea of the boy changing to another profession: Fanny's sister-in-law by her first husband had married a well-to-do Scot named James Lockhart and she had had hopes that he might suggest employment for the boy in Glasgow. Nelson wrote, 'I think if the Lockharts will get Josiah a good place, he has sense enough to give up the sea, although he is already a good seaman',[11] and again, less enthusiastically, 'I wish Mr. Lockhart could get Josiah a good place on shore. I am sure I don't like his going to sea if he can be better provided for and I am certain Josiah would give up the sea for anything we can wish him to do.'[12] In June, he was writing to her almost as though he had had a premonition of conflict with a stepson whose critical awareness and comment might prove a factor in their relationship: 'Josiah . . . is amazingly grown and will be a handsome young man and I have no fears but he will be a good one. He is affectionate but warm in his disposition, which nothing can cool so well as being at sea, where nobody have entirely their own way.'[13]

Soon both husband and son were ashore in Corsica and it proved even more dangerous than the sea. At Bastia, and then at Calvi, Nelson was in charge of naval landing-parties manhandling ships' guns over the beaches and up the mountainsides to batter the defences. Bastia, the first objective, stood above malarial swamps swarming with mosquitoes – although they were not then recognized as the source – and the incubation period broke out into fever when those infected were at Calvi a month later. This combined with heat exhaustion, shot and shell to cause higher casualties than expected. Nelson himself was a survivor, writing to the Duke of Clarence in August:

> It is now what we call the dog-days, here it is termed the Lion Sun; no person can endure it; we have upwards of one thousand sick out of two thousand and the others not much better than so many phantoms . . . I am here the reed

> amongst the oaks: all the prevailing disorders have attacked me but I have not strength for them to fasten upon: I bow before the storm, whilst the sturdy oak is laid low.[14]

Among those lost was Lieutenant James Moutray of the *Victory*, the only son of Mary, and Nelson had a memorial tablet to his memory set in the wall of the church at San Fiorenzo.

Nelson had already suffered a cut in the back at Bastia but now he had to tell Fanny that an enemy shot had struck the breastwork of his battery, flinging dust and stones into his face so that, as he wrote, 'my right eye [is] nearly deprived of sight: it was cut down but is so far recovered as for me to be able to distinguish light from darkness. As to all purposes of use, it is gone; however, the blemish is nothing, not to be perceived unless told.'[15]

Even when Calvi had fallen and the British had a new base at San Fiorenzo, the dangers increased. After another winter at sea, both the *Agamemnon* and her crew were worn out, but a new ordeal awaited them. In March 1795, the French attempted to recapture Corsica with a troop convoy escorted by fifteen sail of the line. In Bath, Fanny received an alarming letter from her husband, sent on the 12th:

> 'We are just in sight of the French fleet and a signal is out for general chase . . . Whatever may be my fate, I have no doubt in my own mind but that my conduct will be such as will not bring a blush on the face of my friends. The lives of all are in the hands of Him who knows best whether to preserve it or no, and to His will do I resign myself. My character and good name is in my own keeping. Life with disgrace is dreadful. A glorious death is to be envied and, if anything happens to me, recollect death is a debt we all must pay and whether now or in a few years hence can be but of little consequence.[16]

Two days later he had written to her again: 'I wrote you a line on the 12th. which I would not send anyone but my better half as it might appear a boasting letter but I flatter myself it will appear from my conduct these last two days to be no boast.'[17] He then described in detail how, in an otherwise indecisive engagement with the French, he had attacked and captured the huge, first-rate *Ça Ira;* he had sent Lieutenant George Andrews – Elizabeth's brother, although he did not mention the connection to Fanny – to take possession of her.

On 1 April, writing from the anchorage at San Fiorenzo, he wrote again:

> I may venture to tell you, but as a secret that I have a Mistress given to me, no less a personage than the Goddess Bellona [the goddess of war]; so say the French [royalist] verses made on me and in them I am so covered with laurels that you will hardly find my little face. At one period I am 'the dear Nelson', 'the amiable Nelson', 'the fiery Nelson'. However nonsensical these things are, they are better than censure and we are all subject and open to flattery.'[18]

He received none from his wife. Her letters were full of family, social and sometimes naval gossip – what his father called 'chit-chat'[19] – and affection; when there was a report that Nelson might be returning, she wrote, 'I never hear the wind but my dear husband and child are fully in my thoughts . . .'[20] Fanny was, above all, ladylike in her attitudes, which were more those of Bath than of Portsmouth, so that while her husband declared that he shared his mother's hatred of the French, she merely declared, 'I wish these French were away, I never liked them.'[21] She was uninhibited only in expressing her own worries and consequent suffering, looking forward to his early retirement from the sea rather than promotion and glory.

Nelson's father would write from Norfolk in summer or Bath in winter – likening his migrations to those of 'the shoals of herring on the Norfolk coast'[22] – about Fanny and 'her time of widowhood',[23] when she was 'a little nervous from anxious expectations, hopes and fears; passions not always under the control of human wisdom'.[24] Indeed, at Bath, she was in the company of other worriers and those who had cause for grief. As he wrote, 'There are here many partners of her apprehensions and many that are really sorrowing under the calamities of war.'[25] It came to the point where, he reported, Fanny was 'continually in a hurry and a fret about him . . . In such a state, the blessings of a marriage union are thus made a torment and most likely the health is destroyed, or the temper soured so as never to be recovered.'[26] Even when she was calmer, she and her father-in-law were, as he told his son, 'often fixing the cottage retirement you are looking forward to'.[27]

It was his zestful descriptions of action and danger that prompted her most acute anguish. 'This winter will be another anxious one,' she had written to her husband. 'What did I not suffer in my mind, the last! . . . My mind and poor heart are always on the rack!'[28] Occasionally, he replied irritably, 'Why you should be uneasy about me so as to make yourself ill, I know not',[29] and, 'Why should you alarm yourself? I am well, your son is well and we are as comfortable in every respect as the nature of our service will admit.'[30] Recovering his good temper, he would later write, 'I grieve to hear such a bad account of yourself. Cheer up, I shall return safe and sound.'[31]

Nelson's irritability with Fanny may, in part, have been due to guilt. His marriage, founded on 'esteem' – a word he had often used when courting – had lacked passion and, after less than a year apart, he seems to have been unfaithful to her. Ashore in Leghorn, the British consul, John Udney, had introduced him to Adelaide Correglia, an opera singer and *demi-mondaine*, who was said to be a useful source of political intelligence. That she became more than that to Nelson is first suggested by an entry for Christmas 1794 in the diary of Captain Thomas Fremantle, himself an officer of coarse-grained morals. 'Dined at Nelson's and his dolly,' he had written; and, the following summer, 'Dined with Nelson. Dolly aboard . . . he makes himself ridiculous with that woman' and again, 'Dined with Nelson and Dolly. Very bad dinner indeed.'[32] Nelson seems to have mixed pleasure with intelligence work, for he reported jocularly to a British diplomat from Leghorn, 'One *old* lady tells me all she hears, which is what we wish,'[33] presumably alluding to Adelaide, and he wrote to her in the French he had tried, and failed, to learn in Saint-Omer, '*Ma chère Adelaide, Je suis partant cette moment pour la mère, une vaisseau Neapolitan partir avec moi pour Livorne; croire moi toujours, votre chère amie Horatio Nelson.*'[34] For whatever reason, he appears to have been paying her rent, for he was writing to the Admiralty agent in Leghorn early in 1795, 'I desired to give my female friend 10 echus in addition to my note left with her and paying her house rent if the letter is not received.'[35] Like other naval officers, he probably rationalized his behaviour as excusable after a long spell east of Gibraltar, while his letters to Fanny during this period included only brief, formal endearments.

When, at the end of 1796, the British fleet was forced to evacuate the Mediterranean – with Nelson himself commanding the rearguard as a commodore – the action became hotter and Fanny's anxiety more desperate. Early in 1797, reports reached London, and then Bath, where Fanny was staying with her father-in-law, that Admiral Jervis had fought a major action with the Spanish in the Atlantic and, as details followed, it was learned that the hero of the Battle of Cape St Vincent on 14 February had been Commodore Nelson. Hauling out of the line of battle without orders to do so, he had steered for the head of the second of the two divisions in which the enemy were sailing, so as to prevent them joining forces. Running his ship – now the *Captain* – alongside one Spanish ship of the line, he had led the boarders that captured her, and then crossed her deck to board a second, capturing her also. The hero of the day, his reward was a knighthood and, as his promotion had just been gazetted, Fanny was now married to Rear-Admiral Sir Horatio Nelson. Glory had been won at last.

Fanny's reaction was to begin a letter, 'Thank God you are well and Josiah. My anxiety was far beyond my powers of expression,' and, after congratulating him, she continued, 'I shall not be myself till I hear from you again. What can I attempt to say to you about boarding? You have been most wonderfully protected: you have done desperate actions enough. Now may I – indeed I do – beg that you never board again. *Leave* it for *captains*.'[36] In her next letter, she returned to this worry: 'I sincerely hope, my dear husband, that all these wonderful and desperate actions such as boarding ships you will leave to others. With the protection of a Supreme Being, you have acquired a character, or name, which all hands agree cannot be greater, therefore rest satisfied.'[37] Old Edmund Nelson was quietly proud, writing what his son wanted to read with his customary whimsicality: 'The name and services of Nelson have sounded throughout the city of Bath from the common ballad-singer to the public theatre. Joy sparkles in every eye and desponding Britain draws back her sable veil and smiles.'[38]

Nevertheless, Fanny was delighted to be the wife of a national hero. Suddenly she was a lioness of Bath society, sought after as a guest at table and able to get tickets for the most exclusive functions; at one such, she told her husband, 'Everybody of title or fashion were there.'[39] After news of the battle had spread, she wrote to him, 'You are universally the subject of conversation.'[40] There might be more to expect than the standard ribbon of the Order of the Bath and Fanny continued, 'I rejoice you have at last begun to be noticed in a proper manner. The Ribbon won't satisfy me. I expect they will give you a handsome pension, if they do not you must ask for it. They cannot refuse. Everybody expects you will have one.'[41] At last, she could see the end of chilly winters at the parsonage or in genteel lodgings; now she could imagine Sir Horatio and Lady Nelson holding court in a country house with a spread of parkland and, perhaps, a town house in Mayfair.

His fantasies of fortune began more modestly than hers, but she was gratified when his letter of early April, which warned, 'As to fortune, we must be content with a little and the *cottage*',[42] was followed at the end of May with ideas 'about a house. Wherever in Norfolk you approve, town or country. You may build upon £5,000 in addition to my half-pay, it may be more . . . I recollect the house in the upper close in Norwich.'[43] He was thinking in squirarchal terms too, writing in June, 'I intend my

Horatio Nelson: hero and charmer. The long-lost smiling portrait in marble of 1797 by Lawrence Gahagan; discovered in Norfolk and presented to the Royal Naval Museum, Portsmouth, by Mr Bryan Hall in 1996.

The mothers: (left) Catherine Nelson (née Suckling) as a young woman. (NATIONAL MARITIME MUSEUM)

(right) Mary Cadogan (formerly Lyon), mother of Emma Hamilton. (ROYAL NAVAL MUSEUM)

(bottom) The parsonage, birthplace and home of Horatio Nelson in Burnham Thorpe, Norfolk, painted by Francis Pocock. (NATIONAL MARITIME MUSEUM) (left) Susannah ('Sukey') Bolton (née Nelson). (PRIVATE COLLECTION)

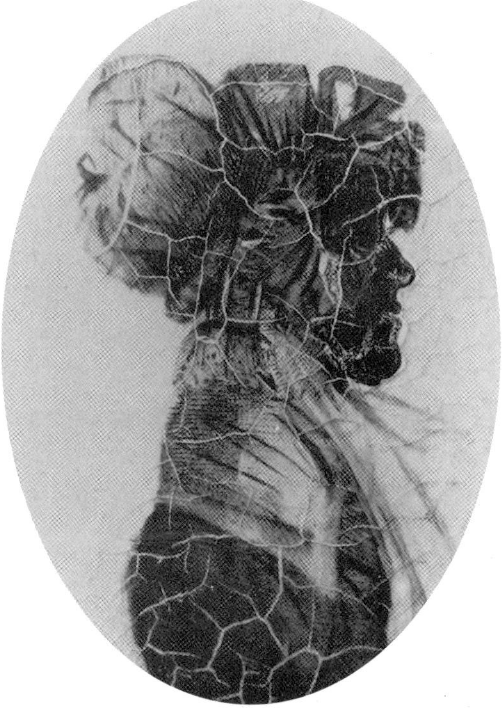

(right) Catherine ('Kate') Matcham (née Nelson), Horatio's youngest and favourite sister. (PRIVATE COLLECTION)

(bottom) 'The Hat Shop', a milliners such as that at Bath where both sisters worked as sales assistants; attributed to John Nixon. (PRIVATE COLLECTION) (top) Susannah's home: the farmhouse at Cranwich in south-west Norfolk as it was in 1998.

(bottom) Kate's home: Barton Hall in eastern Norfolk – one of the elegant houses rented by her and her husband, George Matcham – as it is now.

Elizabeth Andrews, the clergyman's daughter, whom Nelson met in St Omer. (PRIVATE COLLECTION)

Mary Moutray, the young wife of an elderly official, whom Nelson met in Antigua; by John Downman. (PRIVATE COLLECTION)

Frances Nelson (née Woolward; formerly Nisbet), the young widow Nelson met and married in Nevis. (ROYAL NAVAL MUSEUM)

(top) Women as idealised in Nelson's time: a loving daughter cares for her elderly father, a naval officer and possibly Nelson's friend Captain William Locker; painted by Sir David Wilkie. (PRIVATE COLLECTION)

(bottom) Sympathetic womenfolk give alms to a crippled sailor in 'Affliction of Providence Relieved by Attention', painted by Lawrence Cosse in 1804. (PRIVATE COLLECTION)

Nelson afloat: painted after the Battle of the Nile and attributed to Leonardo Guzzardi.
(PRIVATE COLLECTION)

next winter's gift at Burnham to be fifty good large blankets with the letter N wove in the centre that they may not be sold. I believe they may be made for about 15 shillings of the very best quality and they will last . . . for seven years at least.'[44] There were gifts for her too, although not always what she would have chosen: 'I have some Naples sashes to send you and a gown,' he wrote, 'also 5 elegant drawings of the action.'[45] Occasionally his routine expressions of affection became a trifle more elaborate: 'Rest assured, my dear Fanny, of my most perfect love, affection and esteem for your person and character . . . The imperious call of honour to serve my country is the only thing which keeps me a moment from you . . .'[46] Then the words of a loving husband would break through, as when he wrote from Lisbon, 'I shall come, one day or other, *laughing back* when we will retire from the busy scenes of life. I do not mean to be a hermit.'[47]

While Fanny pondered the expectations of a happy return, Nelson's release from duty seemed increasingly unlikely. The beginning of 1797, which had started so brilliantly for the British with the defeat of the Spanish off Cape St Vincent, was to be followed by a sequence of disasters. In April, as the victory was still being savoured and engravings of Nelson's double-boarding of the enemy were being published, came news that was as shocking as it was unexpected. Mutiny had broken out in ships of the Royal Navy at Spithead off Portsmouth and then at the Nore. This had been prompted by bad conditions of service and pay on the lower deck and ignited by the revolutionary spirit that had spread from France and Ireland and, indeed, America. At Spithead, the men's demands were met and they returned to duty; at the Nore, the insurrection was put down by force and the ringleaders hanged. Other squadrons at sea were kept operational by the strong grip of individual admirals, notably Earl St Vincent – as Jervis now was – off Cadiz and Duncan in the North Sea.

Nelson was still with the former, commanding the inshore squadron off Cadiz to watch the Spanish ships that had escaped him in April, when Fanny wrote him a gossipy letter on 19 June. She told him that he was being described as 'our "Norfolk hero"',[48] gave the minor family news and details of 'house hunting'.[49] She told him that his protégé, 'poor Andrews'[50] – Elizabeth's brother George, now a captain – was 'rather better' and that his sister was visiting him; after his health had suffered in Corsica, he had been twice wounded and, Nelson had noted, had 'taken to hard drinking, which would not have suited me'[51]. She still hoped for her husband's early return, writing, 'I am very anxious . . . The time draws near when you thought of returning, it seems just at hand, which most probably increases my feelings and anxiety.'[52] On 3 July, when she could have expected her letter to reach him, Nelson was again engaged in 'service hand-to-hand with swords'[53] in boats off Cadiz; twice his life had been saved by his coxswain parrying blows. Afterwards he wrote, 'My late affair here will not, I believe, lower me in the opinion of the world.'[54]

This scrimmage between boats' crews off Cadiz was a forerunner of worse dangers to come. Later that month, Admiral Nelson was given command of an expedition designed to 'cut out' a Spanish treasure-ship homeward-bound from Manila which was reported to be in the harbour of Santa Cruz on the Atlantic island of Tenerife. This was to involve a direct assault on the port but no undue risk was thought to be involved. The preparations for the attack were watched and described by another naval officer's wife, the former Betsey Wynne, who was on board the frigate *Seahorse* with her husband, Captain Thomas Fremantle. At dinner on the eve of the attack she found Nelson 'very civil and good-natured'[55] and there seemed to be no apprehension. Before going over the side into the boats for the night attack, the officers changed into clean clothes to minimize the risk of infection if wounded, Nelson himself disregarding uniform regulations by putting on blue and white striped stockings. His stepson, now a lieutenant, appeared at Nelson's cabin door, dressed and armed for the attack, to be told, 'Should we both fall, Josiah, what would become of your poor mother?' and ordered to remain on board. Josiah replied, 'Sir, I will go with you tonight, if never again.'[56] What followed, wrote Betsey later, 'proved to be a shocking unfortunate night'.[57]

The assault in the dark in a rough sea with strong currents was a disaster. The Spanish defences had had warning of the attack and the harbour mole, where Nelson himself landed, was swept with grapeshot and musket-fire. As he jumped for the shore, he was hit in the right arm and flung back into the arms of Josiah. In the wild night, the boat pulled back to the *Seahorse*, but Nelson refused to go aboard, saying, 'I would rather suffer death than alarm Mrs. Fremantle by her seeing me in this state when I can give her no tidings whatever of her husband.'[58] Taken to his own ship, the *Theseus*, and down to the surgeon, he suffered the amputation of his right arm above the elbow. Soon afterwards, he heard that the assault had been broken up by the weather, the darkness and fierce Spanish resistance; next morning, that the British survivors had surrendered but were being allowed to return to their ships. The attack on Tenerife had been an unmitigated disaster.

Fanny was spending that summer at Bath, where she had taken lodgings at 17 Upper King Street, a modest stone house dignified by a front door adorned with a pediment and pilasters. Susannah's daughter, Kate, was staying with her and her father-in-law was nearby in Upper Charles Street. She was so attuned to anxiety that when she read in the *Bath Chronicle*, 'Rear-Admiral Sir Horatio Nelson has been dispatched with three sail of the line either for Tenerife, or the Madeiras', she was not unduly alarmed. It was in late August that she received a letter dated 5 August, addressed in untidy, angular and unfamiliar writing but franked as from one of His Majesty's ships. It was from her husband.

'My dearest Fanny,' he began, more affectionately than usual, continuing:

> I am so confident of your affection that I feel the pleasure you will receive will be equal whether my letter is wrote by my right hand, or left. It was the chance of war and I have great reason to be thankful and I know it will add much to your pleasure in finding that Josiah under God's providence was principally instrumental in saving my life.

> As to my health, it was never better and now I hope soon to return to you and my country, I trust, will not allow me any longer to linger in want of that pecuniary assistance which I have been fighting the whole war to preserve to her. But I shall not be surprised to be neglected and forgot as probably I shall no longer be considered as useful. However, I shall feel rich if I continue to enjoy your affection. The cottage is now more necessary than ever . . . I beg neither you, or my father, will think much of this mishap. My mind has long been made up to such an event . . .[59]

On Sunday 3 September 1797, Fanny, Kate and old Edmund went to church. Early that evening, after dinner, they heard horses' hoofs and carriage wheels on the paving and then a familiar voice. At last, Horatio Nelson had 'come laughing home' to his wife. Suffering, war and weather had left their marks: his hair was grey; the half-blinded right eye was milky-blue, its pupil enlarged; his cheeks were lined and sunken and he tended to smile rather than laugh and show his bad or missing teeth; the deeply lined face and firm, sensual mouth illustrated a new air of confidence and command. He was in pain, they learned, from the stump of his right arm, which was still inflamed, and he was suffering from an associated fever. Doctors were summoned, but they were more accustomed to gout and worn-out livers than gunshot wounds and there was little they could do beyond prescribe opium to help him sleep. The stump would have to be washed and dressed daily and that would be Fanny's responsibility. Unaccustomed to any such unpleasantness, she nevertheless did her duty stoically and gently.

London doctors and surgeons – particularly Nelson's old friend Dr Benjamin Moseley, a friend from Jamaica, who was now physician to the Royal Hospital at Chelsea – would be more familiar with such problems and so the couple were in the capital by the middle of the month. Again, it would have to be lodgings, and Nelson had decided ideas about where it was appropriate for an admiral to stay. The streets off the Strand were noisy and reminded him of his visits as a bachelor trying the pleasures of London. He told Fanny that he disliked the long, straight terraces of Baker Street, preferring the smarter residential streets of Mayfair, notably Park Street, where his uncle, Captain Suckling, had lived. They found suitable rooms – first at number 96, then at 141 – Bond Street, a few minutes' walk from the church of St George, Hanover Square.

Bond Street was quiet, for traffic – mostly wagons and herds of livestock being driven to Smithfield Market – poured along Oxford Street, a few hundred yards to the north. But they were woken one October evening by shouting and the shattering of glass. There was a hammering on the front door, which was opened by a servant who was roughly asked why they had not lit the windows with candles to celebrate the great victory of Admiral Duncan over the Dutch off Camperdown. Told that the wounded Admiral Nelson was trying to sleep upstairs, the crowd instantly quietened and drifted away with promises of no more disturbance. It had indeed been just cause for celebration, because Duncan had led his recently mutinous seamen to intercept the Dutch fleet, allied to the French, and in a furious action on 11 October captured thirteen ships. This was the first good news since the Battle of Cape St Vincent at the beginning of the year.

Nelson now felt well enough to accept invitations and quickly found that his failure at Tenerife had not diminished his fame but rather that the loss of his arm had shown him to be a commander who fought alongside his men. He was accompanied by Captain Edward Berry, who had been his first lieutenant at St Vincent, to a levée in St James's Palace, where King George exclaimed, 'You have lost your right arm!' Nelson quickly replied, 'But not my right hand, as I have the honour of presenting Captain Berry.'[60] He called on the new First Lord of the Admiralty, Lord Spencer, and met his handsome, sharp-eyed wife, who wrote of him:

> I saw him . . . in the drawing-room of the Admiralty and a most uncouth creature I thought him. He had just returned

> from Tenerife, after having lost an arm. He looked so sickly it was painful to see him and his general appearance was that of an idiot; so much so that, when he spoke and his wonderful mind broke forth, it was a sort of surprise that riveted my whole attention.[61]

Nelson returned the interest, for he was drawn to intelligent, quick-witted women, and so a friendship was struck. He called her 'the Lady of the Admiralty'[62] and became a regular visitor to Admiralty House.

Nelson sat for the painter Lemuel Abbott and the sculptor Lawrence Gahagan. He visited the College of Arms to decide on a coat of arms which could be engraved on the silver expected to adorn an admiral's table. It still seemed that he would be a retired admiral until, suddenly, the wound healed; the silk ligature, which had been the cause of infection, came away when Fanny was removing a dressing and full recovery was swift. At the beginning of December, he was judged fit for active service by an Admiralty medical board and, on the 8th, he called at St George's, Hanover Square, to leave a note for a prayer to be read on the following Sunday: 'An officer desires to return thanks to Almighty God for his perfect recovery from a severe wound and also for many mercies bestowed upon him.'[63]

All fears of a disabled retirement evaporated when Nelson was summoned to the Admiralty and told that he had been appointed second-in-command to Admiral Earl St Vincent, now lying off Lisbon since the British were still excluded from the Mediterranean. There would, however, be some delay in choosing and making ready a suitable flagship, so there was time for further leave. On 19 December, Nelson attended a service of thanksgiving for naval victories in St Paul's Cathedral attended by the King and himself took part in the procession. He was later presented with the Freedom of the City of London in a flurry of admiring speeches.

There was one more thing to do before returning to sea and that was to settle Fanny in the house he had promised. He had been awarded an annual disability pension of £1,000 and this, together with a rear-admiral's pay and his modest capital, would be enough to buy something suitable. A letter from Sam Bolton, Susannah's brother-in-law, who lived in Suffolk, suggested a substantial new 'gentleman's residence' set in fifty acres of land just outside Ipswich. This was the Roundwood, named after a circular plantation nearby. It was a plain, modern, stucco-fronted house with two reception rooms and four principal bedrooms, standing on high ground in nearly ten acres of garden, with some forty acres of farmland adjoining and let to a farmer. Old elms and sweet chestnuts stood around the house and trees planted when the house had been built would soon provide more seclusion. Nelson and Fanny made a quick visit, decided to bid for the house at auction and, soon afterwards, were happy to hear that their offer of £2,000 had been accepted. So, while he was on active service, she could occupy herself in preparing a suitable haven for his next return from the sea.

A final visit to Norfolk was considered and then postponed in favour of Bath. There Nelson's recovery was marked by some return of his libido and, when offered the use of a box at the theatre in Bath by the Marquis of Lansdowne, he replied roguishly, 'His Lordship did not tell me all its charms; that generally some of the handsomest ladies of Bath are partakers in the box and, was I a bachelor, I would not answer for being tempted. But, as I am possessed of everything that is valuable in a wife, I have no occasion to think beyond a pretty face.'[64]

In March, the Nelsons returned to London, again taking lodgings in Bond Street – at number 96 – while he made final arrangements for his return to duty. On 14 March, he wrote to his father that he had taken leave of the King and expected to be ordered to leave immediately for Portsmouth. Almost every day he had been calling at the Admiralty and he took the opportunity to call on Lady Spencer at Admiralty House next door. As she wrote:

> The day before he was to sail, he called upon me as usual, but, on leaving, he took a most solemn farewell, saying

> that if he fell he depended upon my kindness to his wife – an angel, whose care had saved his life! I should explain that, although . . . no sea captain ever returned without being asked to dinner by us, I made it a rule not to receive their wives. Nelson said that, out of deference to my known determination, he had not begged to introduce Lady Nelson to me; yet, if I would take notice of her, it would make him the happiest man alive. He said he felt convinced I must like her. That she was beautiful, accomplished; but, above all, that her angelic tenderness to him was beyond imagination. He told me that his wife had dressed his wound and that her care alone had saved his life. In short, he pressed me to see her with an earnestness of which Nelson alone was capable.
>
> In these circumstances, I begged that he would bring her with him that day to dinner. He did so and his attentions to her were those of a lover. He handed her to dinner and sat by her; apologising to me by saying that he was so little with her that he would not voluntarily lose an instant of her society.[65]

A reason for their proximity at table was so that she could cut up his food for him and Lady Spencer was so touched by this that she presented him with a combined knife and fork in gold to enable him to eat with one hand.

When Nelson left for Portsmouth, Fanny returned to Bath to join her father-in-law and to meet the Matchams, who were due there, both reaching their destination on 29 March. She was still glowing with the memories of their time together, his recovery and the prospect of preparing the new house. On the morning after her arrival, she wrote to him, 'Unless I write before I have the pleasure of hearing how you are after your journey, you will not in all probability hear from me before you sail as the Portsmouth post comes in at 8 o'clock.' She noted the luggage she had forwarded to his ship from London and more that would be sent from Bath:

> My little blue pillow is sent with your things. If you think it will be of use to you, keep it... I hope you will have everything you can wish to be comfortable. Do tell me if anything is wanting and I will take care and get it myself and send it . . . Pray take care how the box is unpacked that was sent by coach, the one marked china.[66]

Yet the day before, Nelson had written her a short, irritable letter from Portsmouth:

> At half-past five I arrived here and, what you will be surprised to hear, with great difficulty found *one* pair of raw silk stockings. I suppose in some place or other I shall find my linen for there is scarcely any in this trunk. The wind is fair and on Saturday morning I go on board and with the lark on Sunday I am off.[67]

Two days later, he hoisted his flag in the seventy-four-gun ship *Vanguard* at Spithead and sailed to the anchorage in St Helen's Bay at the eastern tip of the Isle of Wight to await a wind that would carry them down-Channel to the Atlantic. During the next week, while lying at anchor, he wrote half a dozen more short letters about plans for sailing, but including reprimands, 'I cannot find my black stock and buckle. I find the weights for your scales are on board this ship'[68] and, two days later, 'My black stock and buckle has not yet appeared, nor are the keys of my dressing stand sent . . . I can very well do without these things but it is a satisfaction to mention them.'[69]

Fanny had been responsible for supervising the packing and dispatch of his clothes and other gear although she had not done the actual packing, so his longer letter of 7 April was even more hurtful.

> I have looked over my linen and find it very different to your list in the articles as follows: thirteen silk pocket handkerchiefs: only six new, five old. Thirteen cambric ditto: I have sixteen. Twelve cravats: I have only eleven. Six

> Genoa velvet stocks: I have only three. You have put down thirty huckaback towels: I have from 1 to 10 . . . ten in all. I only hope and believe they have not been sent. I do not want them. Have you the two old pieces of gold which my father gave me, for I have them not? and yet I am pretty positive I brought them home: if you have them not, they are lost.'[70]

The next day, after he had dispatched that letter, her own in answer to his first complaint arrived in the mail-boat. 'You will, I hope, find all your things; I am much mortified at their being displaced. Have the small paper parcels opened . . . Ryson [the man servant] is quite sure the stock buckle and velvet stocks are in the trunk. Do say if they are found. Have you stockings enough?' She ended, 'As to peace, I most ardently wish for it particularly as you will then be satisfied to live quietly at home. I can't help feeling quite unsettled and a little hurried for when my spirits are not quiet you know I am but a poor creature.'[71]

He replied at once, telling her more softly, 'From my heart, I wish it was peace, then not a moment would I lose in getting to my cottage.' But he could not resist adding, 'I wrote to you this morning about my things. I have bought a *new* stock buckle and double the price of the old one. . .' Finally, as the wind freshened, he wrote, 'the wind is fair and we are getting under sail . . .'[72] Yet the recrimination and apologies over the packing continued and she wrote another long letter about it, ending, 'Another time, I will take more care and hope we shall have proper servants . . . I leave this mortifying subject.'[73]

Fanny's anxiety fed on the newspaper reports and rumours that were coming out of France. Until the beginning of April, the invasion of England or Ireland had been the principal danger. It was known that a French army had been concentrated along the Channel coast for that purpose under the command of General Napoleon Bonaparte, who had swept the Austrians out of northern Italy and overthrown the Venetian Republic. Indeed, at the end of March, Fanny was writing in her first letter from Bath to her husband that the city was 'full with country families supposing it a safe place'.[74] This suggested that Nelson's task would be to operate with the combined Mediterranean and Channel fleets against the threat when there should be safety in numbers.

Early in April, however, a new and puzzling threat came into focus. Another French army seemed to be concentrating on Mediterranean ports – particularly Toulon – where warships and large numbers of transports were being brought into service. As these reports became firmer and more detailed, all questions concerned their destination. They could be preparing to break out of the Mediterranean and join forces with the troops ready to cross the Channel, or to land in Ireland, which was already heaving with political unrest. They might head across the Atlantic to recapture their lost Caribbean islands, or invade the British sugar islands. Or, if they remained within the Mediterranean, they might occupy the Kingdom of the Two Sicilies or seize Malta. Further east, it was suggested they might head for Constantinople as a prelude to taking over the Ottoman Empire, which stretched from Greece to Arabia, or there were persistent rumours that the French intended to annex and colonize Egypt. As the conflicting rumours reached Bath, Fanny told Nelson, 'I was almost done up, seized with violent perspirations, from which I took cold' and a friend had told her that, 'she had never seen any poor creature so affected'.[75]

Since the beginning of the year, Lord St Vincent had been wanting to make a general reconnaissance and, in January, had suggested to the First Lord of the Admiralty, 'In respect of an active squadron taking a range round the Mediterranean, I do not perceive any great obstacle.'[76] Such a mission now seemed far more urgent and word got about that it was to be undertaken. Speculation was that it could be led only by an officer of daring and originality such as Admiral Nelson. So, on the last day of April, when his flagship, the *Vanguard*, joined St Vincent off Cadiz, he was given his orders to take command of a small squadron and 'to proceed . . . up the Mediterranean and endeavour to ascertain by every means in your power, either upon the coast of Provence or Genoa, the object of the equipment. . .'[77]

Unaware of this, at the beginning of May Fanny was following her husband's instructions to move into their new house and at the end of the month she was writing long reports which began, 'The satisfaction I felt was very great in being under your roof.'[78] By the beginning of June, she was aware of what Nelson's task might be and she wrote to him, 'the newspapers say you are with Lord St Vincent, they all mention the great force the French have at Toulon. From the professions of friendship you have had from your chief, I hope he will never send you upon any service without a sufficient force . . .'[79] Fanny had never understood that that very friendship would ensure that St Vincent chose Nelson for the most dangerous duty of all and that he would be grateful for it. Soon afterwards a letter from him arrived at Roundwood, sent from Lisbon on 1 May, which confirmed her apprehension. 'The Admiral probably is going to detach me with a small squadron; not on any fighting expedition, therefore do not be surprised if it should be some little time before you hear from me again. I direct this to our Cottage, where I hope you will fix yourself in comfort . . . England will not be invaded this summer . . .'[80]

With that letter of farewell, he made sail and, in company with two other ships of the line and four frigates, steered east. As a contemporary put it, 'The most important part which Sir Horatio Nelson had to act in the Grand Theatre of the Universe now absorbed every other consideration.'[81]

6
Emma

When Nelson sailed eastward, past Gibraltar and Ceuta – the Pillars of Hercules – he entered a new dimension. Here in the Mediterranean, the rules of London and Bath, the drawing-rooms of Norfolk and the plantation houses on Nevis, did not apply. To Fanny Nelson and her contemporaries, this was the mysterious, even threatening cradle of their world: ancient Egypt, Greece and Rome, where religion, law and the arts had begun. Here young blades with expectations of an inheritance went touring to discover the beauties of art, architecture and landscape, as well as other pleasures they did not discuss with women at home. Here sailors and, sometimes, soldiers went to fight in the endemic wars, for behind the beauty was brutality and refined cruelty. The deep water and its beautiful shores were still haunted by the old gods and goddesses, Mars and Venus, Antony and Cleopatra. Here, had been the perils of Cyclops' thunderbolts and Circe's enchantment.

For Fanny and her like, this was recalled in the mock-classical patriotic verses published monthly in the magazines and in the neoclassical sculptures that decorated English salons and parkland. That this was indeed a place of epic struggle and violence was demonstrated in the first letter Nelson wrote after leaving Gibraltar, dated 24 May, which showed that the Mediterranean still seemed the sea of Zeus, Jehovah and the Almighty:

> I ought not to call what happened to the *Vanguard* by the cold name of accident. I firmly believe that it was the Almighty's goodness to check my consummate vanity . . . I kiss with all humility the rod. Figure to yourself a vain man on Sunday evening at sunset, walking in his cabin with a squadron about him, who looked up to their chief to lead them to glory . . . Figure to yourself this proud, conceited man when the sun rose on Monday morning, his ship dismasted, his fleet dispersed and himself in such distress that the meanest frigate out of France would have been a very unwelcome guest. But it has pleased Almighty God to bring us into a safe port.[1]

He then listed a catalogue of storm damage which had wrecked and almost sunk his flagship when they were struck, almost without warning, that night. The two other ships of the line had survived almost intact but his four frigates had been blown far away and he was not to see them again for months. Worst of all, the huge French fleet of warships and transports which had been gathering in Toulon and in Marseilles, Genoa and other ports along the French and Italian coasts, had escaped, driven by the same wind, and by now might be anywhere. Even when the *Vanguard* was repaired in a Sardinian anchorage, his little force would, without scouting frigates, be almost blind.

Of all the poetic phrases employed to describe Naples, a pearl set in its lustrous shell seemed most appropriate. On the shore of the great bay, below the volcanic cone of Vesuvius, with the dragonback silhouette of Capri out at sea and the scattering of classical ruins and neoclassical villas and churches around it, Naples shone in the sunlight. As Nelson's ships entered the bay, they could see the castles – Sant' Elmo on its hilltop above the city, Nuovo beside the royal palace on the waterfront and Uovo, surf-washed on the rocks offshore. Above the palace, on a spur crowded with lesser palaces and churches, stood the Palazzo Sessa, riding above the rooftops and domes like the prow of a ship. This was the British embassy where were to be found the minister plenipotentiary and his beautiful, beguiling wife, Emma.

Nelson had met Lady Hamilton four years before, when he had come to Naples seeking reinforcements for Toulon, and responded to her enthusiasm, her overt sexuality and the beauty of which he already knew. Emma Hamilton's notoriety had spread throughout Europe and visitors would boast of having met her as they did of having seen the other phenomena of Naples that also occupied her husband's time: the archaeological treasures and its great volcano.

The marriage of Emma and Sir William was already a legend. She was beautiful in the classical taste, voluptuously plump, effervescent, quick-witted, determined yet flawed; he, so much older, was worldly, intellectual, perceptive and also a trifle flawed. She had been a fallen angel from the rough substrata of English society; he was a privileged son of the landowning Scottish aristocracy. He had, in effect, bought her as a concubine from his nephew by making him his heir and she had lived openly with him as such for five years before marriage, but not an eyebrow twitched in the louche court at Naples.

Emma had been born Emily Lyon in the village of Denhall on the flat Wirral peninsula of Cheshire, probably on 26 April 1765. Her father, Henry Lyon, was the village blacksmith but she and her mother, Mary, were to prefer the story that he was really the heir to a local landowner named Cadogan, disinherited for marrying a social inferior. So, when rising through society with her daughter, Mrs Lyon was to use the name Cadogan. As the young Emily grew increasingly beautiful – straight Grecian nose, oval face, cherry-ripe lips – it was almost inevitable that, having followed one of the few careers open to a girl without education, or income, by going into service as a nursemaid, she would gravitate to London, then drift into company that would provide what was euphemistically known as 'protection'. There were to be rumours that she had become a prostitute – she certainly lodged with a brothel-keeper, a Mrs Kelly, in Arlington Street and performed unspecified duties at a dubious clinic that promised cures for impotence – but there was never firm evidence that this was so. She did indeed work as an artist's model for classical subjects painted by some of the most celebrated artists of the day, notably Romney and Hoppner. Not being considered marriageable by the spoilt, rich young men whose eyes she caught, it was again almost inevitable that she – accompanied by her tough old mother – should live 'under their protection' as a mistress. From one of these, Sir Harry Fetherstonhaugh of Uppark in Sussex, she was rescued – when found to be pregnant and discarded – by Charles Greville, a London dilettante, and she and her baby daughter were taken to live with him at his house in Edgware Row. It was he who, short of money and searching for an heiress to marry, conceived the idea of selling her to his uncle, Sir William Hamilton, for the price of the payment of his debts and future inheritance, urging him on with, 'I wish the tea-maker of Edgware Row was yours',[2] and explaining, 'Added to her looks, so cleanly and sweet a creature does not exist.'[3] As Hamilton warmed to the idea, his nephew gave him advice, as if about the handling of a prize pony, stressing that she no longer indulged in 'giddiness and dissipation', and:

> she is prudent and quiet. . . The secret is simple: she has pride and vanity . . . I have shown her that creditable and quiet people will respect her for being from all the society and habits of kept women . . . She has avoided any appearance of giddiness and prides herself on the neatness of her person and on the good order of her house . . . She has vanity and likes admiration but she connects it so much with her desire of appearing prudent that she is more pleased with accidental admiration than that of crowds.[4]

He suggested, 'If you . . . let her learn music or drawing, or anything to keep in order, she will be as happy as if you gave her every change of dissipation.'[5] Finally, Hamilton agreed to the bargain.

When Emma and her mother, 'Mrs Cadogan', arrived in Naples to stay with Sir William at the Palazzo Sessa in 1786, they assumed it was for a holiday. When no arrangements were made for their return, Emma realized what her lover's intention had been and was outraged. This time, there was no possibility of rescue, so she decided to make the best of her situation and settled down to becoming the elderly Sir William's lover. Having himself been unfaithful to his first wife and being at ease in the decadent Bourbon court, Hamilton was a charming, sexually experienced lover but was well aware that one day he would be cuckolded by a younger man. Even so, on a visit to London in 1791, they married and she returned to Naples as Lady Hamilton, the mistress of the Palazzo Sessa.

Emma settled into the role of ambassador's wife with enthusiasm. She had, over the past five years, picked up rapid, if broken, Italian, spoken with traces of a robust rural accent, part Lancastrian, part Welsh. Her effervescence and sheer carnality delighted the King, whose own tastes were those of the Neapolitan *lazzaroni*, the manual workers, fishermen and people of the streets. The volatile Queen she also charmed and became so close a confidante that rumours of a lesbian relationship spread. The prudent tea-maker with neat dress and downcast eyes gave way to a flamboyant hostess, as confident of her position in the raffish society of Naples as she was of her looks. This found expression in her favourite entertainment for her guests, when, with Sir William as master of ceremonies, she struck sculptural 'attitudes', draped in classical robes. By 1798, she was established as one of the sights of the Mediterranean, described in surprisingly admiring and only occasionally mocking terms by even the most sophisticated travellers. Even the occasional woman traveller from the English upper classes, who would formerly have disdained her company, sought to charm the ambassador's lady. One such was the intelligent, socially aware Cornelia Knight, an admiral's daughter aged forty-two who had written a novel and was touring the Continent with her mother, who had herself met Dr Johnson and his circle. While staying at a hotel in Naples, both became friends of Sir William and Lady Hamilton, although more sincerely attached to the former than the latter. Miss Knight kept a mordant eye on the eccentric Neapolitan court, describing how the King 'used to pass our house on his way to the lake where he caught gulls that he sold to the fish-dealers' and that the Queen was subject to 'fits of devotion, at which times she stuck short prayers and pious ejaculations inside of her stays, and occasionally swallowed them'.[6]

When war broke out between France and Britain in 1793, the Kingdom of the Two Sicilies had loosely allied itself to the British, while assuring the French that they would do little to help the Royal Navy, on which they relied for protection. King Ferdinand IV feared revolution himself but had agreed to send troops to help in the defence of Toulon in return for substantial subsidies. His wife, Queen Maria Carolina, a daughter of the Empress Maria Theresa of Austria, was the sister of Queen Marie Antoinette, who had been executed in Paris, and she, having vowed vengeance, was the more militant. When, in September of that year, Nelson arrived to beg for reinforcements, the Hamiltons had entertained him at the Palazzo Sessa and he had entertained them to breakfast in the *Agamemnon*; the three had immediately struck up a friendship, which was kept alive by occasional letters.

The Hamiltons had heard of Nelson's wounding at Tenerife and were thrilled to hear that he was returning to the Mediterranean, because the huge French naval and military force assembling to the north might be used against them. Although Nelson was known to be back, there was alarm when, on 16 June, as Cornelia Knight recorded, 'we perceived a group of lofty masts and sails between the island of Capri and the further point of the coast beyond Posilippo'.[7] This news she transmitted in code to her friend Angelica Kauffmann, the portrait painter, who was living in Rome, then under French occupation. She used a code, written as if about paintings, called the French 'landscape painters', the British 'historical painters' and Nelson 'Raphael'.

But at sunrise next morning a brig was seen approaching and this proved to be the *Mutine*, captured from the French and now Nelson's only small, fast ship available for scouting. Nelson was not on board, for such was the tension over the disappearance of the French that he would not leave his flagship and his squadron and sent Captain Thomas Troubridge ashore to see Hamilton. His aim was to collect whatever intelligence might be available and to ask for royal assent for the British squadron to take on provisions and water, or dock for repairs at any port in the kingdom.

Sir William could tell him that the French were attacking Malta and would presumably sail eastward. Egypt was only one of the possible destinations and Troubridge failed to grasp that, although the ambassador feared for Sicily, he had tangible evidence that their destination was Alexandria. The King and his Prime Minister, Sir John Acton, gave only vague promises of support for the squadron.

Troubridge took with him a letter of greeting from Nelson to Lady Hamilton and the message, 'Tell her I hope to be presented to her crowned with laurels or cypress.'[8] Emma wrote a hurried reply, saying that she had been urging the Queen to persuade her husband to give the British practical help.

> God bless you and send you victorious and that I may see you bring back Bonaparte with you . . . The Queen desires me to say everything that's kind and bids me say with her whole heart and soul she wishes you victory. God bless you, my dear sir. I will not say how glad I shall be to see you so near us.

Then a postscript was scrawled across the bottom of the page: 'I send you a letter I have received this moment from the Queen. *Kiss it* and send it back . . . as I am bound not to give any of her letters.'[9] The Queen's note was said to have promised help at Sicilian ports, a promise given at Emma's prompting and without the King's knowledge. Nelson wrote an immediate reply beginning, 'I have kissed the Queen's letter' and asking Emma to tell her that 'the sufferings of her family will be a Tower of Strength on the day of Battle'.[10] But there was nothing to be gained by delay, so the squadron made sail and, that evening, passed out of sight beyond the jagged headland of Sorrento, sailing south. From this time, only the occasional rumour spread through the port by arriving merchantmen was likely to give news of Nelson's pursuit of Bonaparte until the chase was resolved one way or another.

Nelson was now out of touch with everybody: admirals, family, friends, the Hamiltons and his wife. Fanny had returned from visits to Bath and London and had arrived at Roundwood on 20 May. The letters she now began to write were the antithesis of the bold scrawls of Emma Hamilton, of whose renewed contact with her husband she was, of course, unaware. First Fanny wrote about the house and grounds: the thickness of the walls and the possibility of a new planting of trees giving more seclusion, assuring him that she was 'very comfortably settled'.[11] Susannah Bolton and her husband had been to stay and Nelson's dressing-room had been temporarily converted into a bedroom for one of their daughters. She reported a problem with the Bolton girls: 'When I was ready for church, I called the girls, Kitty answered, "Susannah [a daughter] can't go to church." Upon which, I said, "Why?" "She has no gloves." "And did she come from Ipswich without gloves?" "No, but they are not good enough."'[12] She then described a visit to a nursery to buy plants for the garden:

> The show of carnations (of which I am particularly fond) was very great. I enquired the beauties of two, I next observed the green of one was particularly fine. 'And what are the colours of that?' The gardener's answer: 'Admiral Nelson, a curious plant named last year.' Adml. Reeve then told him who I was . . . You never saw a creature so pleased.[13]

On 16 July, she began to write about neighbours she had met. On that day, Nelson, having passed Malta, made for Alexandria, which he now believed to be Bonaparte's destination – unknowingly overtaking the French armada in the hours of darkness on 25 June – but, finding the port empty, he had steered north towards Turkey and west past Greece on his way back to Sicily. Fanny continued to tell him only that one of the local families 'that drive four horses and still live in great style' had 'been attentive',[14] so, when it was suggested that she join a party of such grandees at an assembly in Ipswich, she stood on her dignity. 'I declined it and took tea with a cheerful party . . .' she explained, having decided 'never to force myself in any titled company that does not seek my acquaintance . . . My spirits are a little fagged, every day I hope to hear from you.'[15]

As the weeks passed without news from the Mediterranean, she continued with her accounts of social visits, including one to a highly unsuitable neighbour, Sir Robert Harland, 'a very gay young man and no gentlewoman ever went to his house'. She explained why:

> We have been to see his beautiful seat . . . A well-behaved man showed us the house and, when he came to the bedrooms, he threw the doors open for us, he remaining outside . . . Mrs. Berry and myself were not at all gratified by the indecent ornaments of a gay young man: fine, naked figures and very handsome looking-glasses at the bottom of the bedstead, so we left his handsome house . . . not much impressed with favourable sentiments of the owner.[16]

Her own house was now decorated with Lemuel Abbott's portrait of her husband and she hung it facing her writing-table. 'My dearest husband, I am now writing opposite to your portrait,' she told him. 'The likeness is great . . . It is my company – my sincere friend in your absence.'[17]

Early in September, rumours of a great sea battle in the Mediterranean began to circulate, but there was no confirmation from the Admiralty. On the 11th, Fanny wrote to Nelson, 'The newspapers have tormented and almost killed me in regard to the desperate action you have fought with the French fleet. How human faculties can be brought to make others intentionally miserable I cannot conceive. In my opinion, a newspaper writer, or fabricator for them, is a despicable creature bearing a human shape.'[18]

A week before, Cornelia Knight had been sitting in the window of the hotel rooms she shared with her mother in Naples. It commanded a magnificent view of the bay from the dark mass of Vesuvius along the Sorrento peninsula to the hard rim of the horizon broken by the heights of Capri. She noted:

> Our telescope was constantly directed towards the entrance of the beautiful bay. At length, one morning, as I was reading to my mother, I happened to turn my eyes towards the sea and thought I discerned a sloop of war in the offing. I consulted the glass and found that I was not mistaken. I also saw that a blue ensign was hoisted but this was no proof that the vessel belonged to the squadron of Sir Horatio Nelson . . . My attention was instantly distracted from my book and my dear mother was rather displeased with my evident preoccupation . . . She rose from her seat and went to the telescope. The sloop was now approaching nearer and nearer to the land. The book was laid aside and we alternately kept an eye at the glass. Presently we saw a boat put out from the shore and pull out to the ship. Two officers were on deck and drew near to the side. We clearly distinguished a gold epaulet on the shoulder and this was quite sufficient to convince us that one was the commander of the sloop and the other a captain going home with despatches. News of a victory, no doubt. We observed the gestures of the officers while they were conversing with the persons in the boat, English residents at Naples. We fancied we could see them, with the commotion natural to sailors and particularly on such an occasion, depict by their action the blowing up of some ships and the sinking of others. Our conjectures were soon happily realised.[19]

The ship was the *Mutine* and the two officers were Lieutenant the Honourable Thomas Capel and Lieutenant William Hoste, both acting captains, the former in command but about to hand over to Hoste when he himself set out for London overland, carrying Admiral Nelson's dispatches to the Admiralty. These reported that, on 1 August, he had sighted and attacked the French fleet in Aboukir Bay to the east of Alexandria, captured nine ships of the line and destroyed two more, only two managing to escape. The French army under Bonaparte had already been landed but was now marooned in Egypt, all dreams of conquest in ashes. They also brought news that Nelson was bringing his damaged flagship to Naples for repairs.

The two young officers went ashore and straight to the Palazzo Sessa, where they gave Hamilton a letter from Nelson. 'Almighty God has made me the happy instrument in destroying the Enemy's Fleet, which I hope will be a blessing to Europe,'[20] he began, then asked for help in hurrying Capel on his way to London. Emma rushed to the Queen with the news, then bundled the two captains into her carriage and, wearing a bandeau inscribed 'Nelson and Victory', paraded them through the streets to shouts of '*Viva Nelson!*' When she could draw breath, she dashed off a long letter to Nelson:

> God, what a victory! Never, never has there been anything half so glorious, so complete. I fainted when I heard the joyful news and fell on my side and am hurt but well of that. I should feel it a glory to die in such a cause. No, I would not like to die till I see and embrace the Victor of the Nile . . . My dress from head to foot is *all a Nelson*. Ask Hoste. Even my shawl is in Blue with gold anchors all over. My ear-rings are Nelson's anchors; in short, we are be-Nelsoned all over.'[21]

At the Palazzo Reale, joy was hysterical. 'How shall I describe the transports of Maria Carolina, 'tis not possible,' wrote Emma to Nelson. 'She fainted and kissed her husband, her children, walked about the room, cried, kissed and embraced every person near her, exclaiming, "Oh, brave Nelson, Nelson what do we not owe to you. Oh, Victor, Saviour of Italy, oh, that my swollen heart could now tell him personally what we owe to him."'[22] When Captain Hoste left in the *Mutine* to rejoin Nelson, the Queen wrote him a letter telling him that she had hung his portrait in her room and added, '*Faites un hip hip hip en mon nom et chantez God saeve die King et puis God saeve Nelson et marine Britannique.*'[23]

Sir William sent him an enticing invitation: 'A pleasant apartment is ready for you in my house and Emma is looking out the softest pillows to repose the few wearied limbs you have left.'[24] Nelson was in need of such cosseting, for, apart from a gashed forehead and concussion, he had a persistent cough and a bout of recurrent malaria: 'My head is ready to split and I am always so sick,'[25] he complained.

As the *Vanguard* slowly sailed north from the Straits of Messina towards Naples, two strange couples waited impatiently to greet the hero of Aboukir Bay. The King with the tastes of the streets and waterfront was now forty-seven, his long, Spanish face deeply lined and his nose so dominant upon it that his nickname was *il Re Nasone* ('The Nose King') to his subjects and 'Old Nosy' to British sailors. The Queen appeared as a coarser version of her sister, the late Queen Marie Antoinette. She was fifty, still proud of her white skin but worn out by the bearing of eighteen children, ten of whom had died; volatile to the point of hysteria, she talked as though her mouth was full of food. More intelligent than her husband, she too was hot-tempered, impulsively generous, her judgement swayed by the mood of the moment.

The Hamiltons were equally curious and regarded as curiosities by all who met them. Sir William, now sixty-seven, was tall and aquiline with the characteristics of a man of the world (he had been a discerning philanderer when young), a man of action (he had been a regular soldier and seen active service), and a scholar (he was a recognized authority on the arts and archaeology – notably, ancient Greek vases found in Italy – and vulcanology, particularly, of course, Vesuvius and the volcanic region north of Naples). Emma Hamilton, now thirty-three, had lost the beautiful, slim body but not the striking face that had complemented it so memorably. She was now fat but, as the

British diplomat Sir Gilbert Elliot described her, 'She tries hard to think size is advantageous to her beauty but is not easy about it . . . She is the most extraordinary compound I ever beheld . . . all Nature and yet all Art; that is to say, her manners are perfectly unpolished, of course very easy, though not with the ease of good breeding but of a barmaid.'[26]

Two of Nelson's ships, the *Culloden* and the *Alexander*, reached Naples before the flagship and the King, accompanied by Hamilton, was rowed out to them. As sailors peered from the gun-ports, Hamilton called to them, 'My lads, this is the King, whom you have saved,' and the reply came, 'Very glad of it, sir – very glad of it.'[27] On 22 September, 'the poor wretched *Vanguard*', as Nelson described her, entered the Bay of Naples and was greeted by another procession of boats, in some of which were brass bands, which had been struggling to learn the tunes of 'Rule Britannia' and 'See the Conquering Hero Comes'. The first boat carried the Hamiltons and, as they approached the *Vanguard*, Emma 'began to rehearse her theatrical airs and to put on all the appearance of a tragic queen'.[28] As they ran alongside, the coxswain was heard to grumble that she had better get aboard quickly for the safety of the boat. They did and, soon after, Nelson described the ensuing scene to a startled Fanny:

> Alongside came my honoured friends: the scene in the boat was terribly affecting; up flew her Ladyship and, exclaiming, 'O God, is it possible?', she fell into my arm more dead than alive. Tears, however, soon put matters to rights, when alongside came the King . . . I hope some day to have the pleasure of introducing you to Lady Hamilton, she is one of the very best women in this world; she is an honour to her sex. Her kindness, with Sir William's, to me is more than I can express: I am in their house . . .[29]

The guests, among them Cornelia Knight, had been entertained to breakfast in the flagship. She noted a white little bird hopping about the table and had been told that it had flown on board the evening before the battle and had decided to stay. With her novelist's eye, she watched Nelson and saw him as 'little and not remarkable in his person either way; but he has great animation of countenance and activity in his appearance: his manners are unaffectedly simple and modest'.[30] His voice was rather high and nasal with a Norfolk accent. That night he was guest at a dinner in the Palazzo Sessa, which was illuminated by 3,000 candles.

The tinselled theatricality of the welcome, stage-managed by Emma Hamilton, was directed at an unsophisticated man. Brought up in a simple parsonage and cramped quarters in damp, wooden warships, Nelson was easily impressed by splendour, whether in Norfolk country houses or Mediterranean palaces. Holkham Hall had once been the grandest house imaginable, but even that memory was dimmed by the sweep of marble staircases and painted ceilings, the red damask walls and draped velvet in the Palazzo Reale. Memories of jolly assemblies in Norfolk market towns were now to be eclipsed by the festivities arranged by Emma to celebrate his fortieth birthday.

His hostess out-dazzled his former ideals of female desirability. She was the most famous beauty in Europe and her sexually charged gaze was now directed at the parson's son from Burnham Thorpe. Fanny's cool gentility could not stand such competition, for hers was the light of the moon dimmed by the glare of the sun. What had seemed an exciting flirtation – her command to kiss and return the Queen's letter had surely been designed to prompt a shiver of anticipation – now became a sexual enchantment.

Nelson's birthday party set the scene for his glorification. The Hamiltons had invited eighty guests to dinner, 800 to supper and nearly 1,800 to dance in a ballroom dominated by what he described to Fanny as 'a rostral column . . . under a magnificent canopy . . . in the front "Nelson", on the pedestal "*Veni, vidi, vici*" ["I came, I saw, I conquered"], anchors, inscriptions . . . were numerous'.[31] Cornelia Knight had written additional verses for the national anthem praising Nelson and these were sung by Emma Hamilton and then transcribed for Fanny.

Indeed, his letters cataloguing the flattery, read in the quiet of

Roundwood, must have aroused mixed feelings. There were eulogies of the Hamiltons – 'The continued kind attention of Sir William and Lady Hamilton must ever make you and I love them and they are deserving of the love and admiration of all the world'[32] – and one particular reference to Emma stung: 'Her ladyship, if Josiah was to stay, would make something of him and, with all his bluntness, I am sure he likes Lady Hamilton more than any female.'[33] Even in her most worried moments, she could hardly have seen this as the first sign of a rift between her husband and son. In his next letter, this was repeated: 'Josiah is well and, could he be here six months, Lady Hamilton would much fashion him, which indeed he wants.'[34] The young man could not fail to notice the attentions paid by his hostess and his stepfather to each other and, drinking too much, he showed his feelings.

The festivities were interrupted by the necessities of war. The French, having occupied Rome, were thought to be threatening Naples, and Hamilton – supported by Nelson – was urging the King to launch a pre-emptive attack. With this in mind, he had already asked for a professional army-commander from Austria, the Bavarian General Baron Karl Mack von Leberich, who was on his way to lead 30,000 Neapolitan troops, although the King himself planned to accompany them to war. More immediately, Nelson himself was going back to sea; his task, to blockade the French garrison of Malta. At the end of September, he wrote a short letter to St Vincent in a mood that might have reflected the aftermath of the celebrations, or his awareness that, for him, Naples was dangerous. 'In a week we shall be at sea,' he told him. 'I am very unwell and the miserable conduct of this Court is not likely to cool my irritable temper. It is a country of fiddlers and poets, whores and scoundrels.'[35] At the beginning of October, he joined the Hamiltons on a visit to the camp where the Neapolitan army was assembling for the march on Rome and it was noticed that Emma 'paraded her conquest over the victor of Aboukir, who, seated beside her in the same carriage, appeared fascinated but submissive to her charms'.[36] The next day, he wrote again to St Vincent, ending, 'I am writing opposite

Lady Hamilton, therefore you will not be surprised at the glorious jumble of this letter. Were your Lordship in my place, I much doubt if you could write so well; our hearts and our hands must be all in a flutter: Naples is a dangerous place and we must keep clear of it.'[37]

Meanwhile, on 2 October, Captain Capel reached London with the news of Nelson's victory at what was called the Battle of the Nile. The triumphant French had not only been halted but humiliated and surely the tide of history had been turned. 'Joy, joy, joy to you brave, gallant, immortalized Nelson!' gushed Lady Spencer. 'May that great God, whose cause you so valiantly support, protect and bless you to the end of your brilliant career! Such a race surely was never run. My heart is absolutely bursting with different sensations of joy, of gratitude, of pride, of every emotion that ever warmed the bosom of a British woman.'[38] Bells were rung, guns were fired, toasts were drunk and cheering crowds gathered in marketplaces across the country; ballads were composed, cartoons were drawn and tableaux were staged in the theatres. In Norfolk, the festivities were intense, culminating in celebratory dinners and balls. One was at the assembly rooms in Swaffham and was attended by Susannah Bolton and her family, as well as that of Captain Hoste, who also lived nearby. This was described by Kitty Bolton in a letter to Fanny:

> They paid Mama the compliment to ask her to begin the Ball but she danced only with Mr. Hoste [the Reverend Dixon Hoste]; it is a dance . . . called *The Vanguard*, or *The Breaking of the Line*. We sent to London for all the songs and we had them and sung . . . Mrs. Hoste's ribbons, which she had from London, were half Navy blue and half red to signify the Knight of the Bath and the Navy. She gave me a medallion of my Uncle, which I wore round my neck at the Ball. Mrs. Micklethwaite had a very handsome cap from London inscribed in gold spangles, 'The Hero of the Nile'.[39]

Nelson expected an earldom for his victory – Jervis had been awarded his for a lesser achievement off Cape St Vincent – but he was created only a baron, hearing the news in late October. He was pleased enough but Emma was outraged and wrote him an extravagant half-furious, half-humorous letter that echoed Edmund Nelson's whimsicality: 'If I was King of England, I would make you the most noble puissant Duke Nelson, Marquis Nile, Baron Alexandria, Viscount Pyramid, Baron Crocodile and Prince Victory. . .'[40] As more honours were announced and the Sultan of Turkey gave him the most extraordinary present of all – a diamond spray, known as a *chelengk* with a star-shaped centre that revolved by clockwork, to be worn in his hat – she wrote a fervent letter of congratulation, adding, 'Sir William and self . . . love you, admire you and glory in your friendship . . . I told her Majesty we only wanted Lady Nelson to be the female *tria juncta in uno* for we all love you and yet all three differently and yet all equally, if you can make that out . . .'[41]

'Hang them I say!' she wrote of the lesser accolade in an effusive letter to Fanny. 'Sir William is in a rage for not having made Lord Nelson a viscount . . . Lord Nelson is adored here. . .' And it jarred when Emma continued, 'Josiah is so much improved in every respect.'[42] This was followed by more criticism of the young man from his stepfather:

> The improvement made in Josiah by Lady Hamilton is wonderful. She seems the only person he minds and his faults are not omitted to be told him but in such a way it pleases him, and his, and your and my obligation are infinite on that score. Not but dear Josiah's heart is good and as humane as was covered by a human breast but his manners are so rough but, God bless him, I love him dearly with all his roughness.

When Fanny read this and considered some of the stories which were beginning to reach her through naval friends, she pencilled at the bottom of the page, 'My son did not like the Hamiltons and would not dance.'[43] What she did not know was that at her husband's birthday party her son had drunkenly expressed his view of his stepfather's behaviour and been led from the room.

Hearing stories that suggested that she was being usurped both as a wife and a mother, Fanny, alone in Suffolk with only the prospect of another visit to Bath with her father-in-law, decided that she should go to Naples. This became determination as further rumours of her husband's entanglement with Lady Hamilton reached her. She sought the advice of his old friend and now his prize agent, Alexander Davison. In December, he wrote a careful letter to Nelson expressing his

> sincere regret at your continuation in the Mediterranean . . . Your valuable better-half writes to you. She is in good health but very uneasy and anxious, which is not to be wondered at . . . Lady Nelson at this moment calls and is with my wife. She bids me to say that, unless you return home in a few months, she will join the Standard at Naples.[44]

Nelson had by now returned from Malta, where he found the French defending Valetta against the Maltese but he was able to capture the island of Gozo. On 22 November, the King and General Mack had led their army out of its camp and were marching on Rome; Nelson's first task was to transport some 5,000 of them by sea to Leghorn. Returning to Naples, he heard that the King had indeed captured Rome but that then the French had counter-attacked and he was now in full flight. The city was sombre and sulphurous. The first of the routed Neapolitan soldiery were streaming into its streets and the King was back and cowering in his palace. The French were marching on Naples and revolution was in the air, 'like a dark cloud announcing a tremendous storm',[45] as Cornelia Knight put it. Yet it was not the revolution of the deprived masses, for the Neapolitan mob,which had laughed and danced with the King on his waterfront frolics, were mostly monarchists. It was primarily the liberal intellectuals – many of the educated middle classes and some from the aristocracy – who wanted a republic. The King was in no mood for another fight and, from the middle of December, the *Vanguard* swung at her anchor in the bay, ready to evacuate the royal family to Sicily, while the admiral himself stayed ashore at the Palazzo Sessa. 'I live as Sir William's son in the house and my glory is as dear to them as their own,'[46] he wrote to Fanny.

As the French approached, the purpose of the British ship in the bay was apparent to all and crowds gathered outside the Palazzo Reale, begging the King to stay in his capital. Escape might be difficult for it might be opposed by loyalists as vehemently as by revolutionaries. Hamilton began, with Nelson's help, to smuggle the royal treasure out to his flagship. First, it was packed into covered farm carts and hauled to the Palazzo Sessa, half a mile away; there, it was unloaded in the *porte cochère*, concealed from view and later, labelled as diplomatic baggage, taken down to the fishing dock at Santa Lucia and loaded into the *Vanguard*'s boats. Tension mounted again when the risk of revolutionaries seizing the waterside forts became such that Nelson ordered his flagship a mile further out to sea, beyond the range of their guns.

Finally, Hamilton reported to Lord Grenville, the Foreign Secretary, 'It needs no great penetration to foresee that in a very short time . . . the kingdom is lost. However, fortunately Lord Nelson is here . . . which will secure our retreat.'[47] This was planned for the night of 21 December, which proved to be dark and stormy. Disinformation was spread and the Hamiltons and the admiral that evening attended a reception given by the Turkish ambassador, who had brought gifts from the Sultan. They had ordered the coach in two hours' time and then supper to be prepared for them at the Palazzo Sessa. In the crush, they slipped away and embarked in one of the *Vanguard*'s boats which was lying at the quay below the Palazzo Reale. Meanwhile, others were to be saved. As Cornelia Knight recorded:

> Just as we were retiring to rest, an officer from Lord Nelson's ship, attended by some seamen, made his appearance and told us that a boat was waiting to take us

> on board. We hastily paid our bill . . . We then accompanied the officer to the shore. Both he and his men were armed. The night was cold . . . and it was between twelve and one before we were in the boat. There were several persons already in it and an English child fell into the water but was taken out unhurt. We had a long way to go for the ships had cast anchor a great distance from the city to be beyond the range of the forts. . .[48]

Lastly it was time to rescue the royal family. Having checked that more boats, guarded by sailors with drawn cutlasses, were waiting below the bulk of the Palazzo Reale, Nelson was led through a small doorway and into a secret passage. As Emma put it, 'Lord N . . . got up the dark staircase that goes to the Queen's room and with a dark lantern, cutlasses, pistols, etc.'[49] Then, as the Queen wrote to her mother, 'We descended – all our family, ten in number, with the utmost secrecy in the dark without our ladies-in-waiting or other attendants. Lord Nelson was our guide.'[50] As the boats were pulled away from the quay into the cold, windy night and choppy sea, they saw other boats lying offshore with silent sailors resting on their oars and manning carronades in the bows to cover their escape. All were embarked in the flagship by midnight. 'If we had remained to the next day,' mused Emma, 'we should all have been imprisoned.'[51] Sir William was in a deep depression, for, as his wife said, they had 'left everything at Naples but the vases and best pictures [these had already been shipped to England], three houses elegantly furnished, all our horses and six or seven carriages.'[52]

The ships had been due to leave for Palermo at dawn but when a watery sun rose on a stormy sea it was too rough to sail and they tossed at anchor all day. That morning, a boat came bouncing over the crests from the shore bringing General Mack to plead with the King to stay, but all knew that Naples was lost. That evening as the wind strengthened, the *Vanguard*, two Neapolitan warships and about twenty merchantmen weighed anchor and turned for the open and rising sea.

7
Dearest Emma

The storm struck the *Vanguard* when she was well clear of land and only the ships of her convoy were able to turn and run for shelter in the Bay of Naples. 'It blew harder than I have ever experienced since I have been at sea,'[1] Nelson was to remember; nobody forgot it. It had been bad enough at anchor in the bay while the ship, crowded and smelling of paint where cabins had been redecorated for the royal passengers, twisted and wallowed at her moorings. The next day, butting into a hurricane of a head-wind and huge seas, tossed by towering crests and plunging into yawning troughs, the passengers were prostrated. Even Hamilton braced himself in his cabin, a pistol in each hand, ready to shoot himself if the ship foundered rather than drown with the 'guggle-guggle-guggle' of salt water in his throat.

The heroine of the storm was Emma Hamilton, who nursed the royal family throughout. To St Vincent, Nelson reported, 'Lady Hamilton provided her own beds, linen, etc., and became their *slave* . . . nor did her ladyship enter a bed the whole time they were on board.'[2] When the Queen's youngest child, six-year-old Prince Albert, managed to eat breakfast on Christmas Day, but then vomited violently and was seized with convulsions, Emma cradled him in her arms until he died. Before dawn on Boxing Day, the *Vanguard* anchored off Palermo and the passengers were put ashore.

Relief mixed with grief and exhaustion. The royal family had escaped the revolution and survived the storm, and now, in loyal Sicily, the sumptuous array of palaces along the waterfront seemed to offer relief. So it did for the royal family, but the great houses were mostly occupied by their owners and the only available accommodation for most was in summer palaces, built for hot weather and so without fireplaces. For the last days of December and the first of 1799, the Hamiltons, the Knights and the other refugees shivered in high-ceilinged, wide-windowed mansions and pavilions. Here they shared and provoked each other's miseries, Emma complaining, 'God knows what yet is to become of us, we are worn out: I am, with anxiety and fatigue; Sir Wm. has had three days a bilious attack . . . My dear adorable Queen, whom I love *better than any person in the world*, is also very unwell, *we weep together* and now that is our only comfort.'[3]

Nelson himself had come to a moment of decision. The recapture of Naples seemed an impossibility and, while the defence of Sicily would be primarily a naval task, there was now no French fleet to fight; also St Vincent was to be replaced as his commander-in-chief by the less sympathetic Admiral Lord Keith. As he told Fanny in a letter, 'There can be no occasion for a Nelson.'[4] There might be no compelling naval purpose in remaining and he was avid to savour his fame in England, yet he was torn between the two women, Fanny and Emma. The former held the key to his acceptance by the upper strata of society at home; only one of the letters she had written since hearing the news of his victory had reached him and he longed to read of the admiration and accolades that must have been lavished upon him.

Yet Emma had, by her resolution during the terrible voyage, showed herself to be more than a seductive hostess. She had proved herself just as he expected one of his young officers to prove himself and his feelings for her entered a new dimension. Yet if he stayed with her and her husband, the probable consequences were clear. The part of him that owed its standards to the Norfolk parson favoured a return home, so he wrote to his wife:

> The first week in March, it is my intention, if I get leave, to quit this situation . . . I shall return much poorer than when I set out, yet my heart is at ease. I must have a house in London, if possible. I should like the one that was Captain Suckling's [his uncle's, in Park Street, Mayfair], or one like it . . . if we have money . . . near Hyde Park but on no account on the other side of Portman Square. I detest Baker Street . . . A neat carriage I desire you will order and, if possible, get good servants. You will see that I am not let down.[5]

Josiah was still making objections to his stepfather's dalliance, relatively innocent as this still was. As if he wanted to deny himself a happy return, Nelson wrote a short, cruel letter to Fanny that January. 'I wish I could say much to your and my satisfaction about Josiah,' he told her, 'but I am sorry to say and with real grief that he has nothing good about him, he must sooner or later be broke, but I am sure neither you or I can help it, I have done with the subject, it is an ungrateful one.'[6] But Josiah's career was not finished. Promotion in the form of a command away from his stepfather was another alternative and, soon afterwards, Captain Nisbet was given command of the fine thirty-six-gun frigate *Thalia*, far from the snares of Palermo.

The worry was beginning to show and Nelson had not fully recovered from his head wound, which may have affected his brain and even brought about some changes in character, or, at least, in temper. He was tired and irritable, his head ached and he had to wear his cocked hat pushed back from the tender scar of his forehead. 'My health is such that without a great alteration, I will venture to say a very short space of time will send me to that bourne from whence none return,' he wrote to Lady Parker, his friend in Jamaica. 'After the action I had nearly fell into a decline . . . I am worse than ever: my spirits have received such a shock that I think they cannot recover . . . You, who remember me always laughing and gay, would hardly believe the change; but who can see what I have and be well in health?'[7] Added to the strain was the new pattern of life ashore, accompanying the Hamiltons to routs and dinners and, when Sir William had retired to bed, sitting up late with Emma, eating and drinking.

The mood was darkened by bad news for the King and Queen, the Hamiltons and for Nelson himself. At the end of January it was confirmed that the French had entered Naples on the 23rd and that a Vesuvian or Parthenopean (Parthenope was the classical name for Naples) Republic had been proclaimed. Then Hamilton heard that the *Colossus*, in which half his collection of vases was being shipped to England, had been wrecked and lost off the Scilly Islands. Nelson was told that part of his responsibilities in the eastern basin of the Mediterranean were to be transferred to a junior officer, Captain Sir Sidney Smith, a brilliant but difficult officer, who could be as charming, brave, vain and ambitious as himself.

Meanwhile, Nelson lived ashore with the Hamiltons and Mrs Cadogan in the Palazzo Palagonia and there they began to hold court. Lord Montgomery and his tutor, Pryse Lockhart Gordon, were invited to dine and, when introduced to Emma, the latter was to recall:

> She rehearsed in a subdued tone a *mélange* of Lancashire and Italian, detailing the catalogue of her miseries, her hopes and her fears with lamentations about the dear Queen, the loss of her own charming palazzo and its precious contents, which had fallen into the hands of the republicans. During this interesting conversation, the Lady discovered that she was Lord Montgomery's cousin, 'A'nt us, Sir William?' His Lordship made his bows and acknowledgements.

After dinner, a Turkish messenger arrived with a letter from the Tsar of Russia and, before admitting him, Emma told Nelson to put on the hat adorned with the *chelengk* and the fur-lined cloak that the Sultan of Turkey had sent him. As soon as the messenger saw the *chelengk*, 'the slave was prostrate on the earth, making the grand *salaam*,' reported Gordon. 'Lady H., by means of a Greek interpreter belonging to the Embassy, flirted with the Turk, a coarse, savage monster, and he was invited to dinner the following day.' Then, he continued:

> The Turk, drunk with rum, drew his scimitar and boasted to Emma, 'With this weapon, I cut off the heads of twenty French prisoners in one day! Look, there is their blood remaining on it!' This was translated and her Ladyship's eye beamed with delight and she said, 'Oh, let me see the sword that did this glorious deed!' It was presented to her; she took it into her fair hand covered with rings and, looking at the encrusted Jacobin blood, kissed it and handed to her hero of the Nile!

This was 'applauded by the toad-eaters ... but many cried "Shame!" loud enough to reach the ears of the Admiral, who turned pale, hung his head and seemed ashamed. Lord N. got up and left the room and I speedily followed. Poor Nelson was to be pitied.'[8]

Then word came from another world that had been his own. On 9 April, the mail from England at last arrived via Venice and it included the letters Fanny had written in December, in which she announced her intention of joining him in Palermo. He replied next day, apologizing for having written so little on the grounds that he had to write so many official reports and had no time. He did his best to dissuade her from coming:

> You would, by February, have seen how unpleasant it would have been had you followed any advice which carried you from England to a wandering sailor. I could, if you had come, *only* have struck my flag and carried you back again for it would have been impossible to set up an establishment at either Naples, or Palermo. Nothing but the situation of affairs in this country has kept me from England; and, if I have the happiness of seeing their Sicilian Majesties safe on their throne again, it is probable that I shall yet be home in the summer. Good Sir William,

> Lady Hamilton and myself are the mainsprings of the machine which manage what is going on in this country. We are all bound to England when we can quit our posts with propriety.[9]

Then in the hope of mollifying her, he made a rather more kindly reference to her son, whose resentment was showing itself in heavy drinking and antagonizing his own officers. In one quarrel with the navigating master of his ship, Captain Nisbet had dismissed him with, 'If you don't leave the ship, I shall make her a hell for you. I want no master but a broomstick, who I can make do as I think proper.'[10] This was the antithesis of Nelson's way with subordinates, yet he wrote, 'Josiah is now in full possession of a noble frigate. He has sent to say that he is sensible of his youthful follies and that he will alter his whole conduct.'[11]

Fanny was loyal to both her men, having written to Josiah in February:

> I have received a letter from Lord Nelson . . . where he mentions your improvements with tenderness and kindness. His love for you is very great. He flatters himself he shall see you a good and great man. It is in your power to be both. Therefore, God bless you and disappoint us not. You are very young and cannot know the world, be satisfied of this truth and implicitly follow the directions of my husband, who is truly a good man and his military achievements have stamped his character great all over the world. You are more conspicuous than you imagine. Be assured you are much envied from having such a father to bring you forward, who has every desire to do it.[12]

Bereavement again clouded the lives of the Nelsons, when, on 3 April 1799, Suckling died at Burnham Thorpe. Since the failure of his shop-keeping at North Elmham, he had read for the priesthood at Cambridge University, been ordained and returned to Norfolk as his father's curate. Hitherto, his principal interests had been greyhounds, hare-coursing, gambling and drinking. Of Edmund's sons there remained William, the rector of Hilborough, and Maurice, the shy civil servant in the Navy Office, who had been surprised and flattered to be invited to represent his brother at a dinner in London to celebrate the Battle of the Nile. Susannah had been living near Ipswich, her husband, Tom Bolton, arousing concern because of his tendency to overspend, particularly in buying a farm at Cranwich, near Hilborough, with a handsome, long, low farmhouse, dignified by a pillared porch. Kate was staying happily with her handsome, well-to-do husband, George Matcham, at Bath. The family's eyes were fixed upon Horatio, in whose reflected glory they all basked.

Despite the apparent lethargy in Palermo, vigorous plans for the recapture of Naples were in hand. The driving force of the counteroffensive was an extraordinary Calabrian nobleman, Fabrizio Ruffo, a former treasurer and war minister to the Pope who had been rewarded by being appointed cardinal in a minor order. He planned to land in Calabria, raise the peasantry through the combined influence of landowners and ecclesiastical friends and march on Naples. Although Nelson dismissed him as a 'swelled-up priest',[13] he was surprisingly effective. He and a small staff had landed on the mainland in February and soon he was leading 17,000 men northwards under the banner of the Christian Army of the Holy Faith. His prospect improved when, in March, Austria had again declared war on France, the Turks and Russians offered naval support and General Bonaparte, trying to lead his army back to France overland, was stopped by Captain Sir Sidney Smith's defence of the Levantine coastal city of Acre. Ruffo made such rapid progress that Nelson sent Troubridge with four ships to take the islands of Capri and Ischia and blockade Naples.

By the end of April, the royalist hordes were nearing the city, looting and murdering those suspected of treason, while Troubridge had taken the islands. The bulk of French troops withdrew from the city, leaving a garrison in the hilltop fortress of Sant' Elmo to stiffen the 20,000 men of the Parthenopean

Republic's civil guard. But at the same time a naval crisis suddenly threatened. A strong French fleet escaped from Brest and, eluding Lord Keith in the Atlantic, entered the Mediterranean, followed by a Spanish fleet from Cadiz. If the two could combine the British would be faced by an overwhelming force of forty-two ships of the line. On 12 May, Nelson received orders to take his entire force into the western Mediterranean, but he was reluctant to leave Sicily, writing to St Vincent, who was ashore, sick, at Gibraltar, 'You may depend upon my exertion and I am only sorry that I cannot move to your help; but this island appears to hang on my stay. Nothing could persuade the Queen this night but my promise not to leave them unless the battle was to be fought off Sardinia.'[14] But he did send ten sail of the line to Minorca and then deployed the rest of his ships for the defence of Sicily.

At Naples, the royalists had invested the three castles and Ruffo had demanded their surrender. On 12 June, Emma wrote to Nelson:

> I have been with the Queen this evening. She is very miserable and says that, although the people of Naples are for them in general, yet things will not be brought to that state of quietness and subordination till the fleet of Lord Nelson appears off Naples. She therefore begs, entreats and conjures you, my dear Lord, if it is possible to arrange matters so as to be able to go to Naples . . . For God's sake, consider it and go.'[15]

On the same day, Nelson wrote to St Vincent, 'Tomorrow morning I receive on board . . . 1,700 troops and sail for the Bay of Naples.'[16] His plan was delayed by reports that the French fleet might be approaching, but they had in fact run for Toulon and the Spanish for Cartagena; there would be no confrontation at sea. Meanwhile, Captain Foote of the *Seahorse* had been sent ahead and arrived off Naples to see fires and fighting ashore.

When Nelson finally did sail for Naples in his new flagship, the *Foudroyant*, on 20 June, he took the Hamiltons with him, having suggested to Emma, 'If you both thought the sea air would do you good, I have plenty of room. I can make you private apartments and give you my honour the sea is so smooth that no glass was ever smoother.'[17] Emma was delighted, but not for the sake of her health: she saw herself as the Queen's special emissary to Naples.

Nelson was in an ugly mood, far removed from his characteristic humanity. When Troubridge wrote asking for a judge to be sent urgently to try captured insurgents, he replied, '*Minerva* shall bring the troops and the judge. Send me word some proper heads are taken off, this alone will comfort me.'[18] On 24 June, the British squadron anchored off Naples. As soon as contact was established with the shore, Sir William sought news of the Palazzo Sessa and his collection and was enraged to hear that it had been looted by the *lazzaroni*, the royalist mob. Emma was infected by the vengeful excitement and filled with self-importance as she insisted that Queen Maria Carolina had asked her to act in Naples on her behalf; indeed, she had already written to Emma, 'I recommend Lord Nelson to treat Naples as if it were a rebellious city in Ireland.'[19] Emma wrote to her former lover, Charles Greville:

> The Queen is not come. She sent me as her Deputy; for I am very popular, speak the Neapolitan language and am considered, with Sir William, a friend of the people . . . The head of the Lazerony [sic], an old friend, he came in the night of our arrival and told me he had 90 thousand Lazeronis ready, at the holding up of his finger . . . Lord Nelson, for whom I interpreted, got a large supply of arms for the rest and they were deposited with this man.[20]

The mobs were already raging through Naples, murdering suspected liberals and looting. It was too dangerous for the Hamiltons to venture ashore, even among those they considered their friends and their former friends, many of whom were being hunted through the streets. Meanwhile, Nelson, who did not speak Italian, was reliant on the Hamiltons as interpreters and, more importantly, advisers.

At once a confrontation between Nelson and Ruffo began. Captain Foote had written to the admiral that the cardinal had been treating with the rebels in the city and its three castles and that a truce had been agreed. Under this, there would be a general amnesty and republicans wishing to leave the city could embark in ships which would be allowed to sail for Toulon. Nelson was outraged. He saw the revolution in terms of the Reign of Terror in Paris and the republicans as bloody regicides rather than idealistic reformers. Hamilton's advice was that, as the terms of the truce had not been authorized by the King, they were therefore invalid and he wrote to Ruffo declaring the agreement void. Meanwhile, Nelson repeated his view to Foote, adding, 'Your news of the hanging of thirteen Jacobins gives us great pleasure.'[21] So the garrisons of the forts were ordered to surrender unconditionally and the flotilla of coastal craft, loaded with refugees bound for Toulon, were brought under the guns of the fleet. All prisoners, Nelson announced, would be expected to throw themselves on the King's mercy, although he must have known how unsparing that would be. One of the first prisoners to be tried for treason was the Neapolitan admiral Prince Carraciolo, who had supported the revolution: court-martialled on 29 June, he was condemned to death, Nelson confirming the sentence.

After the sentence of death by hanging had been passed, the condemned man begged the British naval officer commanding his guard to ask Lady Hamilton to intercede with Nelson to commute the sentence to the less degrading execution by shooting. She could not be found and Carraciolo was hanged from the yardarm of a Neapolitan frigate at five o'clock that afternoon. It was to be rumoured that Emma had watched the hanging, but in fact she and her husband were dining with Nelson in the *Foudroyant* at the time. One of her enemies spread the story that when the admiral's secretary carved off the head of a roasted pig, which was served at table, she had fainted and, on recovering, made a joke about this having reminded her of Carraciolo. Probably they did hear the report of the signal gun that announced the execution.

Meanwhile, ships crowded with surrendered rebels lay alongside the British ships in the bay, the prisoners – men, women and children – awaiting their fate. What this might be became increasingly apparent, for the Queen instructed Emma by letter to treat the leaders with 'a rigorous severity' and 'the females who have distinguished themselves in the revolution' were 'to be treated the same way and without pity . . . This is not pleasure but absolutely necessary . . . I recommend to you therefore, my dear Lady, the greatest firmness, vigour and severity . . .'[22]

The British ships' companies were horrified. One midshipman, George Parsons, described fugitives from Ruffo's bloodthirsty irregulars vainly pleading for mercy:

> Many, very many of Italy's beauteous daughters, and those of high rank, have I seen prostrate on our deck, imploring protection from these bloody ruffians, by whom their natural protectors had been murdered. Their graceful forms bent with misery – their dark eyes and clasped hands raised to the Father of all for mercy – their clear, olive complexions changing to a sickly hue from anguish of mind. How could men, possessing human hearts refrain from flying to their relief? Yet, I am sorry to say, they were placed (without regard to their feelings) in polaccos [coastal craft] under the guidance of young English midshipmen, there to let their afflicted hearts break at leisure . . . I grieve to say, that wonderful, talented and graceful beauty, Emma Lady Hamilton, did not sympathise in the manner expected from her generous and noble nature. . .'[23]

Emma was well aware of what was happening and was about to happen in the city. One letter from an English friend ashore told her, 'The great question is, who is to be hanged and who is to be beheaded. Few, or none, dispute that they don't merit death but then to prolong the moment, each produces his privilege, just as if it was of any consequence whether a man goes to

Heaven in a coach and six, or in a wheelbarrow.'[24]

Seeing Nelson as King Ferdinand's representative at Naples – until the latter arrived in the bay at the beginning of July and wisely did not venture ashore – and herself as the Queen's, Emma revelled in the power she undoubtedly possessed. She compiled a list in her own hand of the surrendered Jacobins in the ships and those still believed to be at large in the city and she wrote to Greville that she sent daily reports to Palermo.

Nelson, as infected as the Hamiltons by a zest for vengeance, proudly wrote to her mother, also in Palermo, that she 'has her time so taken up with excuses from rebels, Jacobins and fools that she is most heartily tired'.[25] Many of these were old friends, the cultivated, often aristocratic Neapolitans whose palaces they had frequented and who had, in turn, admired Sir William's collections. One of the pleading letters that reached her was from Domenico Cirillo, a doctor, Professor of Botany at Naples University and a member of the Royal Society in London.

He had indeed been a member of the revolutionary council, pleased that he had been elected to the legislative council of the short-lived republic, but he had treated the wounded from both sides and saved the English garden in the royal palace at Caserta from destruction. Emma passed his appeal to Nelson, who declined to intervene, and Sir William was to write to his nephew, Greville, 'Many of all classes have suffered death by having been beheaded, or hanged; among the latter we have seen with regret the name of Doctor Domenico Cirillo, one of the first physicians, botanists and naturalists in Europe.'[26]

As the *Foudroyant* lay at anchor in the bay, letters arrived for Nelson from Fanny, telling him of the death of his brother Suckling, and about a gift to him of money from the East India Company; he wrote a polite reply, asking her to divide it between his brothers and sisters. He told her that now that 'the kingdom of Naples is liberated from thieves and murderers' he had celebrated this – and the anniversary of the Battle of the Nile on 1 August – by giving a dinner party for the King on board his flagship. 'In the evening there was a general illumination,' he continued. 'A large vessel was fitted out like a Roman galley; on the oars were fixed lamps and in the centre was erected a rostral column with my name, at the stern, elevated, were two angels supporting my picture. In short, the beauty of the thing was beyond my powers of description.' But he did try to describe it:

> More than 2,000 variegated lamps were fixed round the vessel, an orchestra was fitted up and filled with the very best musicians and singers. The piece of music was in great measure my praises, describing their distress, but Nelson comes, the invincible Nelson and we are safe and happy again. This must not make you think me vain, so far, very far from it, and I relate it more from gratitude than vanity.'[27]

Meanwhile, the executions continued ashore and, on 4 August, he escorted the King and the Hamiltons back to Palermo.

It was at this time that the debate over Nelson's behaviour at Naples in the summer of 1799 began: was he simply putting into action the rough demands of politics and war, or in thrall to the vengeful Emma Hamilton and her husband or had the head-wound suffered in Aboukir Bay temporarily affected his character and judgement? That such wounds could have various lasting effects was illustrated when his friend Captain Hardy remarked, 'If they push the bottle fast, I shall not forget to mention my unfortunate wound in the head that always makes me *mad* after the first bottle.'[28]

They arrived at Palermo four days later and the King at once showed his gratitude to Nelson by raising him to the Sicilian aristocracy, creating him Duke of Bronte. His estate, which had originally belonged to a monastery, was named after a small town on the black, volcanic western slopes of Etna, giving him an estate of 30,000 acres that was said to be the finest corn-growing land in Europe but was in fact a rocky wilderness of lava. The name, derived from the mythological giant who forged thunderbolts for Jupiter, was Italian for thunder. Nelson played with versions of his new signature – 'Bronte Nelson', 'Bronte Nelson of the Nile', 'Nelson and Bronte' – while Emma jokingly called him 'My Lord Thunder'.[29]

The triumph was celebrated on 3 September with a party culminating in a firework display in the gardens of the royal palace. The officers of the British ships were invited and the sarcastic Midshipman Parsons described

> the fairy scene presented by the illuminated palace and the gardens, the assembled royal family, the great in rank, the bold in arms, with Italy's nut-brown daughters, their lustrous black eyes and raven tresses, the elegant and voluptuous forms gliding through the mazy dance; and the whole presided over by the genius of taste, whose attitudes were never equalled and with a suavity of manner and a generous openness of mind and heart, where selfishness with all its unamiable concomitants, pride, envy and jealousy would never dwell – I mean Emma, Lady Hamilton.'[30]

The centrepiece of the garden party were life-sized waxworks of Nelson and the Hamiltons in an allegorical tableau within a mock-classical temple. The figure of Nelson was dressed in the coat the admiral had worn at the Battle of the Nile and wore a laurel wreath; beside him, 'Emma', dressed in 'royal purple, on which was embroidered in letters of gold an inch long the names of the ten captains who achieved the victory' and holding a trumpet, represented Fame. Then, as a British visitor put it, rockets were fired and the crown prince, dressed as a British midshipman, 'advanced from the royal group to the temple and, with a grace and modesty becoming his years, raised from the brow of the waxen admiral the wreath of laurel and placed it on that of the living one! I was in hopes that this melodramatic farce might have closed here,' continued the visitor. 'But the crowned hero with his satellites continued to march about the gardens for three hours ... followed and gazed at by the multitudes.'[31] Midshipman Parsons noted that Lord Nelson was moved to tears by the spectacle but 'his trusty aides-de-camps could do no less than apply their handkerchiefs though, in some, from a contrary feeling of mirth.'[32]

The adulation had gone to Nelson's head and he was delighted to hear that the fashionable Irish portrait-painter, archaeologist and aspiring diplomat Robert Fagan had called for the erection of his statue, or a rostral column to his triumphs, in Rome, when that was possible. Fagan seems to have suggested this in the hope that Sir William Hamilton might arrange with the King for a grant of rights to excavate the antiquities. But enthusiasm was premature. Nelson had written to Fagan of his gratification that 'my actions have contributed to preserve the works which form the School of Fine Arts in Italy, which the modern Goths wanted to carry off and destroy'.[33] But Fagan, on second thoughts, had to dampen his enthusiasm because, 'It would be impossible, I fear, to have it erected on the Capitol without removing the statue of Marcus Aurelius, as the vicinity of each to the other would prejudice the effect of both.'[34]

It was all so very different from the quiet of Burnham Thorpe, where Fanny had been spending a month with her father-in-law. There had been little news to tell her husband in her dutiful letters. There had been trouble with a dishonest coachman, whom she had had to dismiss when he was thought to be guilty of theft and the rector had warned him that such behaviour led to the gallows. There had been worries about the Bolton family because Susannah's husband had, as feared, run into debt by moving to Cranwich, Fanny reporting that it had been put about that he had a brother-in-law, 'a great lord, that is to pay all his debts, therefore he will be trusted'.[35] There was gossip about neighbours, naval friends and, when relations came to stay, who would sleep in which spare bedroom. There was no more talk of coming to Palermo.

In July 1799, the French and Spanish fleets had abandoned the Mediterranean, sailing into the Atlantic, pursued by Lord Keith; the former making for Brest, the latter for Cadiz. Keith had now been confirmed as St Vincent's successor as commander-in-chief and, in his absence, Nelson was ordered to take supreme command from Gibraltar to the Levant. As he saw it, Palermo, midway between the extremities, was the perfect headquarters and more effective than a flagship at sea. He had that same month ignored an order from Keith to move his ships to Minorca on the grounds that he considered the defence of Sicily of greater strategic importance. The strategy also suited his private life, which became increasingly fervid.

Living ashore with the Hamiltons, this had begun happily, with Sir William writing, 'Lord Nelson and I, with Emma, are the *Trio Juncta in Uno* . . . I glory in the hospitality I have had in my power to show Lord Nelson and almost all the Heroes of the Nile.'[36] But at the end of the year he was writing to Charles Greville, 'Lord Nelson continues to live with us so that my house is always full of marine officers and altho' I must own that I am a little tired of keeping open house so long as I have and which I really could not do without Emma's doing the honours so well as she does.'[37] He hankered after England but concluded, 'Without me, Lord Nelson would not stay here and, without Lord Nelson, their Sicilian Majesties would think themselves undone.'[38] He stressed the Queen's affection for Emma as a major influence, but this view was not always shared. Visiting Palermo, the tart-tongued Lord Elgin, newly appointed ambassador to Constantinople, remarked:

> You never saw anything equal to the fuss the Queen made with Lady H. and Lord Nelson, wherever she moved was always by her side. I am told the Queen laughs very much at her to all her Neapolitans but says her influence with Lord N. makes it worth her while making up to her. Lady H. has made him do many very foolish things.[39]

Of Emma herself, he sneered, 'She looked very handsome at dinner, quite in an undress – my father would say, "There is a fine woman for you, good flesh and blood." She is indeed a whapper! and I think her manner very vulgar. It is really humiliating to see Lord Nelson. He seems quite dying and yet as if he had no other thought than her.'[40] The compliments he paid to her were widely repeated; when he wrote to the British consul at Leghorn, asking him to send him 'the handsomest coral necklace, earrings and bracelets which can be procured', he added that they were 'for the most beautiful woman in the world, Lady Hamilton'.[41] Without Emma, Nelson's enthusiasm for Palermo would have waned: Sir William had been unwell, bilious and suffering from diarrhoea, and he himself spent his evenings and, increasingly, much of his nights with Emma. Night after night he would be seen beside her, sometimes asleep, while she gambled and drank.

Rumours spread far beyond Palermo through naval officers frequenting the admiral's shore headquarters and worried his friends. One of them, Captain Troubridge, decided to face the crisis and wrote to him, 'If you knew what your friends feel for you, I am sure you would cut out all the nocturnal parties; the gambling of the people at Palermo is talked of everywhere. I beseech your Lordship, leave off. Lady H—'s character will suffer; nothing can prevent people from talking; a gambling woman in the eyes of an Englishman is lost.'[42] He added ominously, 'Some person in Sir William's house sends accounts. I have frequently heard things, which I know your Lordship meant to be kept secret.'[43] A tightening of the reins came at the beginning of 1800, when Lord Keith returned to the Mediterranean, resumed command and ordered Nelson to meet him off Leghorn.

On 20 January, 1800, the two admirals met and then sailed for Palermo on their way to Malta, where the French garrison of Valetta was still holding out. Sailing south, Nelson was, despite the responsibilities of command and conscious of being under the eye of a disciplinarian commander-in-chief, obsessed by Emma. On the 29th he began a distracted letter to her: 'Separated from all I hold dear in this world, what is the use of living if indeed such an existence can be called so . . .' Next morning, six days out of Leghorn, he continued:

> I shall run mad. We have had a gale of wind; that is nothing but I am 20 leagues farther from you than yesterday

> noon . . . Last night I did nothing but dream of you, altho' I woke 20 times in the night. In one of my dreams, I thought I was at a large table, you was not present – sitting between a princess, who I detest, and another. They both tried to seduce me and the first wanted to take those liberties with me, which no woman in this world but yourself ever did. The consequence was I knocked her down and in the moment of bustle you came in and, taking me in your embrace whispered, 'I love nothing but you, my Nelson'. I kissed you fervently and we enjoyed the height of love. Ah, Emma, I pour out my soul to you.[41]

The squadron arrived off Palermo on 3 February and Nelson escorted his commander-in-chief ashore. Admiral Keith was a tough, reliable, unimaginative Scotsman of fifty-four and he arrived in his flagship accompanied by his wife, 'Queenie'; the daughter of Mrs Hester Thrale, who, as a child, had known Dr Samuel Johnson. She took to Cornelia Knight, who had been staying with the Hamiltons since her mother's recent death, rather than Emma. Lord Keith disliked everything he saw, declaring, 'The whole was a scene of fulsome vanity and absurdity', and determining to take Nelson on to Malta away from 'Palermo and its allurements.'[45] They were to sail on 12 February and, that day, Nelson was alone with Emma. Their farewell was such that he was to write, 'I did remember well the 12th. February and also the months afterwards. I shall never be sorry for the consequences.'[46]

On 18 February, Nelson was hunting two fugitive ships of the line from Aboukir Bay, writing to Emma from his flagship, 'I feel anxious to get up with these ships and shall be unhappy not to take them myself . . . If it be a sin to covet glory, I am the most offending soul alive. *But here I am* in heavy sea and thick fog!'[47] Then the fog lifted, a masthead lookout sighted the topsails of a ship of the line and Midshipman Parsons, standing near Nelson on the *Foudroyant*'s quarterdeck, heard a the lookout shout, 'Deck there! The stranger is a line-of-battle ship, my lord, and going large on the starboard tack.' It could be one of the two fugitives from Aboukir Bay, *Le Généreux* or the *Guillaume Tell*, and Nelson said to Captain Berry, his flag-captain, 'The signal for a general chase, Sir Ed'ard. Make the *Foudroyant* fly!'[48] She was *Le Généreux* and, after a sharp action, she struck her colours. Now only the *Guillaume Tell* remained of the French fleet and, six weeks later, Berry captured her too.

Insisting to Keith that he return to Palermo because of poor health, Nelson was accorded another hero's welcome. After he joked about his prize to Cornelia Knight – 'Ah! she knew that she belonged to us and her conscience would not let her stay away any longer'[49] – she had written an extra verse for singing to the tune of the national anthem (to add to the hymn of praise she had written about the Battle of the Nile):

While thus we chant his praise,
See what new fires blaze!
New laurels spring!
Nelson! thy task's complete;
All their Egyptian fleet
Bows at thy conqu'ring feet
To George our King![50]

Nelson waited until the commander-in-chief had departed for Genoa and then embarked the Hamiltons for a cruise to Malta. In the great cabin of the *Foudroyant* they found monthly magazines sent from London by Fanny and it was cluttered with the admiral's trophies, including the huge wooden plume of feathers taken from the masthead of the *Guillaume Tell*. These inspired Cornelia Knight, who was of the party, to compose another eulogy to be sung to the tune of 'Heart of Oak', in which the name Emma was changed to Delia for propriety's sake and which ended:

Then cheer up, fair Delia! remember thou'rt free;
And ploughing Britannia's old empire, the sea,
How many in Albion each sorrow would check,
Could they kiss but one plank of this conquering deck.[51]

They sailed on 23 April in what Midshipman Parsons described as 'this Noah's ark',[52] arrived off Valetta and anchored at night. A wind got up, the ship dragged her anchor; at dawn, they found themselves nearer to the city than expected and within range of French guns.

> At peep of day, he made us a target for all his sea batteries to practice on. 'All hands up!', 'Anchor ahoy!' resounded fore and aft and we hove short to the music of the shot, some of them going far over us. Lord Nelson was in a towering passion and Lady Hamilton's refusal to quit the quarterdeck did not tend to tranquillise him.'[53]

Eventually, decks wet with splashes from falling shot, the ship was warped out of their range. Then, as Parsons put it, 'Lady Hamilton, finding that the French governor would not surrender until he had made a meal of his shoes, influenced Lord Nelson to turn her head for Palermo . . . where the balls were not all of iron.'[54]

On passage, they encountered Lord Keith, whose flagship, the *Queen Charlotte*, had been destroyed by an accidental fire and who had decided to take over Nelson's flagship. 'This caused many long faces on our quarterdeck,' noted Parsons, 'and even Lord Nelson's countenance wore an expression of vexation as he arrayed himself in his paraphernalia of stars and diamonds to wait on his senior officer.'[55] The scene was changing. Not only was Nelson now under the direct command of an unsympathetic admiral but he had received a brusque letter from Lord Spencer, the First Lord of the Admiralty, who, having heard that he had had to return to Palermo 'on account of the state of [his] health', thought it would be best if he returned to England instead of being 'obliged to remain inactive at Palermo . . . you will be more likely to recover your health and strength in England than in an inactive situation at a foreign Court, however pleasing the respect and gratitude to you for your services may be'.[56]

Also, Hamilton had been told that he was to be replaced as

ambassador. He and Nelson had seen their partnership as essential to the survival of the Kingdom of the Two Sicilies and there was the current joke that Lady Hamilton was the real Commander-in-Chief of the Mediterranean Fleet. Therefore, a return home became inevitable. But there or abroad, a new problem would have to be faced: Emma was pregnant with Nelson's child.*

What form that home would be seemed problematical. From England, Fanny had been writing bravely cheerful letters, hoping that all was well in Palermo: 'I hear the weather is delightful there. The sun does shine upon us today, it's quite a treat.'[57] It had been chilly in England, she had been wearing two layers of undergarments and was sending 'Lady Hamilton a cap and a kerchief such as are worn this cold weather'.[58] Smart society was at last seeking her company and one particularly grand lady was showing 'her extreme anxiety for the honour of my acquaintance'.[59] There was family news – the Matchams were trying to sell their house in Hampshire – and she had given some seeds her husband had sent her from Sicily to the gardener at Roundwood, who 'will raise a few for us'.[60] In London, she had been to Court and wrote, 'I shall make you smile at my economy. My birthday suit could not be worn after Easter, therefore I took the first tolerable Thursday to pay my respects at St. James's . . . Our gracious King thought it was a long time since I heard from you and told me the wind was changed therefore he hoped I should hear from you very soon.'[61] She had heard the latest news of his success at sea – 'I thank God for the preservation of my dear husband and your recent success off Malta' – and had hopes for their reunion: 'I can with safety put my hand on my heart and say it has been my study to please and make you happy and I still flatter myself we shall meet before very long.'[62]

Nelson and the Hamiltons planned to travel home together but, as Lord Keith refused to allow him to take his flagship out

* It has been suggested that Emma became pregnant while on board the *Foudroyant*. Nelson sometimes used a double easy chair that unfolded to become a wide bed; one such, from the *Victory*, was handed down in the Gatty family, who are descended from one of Nelson's chaplains.

of the Mediterranean, they would sail to Leghorn and make their way via Vienna – whither the Queen was bound – and on across the Continent to Hamburg in the expectation of being met by a ship of the Royal Navy for a passage to England.

Emma's departure from Palermo was almost as uncomfortable as her arrival. She was suffering from morning sickness, the sea was rough and, in contrast to her resolution on the voyage from Naples, she 'began to wail and roll about'.[63] On arrival at Leghorn all was seemly again and the Queen distributed presents to her British friends. But worrying news awaited them: General Bonaparte had again invaded northern Italy and had defeated the Austrians at Marengo, so to travel overland to Vienna would be fraught with danger. Now Lord Keith arrived at Leghorn and refused Nelson's request that he escort the Queen back to Palermo, saying his ships were needed urgently for operations elsewhere and they would have to make use of Austrian frigates also in port. This the Queen refused, saying she would take passage only in a British warship. Nelson agreed and an appalled British witness noted, 'His zeal for public service seems entirely lost in his love and vanity and they all sit and flatter each other all day long.'[64] Lord Keith was adamant, muttering, 'Lady Hamilton has had command of the fleet long enough.'[65] The Queen became hysterical but to no avail and finally calmed sufficiently to agree to the one remaining option, to travel overland, via Florence, to Ancona, take a ship to Trieste and then proceed from there to Vienna, avoiding capture by the French if they could.

The Queen left for Florence in a cavalcade of eighteen carriages and baggage-wagons on 12 July and Nelson, the Hamiltons and Cornelia Knight followed the next day. Reaching Florence safely, they were heading into the Apennines when, at Arezzo, the coach in which Nelson and the Hamiltons were travelling overturned and was damaged. The French were close to the north and it was too dangerous to risk Nelson or Sir William, so Mrs Cadogan – dignified by Nelson with the title of *Signora Madre* – and Cornelia Knight were turned out of their carriage, in which the others continued their journey, while they waited three days for the damaged coach to be repaired. As a chivalrous gentleman, Sir William was distressed at such an ungallant necessity, but, noted Cornelia Knight, 'his wife and Nelson were too much wrapped up in each other to care'.[66] Yet all reached Ancona without further mishap, boarded Russian frigates lying there and, on 1 August, arrived at Trieste to find the city celebrating the second anniversary of the Battle of the Nile. They paraded the streets to shouts of, '*Viva Nelson!*' and, much happier, took the road to Laibach in Slovenia, then through the mountain passes to the Austrian towns of Klagenfurt and Graz and finally to Vienna.

There, at the Court of the Empress Maria Theresa, the Queen introduced her British friends to the gentle pleasures of her capital, which were such a contrast to the turgid temptations of Naples and Palermo. There was plenty to distract Nelson from thoughts of his eventual arrival in England and what would transpire. In April, Fanny had written to him saying that she expected, when Malta surrendered and King Ferdinand was restored to Naples, he would 'feel himself at liberty to think of your health and affairs and to show yourself in England. John Bull's eyes sparkle at the sound of the Battle of the Nile', yet she did not present herself attractively, adding, 'I have been confined from going into hot rooms owing to a rash, which was very troublesome.'[67]

Here in the cool baroque drawing-rooms of Vienna, Nelson and the Hamiltons, who had become as much part of the scene in Palermo as the tinselled puppets of the street theatres, seemed grotesque. Emma was, 'coarse, ill-mannered, disagreeable'[68] . . . 'the fattest woman I've ever set eyes on'[69]; Sir William, 'old, infirm, all admiration of his wife',[70] and Nelson himself, 'a gig from ribbands, orders and stars',[71] a comic-operatic figure whom Emma led 'like a keeper with a bear . . . It is plain that Lord Nelson thinks of nothing but Lady Hamilton . . . She puffs the incense full in his face but he . . . sniffs it up very cordially.'[72] The trio 'looked like a troupe of strolling players'.[73] As a final touch they were accompanied by the statuesque Fatima, Emma's Nubian maid.

There was a round of entertaining and sightseeing. The composer Joseph Haydn dined with them and accompanied Emma on the piano when she sang in her loud, fruity voice Cornelia Knight's 'Ode on the Battle of the Nile' and the exploding of *l'Orient*:

> . . . The dire concussion shakes the land
> Earth, air and sea, united groan.
> The solid Pyramids confess the shock
> And their firm bases to the centre rock.

Lavish entertainment – hunting, dancing, dining – arranged by Prince Esterhazy culminated in a firework display and the toasting of Nelson 'with a flourish of trumpets and firing of cannon'.[74] Then Haydn again played in a concert, but Emma ignored the music and decided to gamble, sitting at the faro table, playing Nelson's cards for him and winning handsomely. Yet the composer did sense greatness in Nelson and, for a finale concert, had, noted Cornelia Knight, 'composed a finale so melancholy, so touching, that it drew tears from many of the audience and he had given orders that while it was playing the lights should be gradually extinguished. . .'[75] This he had named 'The Nelson Mass'.

While in Vienna, Nelson had his portrait painted by Friedrich Füger and permitted his face to be covered with plaster – while he breathed through straws inserted into his nostrils – for the casting of a 'life mask'. Both were flattering images and very different from the description given by an Austrian, who saw the trio:

> Lady Hamilton never stopped talking, singing, laughing, gesticulating and mimicking while the favoured son of Neptune appeared to leave her no more than her shadow, trying to meet with his own small eyes the great orbs of his beloved and, withal, as motionless and silent as a monument, embarrassed by his poor figure and by all the emblems, cords and crosses with which he was bedecked.

> In a word, the Lord of the Nile seemed as clumsy and dim on land as he is adroit and notable at sea.[76]

Their coach rumbled on to Prague where they boarded river-boats for the journey to Dresden. There another sharp-eyed observer recorded their arrival:

> Nelson is one of the most insignificant figures I ever saw in my life. His weight cannot be more than 70 pounds. A more miserable collection of bones and wizened frame I have never yet to come across. His bold nose, the steady eye and the solid worth revealed in his whole face betray in some measure the great conqueror. He speaks little and then only English and he hardly ever smiles . . . he was almost covered with orders and stars . . . Lady Hamilton . . . behaved like a loving sister towards Nelson; led him, often took hold of his hand, whispered something into his ear and he twisted his mouth into the faint resemblance of a smile.[77]

Continuing on the river Elbe to Dessau, where an artificial hillock was named the Nelsonberg, a more fastidious member of the party recorded, 'Lady Hamilton began bawling for a Irish stew and her old mother set about washing the potatoes . . . They were exactly like Hogarth's actresses dressing in a barn.'[78] At Magdeburg, another visitor recorded that Emma – 'a woman full of fire, in whom one can still clearly see the beauty of youth; she is somewhat stout' – helped the one-armed Nelson with his food. But he also noticed that 'nothing was noticeable about his eye and he even seems to be able to see with it'.[79]* Finally they arrived at Hamburg, hoping to find at least a frigate of the Royal Navy waiting to take them home; none was there.

*The sight of the eye damaged in Corsica had improved, but Nelson worried about the deterioration of his left eye and, in bright sunlight, wore a green eyeshield over it.

While waiting in the hope that a ship would arrive, Nelson asked Cornelia Knight to come shopping for 'magnificent lace trimming for a court dress'[80] for Fanny. When no frigate appeared, they decided to make their own way to England and, on 31 October, boarded the mail-packet *King George*. Butting into rough sea and squalls, they sailed into the North Sea, bound for Nelson's native Norfolk and the inevitability of disaster, one way or the other.

8
Fanny Meets Emma

Fanny had planned to greet her returning husband at their new house in Suffolk. She would sit writing to him at her escritoire, glancing up at Lemuel Abbott's reassuring painting, which showed him as the sensitive, reliable man she had remembered during his three years' absence. Everything was ready for him. 'Roundwood is in good repair,' she wrote, 'even the shrubs are trimmed up, and look smiling, all ready to receive my lord', and the carriage he had ordered was 'really elegantly neat'.[1] But Roundwood in winter did not suit her health any more than Burnham Thorpe. The previous winter, she had complained that she was 'teased with a sad cough',[2] as was her father-in-law, who had come to stay; so they decided on spending the cold months in London where, she explained, 'I hope going to a warmer air will be of service, at least the variety of St. James's Street'.[3]

She had heard that her husband was travelling home overland with the Hamiltons but did not know when to expect him; then he had written from Vienna to suggest they meet in London. She did not know where he might land if he sailed from Hamburg. It was likely to be one of several East Anglian ports – perhaps Harwich or Great Yarmouth – within easy reach of their house, but equally he might arrive in the Thames estuary and be taken up to London. When she heard that he had reached Hamburg on 21 October, she wrote, inviting him to bring the Hamiltons to Roundwood. As time passed with no further word, she began to guess at other ports of arrival and decided that it would be better to await him in London. The decision would have come as a relief because, from what she knew of Lady Hamilton and the rumours she had heard, she can have had no wish to allow the gentility and, indeed, the sanctity of the house prepared for the resumption of their marriage to be tainted by such a visitor. So, leaving word of her plan with the servants at Roundwood, in case he arrived there after all, she travelled to London and took rooms for herself and her father-in-law at Nerot's Hotel in King Street, off St James's Street.

Meanwhile, Nelson, his mistress – now seven months pregnant – and her husband had landed at Great Yarmouth on 6 November to a tumultuous reception. 'I am a Norfolk man and glory in being so,'[4] he told the crowd as they took the horses from the traces of his carriage and hauled it through the streets, cheering. Finally receiving Fanny's letter, he decided that they would leave for Ipswich the following day, arriving at Roundwood in time for dinner. Dreading the immediate future, he also wrote to the Admiralty, asking for immediate employment at sea. The next day, they departed with an escort of Norfolk yeomanry and, that afternoon, the carriage swept up the gravel drive to his own front door. But Fanny was not there, a servant explained that she awaited them in London and Nelson regarded the muddle as another example of his wife's inefficiency. He walked through the house but could not bring himself to stay there and, after an hour, ordered the coachman to drive on to London.

There, Fanny, old Edmund and Nelson's friends were becoming impatient. On the 8th, Nelson's former flag captain Thomas Hardy wrote:

> Notwithstanding all the newspapers, his Lordship is not arrived in town and when he will God only knows. His father has lost all patience, her Ladyship bears up very well as yet but I much fear she also will soon despond . . . Should he not arrive tomorrow I think I shall set off for Yarmouth *as I know too well the cause of his not coming*.[5]

Next day, he did arrive.

Sunday 9 November 1800 was wet and stormy. Trees had been blown down and the streets were slippery with mud and wind-blown leaves. At Nerot's Hotel, 'the gallant hero of the Nile . . . was met by his venerable father and his amiable lady', as the *Morning Herald* reported. 'The scene which took place was of the most graceful description and is more easily conceived than described.'[6] Indeed, it could only be imagined since it was in private. Nelson, wearing full naval uniform with decorations, escorted Sir William and Lady Hamilton ('Emma grown fat, Sir William thin – like Jack Sprat and his wife,'[7] noted a friend), followed by Fatima, the Nubian maid, into the hotel. There, Fanny, chilled with apprehension, radiated what Emma was to call an 'antipathy not to be described'.[8] The introductions were coldly formal and dinner at five o'clock so tense that Nelson left as soon as he could for an official visit to the Admiralty. Each woman found that the other fulfilled her worst apprehensions: Fanny recognized Emma's sexual energy and the residue of her beauty as qualities with which she could not compete; Emma saw Fanny as the English lady whose poise and manners she could never emulate and, once out of earshot, reacted violently, describing her as a 'Creole with her heart black as her fiend-looking face'.[9] Later, the Hamiltons continued to a large new house – 22 Grosvenor Square – which they had been lent by Sir William's rich, dilettante cousin, William Beckford, while Fanny remained at the hotel because the house rented for them by Alexander Davison in Dover Street was not ready.

Cornelia Knight and Mrs Cadogan were to stay at Lothian's Hotel in Albemarle Street and, soon after they arrived, Nelson's friend Captain Troubridge called upon the former with a warning. Bluntly, he told her what she already expected, that Lady Hamilton was unacceptable in polite society – let alone the court, where she herself had useful connections – and that she should distance herself from them as soon as possible. Seeking the advice of a friend, Margaret Nepean, the wife of the Secretary to the Admiralty, she found the warning endorsed and accepted an invitation to stay with them. She saw the Nelsons and the Hamiltons once more, when she dined with them at

Grosvenor Square, but, she recorded, 'Most of my friends were very urgent with me to drop the acquaintance but . . . I feared the charge of ingratitude, though greatly embarrassed as to what to do for things became very unpleasant. So much was said about the attachment of Lord Nelson to Lady Hamilton . . . Mischief was made on all sides.'[10] Next evening, she refused an invitation to join the party at the theatre and others that followed. Her defection was quickly noticed and Emma reacted angrily, scrawling on the flyleaf of a book Cornelia had given her, 'Given to me by Miss Knight, whom I thought good and sincere . . . We gave shelter to Miss K. for near two years. We brought her free of expense to England. What has she done in return? . . . She is dirty, ill-bred, ungrateful, bad-mannered, false and deceitful.'[11] Nelson simply snarled, 'that bitch Miss Knight".[12]

Fanny, however, was determined to remain the lady, continuing to regard Nelson as her husband and Emma as his unsuitable friend; she even invited the Hamiltons to stay with them at Roundwood when the pressure of activity allowed. He, of course, was instantly engulfed in a round of official visits and ceremonial festivity. On Monday morning, he called on the Admiralty Board in Whitehall and then, in full uniform, walked along the Strand to the Navy Office in Somerset House through excited crowds. There was a royal levée at St James's Palace, a banquet at the Guildhall and another dinner in St James's Square, at which Nelson met William Pitt, the Prime Minister, and the gross Prince of Wales, who angered him by casting a lusty eye over Emma. Four days after his arrival, Lord and Lady Nelson again dined with the First Lord of the Admiralty, Lord Spencer, and his wife. Well remembering that, on the last such occasion, the couple had behaved towards each other as lovers, Lady Spencer was shocked. As she told a friend:

> Such a contrast I never beheld! A trifling circumstance marked it very strongly. After dinner, Lady Nelson, who sat opposite to her husband (by the way, he never spoke during dinner and looked blacker than all the devils),

> perhaps injudiciously, but with a good intention, peeled some walnuts and offered them to him in a glass. As she handed it across the table, Nelson pushed it away from him so roughly that the glass broke against one of the dishes. There was an awkward pause; and then Lady Nelson burst into tears! When we retired to the drawing-room, she told me how she was situated.[13]

Worse was to follow. The Nelsons had now moved into 17 Dover Street, the house rented for them by Alexander Davison, and there they planned to entertain the Hamiltons. The two couples twice went to the theatre. Sitting together in a box, they formed a striking tableau: Nelson in the centre with Emma on his right and Fanny on his left. A newspaper reported, 'Lady Nelson appeared in white with a violet satin head dress and a small white feather. Her ladyship's person is of a very pleasing description; her features are handsome and exceedingly interesting and her general appearance is at once prepossessing and elegant.' These were the qualities that so filled Emma with jealousy, while she was reported as being 'rather *embonpoint* but her person is nevertheless highly graceful and her face extremely pretty. She wore a blue satin gown and head dress with a fine plume of feathers.'

Both performances were accompanied by the singing of patriotic and nautical songs and both by the collapse of one of the two ladies. On one occasion, the heavily pregnant Emma, overcome by the heat and excitement, fainted and was helped from the box by Fanny, who then may have discovered the biological reality. On the other, the play was *Pizarro* and, towards the end of the third act, came the words, 'How a woman can love, Pizarro, thou hast known . . . how she can hate, thou hast yet to learn . . . wave thy glittering sword, meet and survive an injured woman's fury', and at this Fanny fainted. She was carried from the box but recovered before the end of the performance. 'We understand,' reported the newspaper, 'that she has for some days been in a very indifferent state of health.'[14] Soon afterwards, Fanny invited the Hamiltons to dine at Dover Street and again it was

Emma who collapsed, rushing from the dining-room to vomit. Fanny did not immediately follow but Nelson ordered her to do so, himself leaving the room to comfort his mistress as she was sick into a bowl held by his wife.

After their guests had departed, the tensions between Nelson and Fanny became unbearable and he left the house to walk the streets for hours, finally knocking on the door of the Hamiltons' house in Grosvenor Square at dawn, physically and emotionally exhausted. Admitted by a startled servant, he was shown into the Hamiltons' bedroom and, sitting on the edge of a bed, pleaded with them to allow him to stay with them. Emma worried about public reaction to that, but Sir William said he did not care what anybody thought. Even so, Nelson returned to Dover Street. It was only to be a fleeting return.

In the hope of escape to sea, he had again asked the Admiralty for employment, but they were not to be hurried. Meanwhile, the social season of Christmas and the New Year lay ahead. Already it had become clear that Fanny would be received at Court but that Emma would not. Pleading by Nelson and Hamilton was ignored, as was a letter of recommendation from Queen Maria Carolina. Then Sir William's cousin, William Beckford, came to the rescue. A homosexual of exotic tastes he could indulge thanks to a West Indies sugar fortune, he was about to celebrate the near-completion of a monstrous folly, Fonthill Abbey. This was a gigantic, mock-ecclesiastical, Gothick building with a tower rising nearly 300 feet, designed for entertaining in the depths of his beautiful Wiltshire estate of wooded hills and lakes. He had invited Nelson and the Hamiltons to stay for Christmas – pointedly, Fanny was not included – for 'a few comfortable days of repose, uncontaminated by the sight and prattle of drawing-room parasites'.[15] The party, accompanied by Emma's mother, travelled to Wiltshire on 19 December.

They stayed at Fonthill Splendens, the Palladian mansion built near a lake and below the hill upon which the architectural fantasy loomed. The other guests were often more amusing than those they might have met at a more conventional gathering.

They included Benjamin West, the American-born President of the Royal Academy; Dr John Walcott, the satirical writer; James Wyatt, the architect of Fonthill Abbey; and Madame Banti, the singer, whom the Hamiltons had known in Naples. The climax of the stay was an evening entertainment at the Abbey on the 23rd that wrapped them in a Gothick spell of high theatricality. The procession of carriages ascended the hill through dark woods in which torches flickered and music was played by unseen musicians. Entering the Abbey itself, the high, pillared hall – its vaulting, eighty-feet high, lost in gloom above the flaring torches – a mock-monastic meal was served – sadly, for gourmands like Emma, 'unmixed with the refinements of modern cookery'.[16] However, before returning to Fonthill Splendens for supper, Emma appeared in an 'Attitude' as Agrippina carrying the ashes of Germanicus. Her Attitudes were not quite what they had been, for she was nearly forty, fatter and heavily pregnant. However, as a newspaper report put it, she still displayed

> a superior, graceful animation of figure, now a little on the wane from too great a propensity to the *en bon point*. Her attitudinarian graces, so varying in their style and captivating in their effect, are declining also under this unfortunate personal extension . . . Her conversaziones, if not solid and argumentative, are at least sprightly and unceasing.[17]

The party broke up on Boxing Day and Nelson returned to London and Fanny. The crisis broke soon afterwards. Their solicitor, William Haslewood, was breakfasting with them, when Nelson mentioned 'dear Lady Hamilton' and Fanny snapped, 'I am sick of hearing of dear Lady Hamilton and am resolved that you shall give up either her or me!' According to Haslewood, Nelson replied quietly, 'Take care, Fanny, what you say. I love you sincerely but I cannot forget my obligations to Lady Hamilton and speak of her otherwise than with affection and admiration.' Fanny then rose and, 'muttering something about her mind being made up', left the room.[18]

Now the Admiralty came to the rescue. Promoted to vice-admiral, Nelson was appointed second-in-command of the Channel Fleet and ordered to join his flagship, the *San Josef* forthwith. Before leaving in the early morning, he visited Fanny, who was still in bed; it was reported that she held out her hand to him and said, 'There is not a man in the world who has more honour than you. Now tell me, upon your honour, whether you have ever suspected, or heard from anyone, anything that renders my own fidelity disputable.' He said that he had not. Then he walked out of her life.

The final parting had not been acrimonious; indeed, that night he wrote to her from Southampton, 'We have arrived heartily tired; and, with kind regards to my father and all the family, believe me, your affectionate Nelson.'[19] There was another friendly note from him, thanking her for forwarding letters, and then a spate of complaints about the inefficiency of the packing of his gear, for which he held her responsible. 'I find myself without anything comfortable or convenient,' he wrote to her, listing the missing furniture, cutlery and china. A few days later he wrote, 'It was never my intention to find fault but the fact is I have nothing and everything. If I want a piece of pickle it must be put in a saucer, if a piece of butter on an earthen plate . . . Large nails drove through the mahogany table and drawers to fasten the packing cases.' There were missing keys to a trunk and a wardrobe, lost decanters and on an ornamental silver centrepiece for his dining-room table 'the trident of Neptune is bent double from ill package'.[20]

Fanny had gone to Brighton in the hope of easing the strain and there she received a final letter, telling her that Nelson would be visiting the Admiralty but that on no account was she to return to see him in London, or in Portsmouth, while his ship might be there. He now knew that he was bound for the Baltic but did not mention this.

Fanny did not give up hope. Roundwood was to be sold but Nelson had taken a year's lease on 17 Dover Street and was making her a generous allowance to maintain her social position in London.

Her friendship with her father-in-law was close and she was friendly with her brothers- and sisters-in-law friendly. Now that Nelson had left the halls of distorting mirrors in Naples and returned to the practicalities of life in England, she still hoped that the infatuation with Lady Hamilton would pass. In truth, Nelson was longing for domestic tranquillity – but not with his wife – and was given a poignant reminder of this when, in April, he dined with Cuthbert Collingwood and his wife and daughter at Plymouth. 'How surprised you would have been to have popped in to the Fountain inn,' wrote Collingwood to his old friend Mary Moutray, now living in Ireland, 'and see Lord Nelson, my wife and myself sitting by the fire cozing and little Sarah teaching Phyllis, her dog, how to dance.'[21]

Yet he was in no mood for such felicities, being obsessed and seething with love, lust and jealousy. Flying his flag in the *San Josef*, he wrote to Emma, often several times a day, sometimes as himself, often as if writing on behalf of one of his ship's company, named Thompson, or Thomson, who, beset by love and anxieties, 'is so agitated . . . he cannot write'.[22] The improbable story was that Thompson was an illiterate sailor whose sweetheart ashore was about to give birth to his child and that the admiral had agreed to write letters for him, addressing Lady Hamilton as 'Mrs. Thompson' although the fictitious girl was unmarried. Whether writing as 'Thompson', as himself, or in a muddled mixture of the two, his were the symptoms of a manic depressive, writing to her, 'When I consider this day, nine months, was your birthday and that, although we had a gale of wind, yet I was happy and sung 'Come, Cheer Up, Fair Emma', etc. Even the thoughts . . . make me melancholy, my heart is somehow sunk within me.'[23] But then his obsessive fear of the attentions of the Prince of Wales, who had eyed Emma at Alexander Davison's party in St James's Square, erupted, as he speculated that Sir William might begin to curry royal favours:

> I own that I wonder that Sir Wm. should have a wish for the Prince of Wales to come under your roof; no good can come of it but every harm . . . We know he is dotingly fond

> of such women as yourself and is without . . . honour in those respects and would leave you to bewail your folly. But, my dear friend, I know you too well not to be convinced you cannot be seduced by any prince in Europe. You are, in my opinion, the pattern of perfection.[24]

Yet he suffered lurking doubts about Emma's fidelity, also writing, 'I own I sometimes fear that you will not be so true to me as I am to you, yet I cannot, will not, believe you can be false. No, I judge you by myself.'[25]

On 29 January, Emma gave birth to twin daughters at 23 Piccadilly. The news was discreetly sent to Nelson, who was told, untruthfully, that only one had survived. In fact both girls were healthy, but Emma had decided that one was appropriate while two would destabilize the balance of their liaison; one baby might be concealed but two could not. Sir William did not choose to recognize the event, or even that he was aware of it.

Three days later Nelson replied, again writing about 'Thompson', declaring:

> I believe poor dear Mrs. Thompson's friend will go mad with joy. He cries, prays and performs all tricks, yet dare not show all or any of his feelings, but he has only me to consult with. He swears he will drink your health this day in a bumper and, damn me, if I don't join him despite of all the doctors in Europe for none regard you with truer affection than myself. . . I cannot write, I am so agitated by this young man at my elbow. I believe he is foolish, he does nothing but rave about you and her. I own I participate of his joy and cannot write anything.[26]

He was again writing to 'Mrs. Thompson' two days later, declaring that her lover

> hopes the time may not be far distant when he may be united for ever to the object of his wishes, his only, *only* love. He swears before heaven that he will marry you as

> soon as it is possible, which he fervently prays may be soon. He charges you to say that . . . you must, on every opportunity, kiss and bless for him the dear little girl, which he wishes to be called Emma, out of gratitude to our dear, good Lady Hamilton . . .[27]

Emma was to comply – although Nelson was soon to change his mind about the name – and the baby to be discarded was called Emma, although her father would never know it.

Yet three days later, on an upsurge of jealousy, he was writing, 'Sir William should say to the Prince that, situated as you are, it would be highly improper for you to admit H.R.H. . . . I know his aim is to have you for a mistress. The thought so agitates me that I cannot write.'[28] Jealousy brought him to the edge of hysteria, writing again in a long letter, 'Hush, hush, my poor heart keep in my breast, be calm. Emma is true but no one, not even Emma, could resist the Serpent's flattering tongue . . . Oh, I could thunder and strike dead with my lightning . . . the villain. Don't scold me, indeed I am not worth it and am to my last breath yours.'[29] Then he was again writing about the Thompsons, this time in the guise of Thompson himself, about the child that had apparently been born to the sailor and his girl:

> It is not usual to christen children until they are a month, or six weeks, old; and as Lord Nelson will probably be in town, as well as myself, before we go to the Baltic, he proposes then . . . that myself and Lady Hamilton should be two of the sponsors . . . Its name will be Horatia, daughter of Johem and Morata Etnorb. If you read the surname backwards and take the letters of the other names, it will make, very extraordinary, the names of your real and affectionate friends Lady Hamilton and myself.[30]

On the same day, he drew up a memorandum specifying handsome bequests to 'a child . . . in whom I take particular interest and, as Emma Hamilton is the only person who knows the parents of this female child, I rely with the greatest confidence on her unspotted honour and integrity that she will regard this child as mine ... bringing it up as the child of her dear friend Nelson. . .'[31]

A week after the birth of the twins, Emma took a closed carriage from Piccadilly to 9 Little Titchfield Street, a modest house just to the north of Oxford Street, carrying a well-wrapped infant. This was Horatia, whom she was putting into the care of a foster-mother, Mrs Gibson. At about the same time, the twin, Emma, was delivered to a nurse with instructions that, after two months, she should be given to the Foundling' Hospital* in Holborn. Nelson, not knowing that both children had survived, looked to the future with optimism and arch sexual imagery, writing to Emma in the Thompson guise, 'I dare say twins will again be the fruit of your and his meeting. Have the dear thatched cottage ready to receive him and I will answer that he would not give it up for a queen and a palace.'[32] Shifting his adoration into another dimension, he wrote to her, 'As truly as I believe in God, I believe you are a saint and in this age of wickedness you set an example of real virtue and goodness.'[33] He even composed and sent her a prayer that used the facility of pious words he had learned at his father's services, 'O God, who knows the purity of my thoughts and the uprightness of my conduct, look down, I beseech Thee, on me . . .'[34]

He had shifted his flag to the *St George* and sailed to Spithead, which was a day's journey from London, and there he received a letter from Emma confirming that his daughter had indeed been named Horatia. 'You win my heart for ever,' he replied. 'I am all soul and sensibility.' He was all devotion, too, adding, 'With my present feelings, I might be trusted with fifty virgins naked in a dark room.'[35] Soon afterwards, he was writing again:

*Moved to Berkhamstead in 1926 and the original buildings demolished; the organization continues as the Thomas Coram Foundation for Children.

> My longing for you, both person and conversation, you may readily imagine. What must be my sensations at the idea of sleeping with you! It sets me on fire, even the thoughts, much more would be the reality. I am sure my love and desires are all to you and if any woman naked were to come to me, even as I am at this moment from thinking of you, I hope it might rot off if I would even touch her with my hand. No, my heart, person and mind is in perfect union of love towards my own, dear, beloved Emma.[36]

Granted three days' leave, he set out to see his daughter for the first time but, in his neurotic anxiety, feared that Fanny might burst on to the scene. He knew she had been staying in Brighton and so wrote to her, 'I am sent for to town on a very particular business for a day or two. I would not have you come to London but rest quiet where you are. Nor would I have you come to Portsmouth for I never come on shore.'[37] He hurried to London for a passionate reunion and the visit to Little Titchfield Street to see Horatia. 'A finer child was never produced by any two persons!' he exulted. 'In truth, a love-begotten child!'[38] The meeting was short. He knew that he was going on active service, as second-in-command to Vice-Admiral Sir Hyde Parker, who was bound for the Baltic to deter the alliance of Russia, Denmark, Sweden and Prussia from acting in support of France.

Emma now had a confidante in Sarah Nelson, William's wife, in whom she recognized social ambition, which could be harnessed to her own aims. Sarah, she saw, was resentful of the ladylike Fanny Nelson and it was to her that she first used the latter's cruel nickname 'Tom Tit', arising from the latter's stiff, bird-like gait, and calling Josiah 'The Cub'. In February, she had written to Sarah, 'You and I liked each other from the moment we met. No so with *Tom Tit*, for there was an antipathy not to be described.'[39] Now she wrote again about her reunion with Nelson, giving her a day-by-day account: 'We had a pleasant evening', then writing and erasing the words 'and night'. He had now left for Great Yarmouth to embark and she continued, 'He goes off tonight and is to sail immediately. My heart is fit to burst quite with grief. Oh, what pain, God only knows . . . I shall go mad with grief. Oh, God only knows what it is to part with such a *friend, such a one*. We were truly called the *Tria Juncta in Uno* for Sir W., he and I have but *one heart in three bodies*.'[40] She was relieved that Fanny had remained in Brighton but she wrote to Sarah Nelson, 'Tom Tit does not come to town. She offered to go down but was refused. She only wanted to do mischief to all the great Jove's relations. 'Tis now shown all her ill treatment and bad heart, Jove has found it out.'[41]

On 4 March, Nelson did write again to Fanny, reminding her that, due to his patronage, Josiah had been given command of a frigate:

> I have done *all* for him. And he may again, as he has done before, wished me to break my neck and be abetted in it by his friends, who are likewise my enemies. But I have done my duty as an honest, generous man and I neither want, or wish, for anybody to care what become of me, whether I return, or am left in the Baltic, seeing I have done all in my power for you. And, if dead, you will find I have done the same.* Therefore my only wish is to be left to myself. . .'[42]

Desperate for advice, Fanny consulted her brother-in-law, the solemn, reliable Maurice, sending him his brother's letter, and, when he replied, wrote across the top, 'This is my Lord Nelson's letter of dismissal, which so astonished me that I immediately sent it to Mr Maurice Nelson, who was sincerely attached to me, for his advice; he desired me not to take the least notice of it as his brother seemed to have forgot himself.'[43]

Wrapped in his own love, lust, jealousy and guilt, Nelson was, however, sharply aware of other men's relationships with women. In Plymouth he had been aware of Cuthbert

*Nelson had indeed made provision for Fanny, with, initially, an annual income of £1,600 and a legacy in his will.

Collingwood's happy marriage to the charming Sarah, complicated only by his absences at sea. At Portsmouth, he noted in a letter to Emma that the port admiral's wife was 'dressed old ewe-lamb fashion'[44] and that the dockyard commissioner's wife 'likes a drop and looks like a cook-maid'.[45] Now, in Yarmouth, he called on Admiral Hyde Parker, newly married to a plump young wife – nicknamed 'the batter pudding' – one morning at the inn, where they were staying. When told that the couple were not yet down from their bedroom, he remarked in a letter to Captain Troubridge, 'Consider how nice it must be laying in bed with a young wife, compared to a damned cold, raw wind.'[46]

While he was awaiting the departure of Admiral Parker's fleet from Yarmouth roads, the nightmares of jealousy returned at the thought of Emma as hostess when her husband entertained in London and he was writing to her:

> What can Sir William mean by asking you to launch out into expense and extravagance? He that used to think that a little candle-light and iced water would ruin him? . . . You are at auction, or rather to be sold by private contract. Good God! my blood boils . . . I cannot bear it. Aye, how different I feel. A cottage, a plain joint of meat and happiness, doing good to the poor and setting an example of godliness, worthy of imitation even to kings and princes.[47]

Then he would become calm and loving: 'I worship – nay, adore you and if you was single and I found you under a hedge, I would instantly marry you'[48] and 'the thought of Horatia cheers me up'.[49] Then again the jealousy would surge and he wrote, 'I see clearly, my dearest friend, that you are on SALE. I am almost mad to think of the iniquity of wanting you to associate with a set of whores, bawds and unprincipled liars. Can this be the great Sir William Hamilton? I blush for him.'[50]

The next day, 12 March 1801, the fleet sailed for the Baltic. Once he was away on active service, his letters to her became almost serene: 'I have much to do here, exactly what you said in

London. May God, whom I worship, protect and send me victorious. Amen, if it be His good pleasure. May the heavens bless you.'[51] Despite his passion, he was aware of his own enthralment, telling her, 'It is your sex that makes us go forth and seem to tell us, none but the brave deserve the fair . . . It is your sex that rewards us, it is your sex who cherish our memories.'[52] Self-pity was limited to, 'It is dreadfully cold . . . we Mediterranean people are not used to it.'[53]

When Hyde Parker's fleet disappeared into the North Sea, there was much speculation about the outcome. Would he attack Copenhagen as he forced his way into the Baltic, or make straight for the powerful Russian fleet and destroy it? Those who knew Nelson expected the latter, but he was, of course, only second-in-command. Such speculation was bandied about in London, but the long wait for news of a departed expedition was normal and anticipation served to heighten the excitement of social life. In London, Nelson's fears of a predatory Prince of Wales and faithless Emma proved unfounded, but he would have winced at the thought of her former lover, Sir William's nephew, Charles Greville, as a guest at one of the many dinner parties at 23 Piccadilly. This was held on 15 April and among more than a dozen other guests were two dukes (Gordon and Queensberry), a Neapolitan duke, the actor Charles Kemble, William Nelson, up from Norfolk, and Nathaniel Wraxall, a friend of Sir William with particular knowledge of Denmark.

On that day, news had reached London that Nelson had destroyed the Danish ships and batteries off Copenhagen on 2 April and that the city had surrendered to him. The dinner party became a wild celebration. It began with Emma singing patriotic songs and accompanying herself on the harpsichord, then dancing a tarantella, which Wraxall described as

> an Apulian dance . . . a copy of the Bacchant amusements of antiquity, demanding no slender portion of animal strength and spirits. Sir William began it with her and maintained the conflict, for such it might well be esteemed,

during some minutes. When unable longer to continue it, the Duke de Nöia [Duca di Noja] succeeded to his place, but he, too, though nearly forty years younger than Sir William, soon gave in from extenuation. Lady Hamilton then sent for her own maid-servant, who being likewise presently exhausted, after a short time another female attendant, a Copt, perfectly black, whom Lord Nelson had presented her on his return from Egypt, relieved her companion. It would be difficult to convey any adequate idea of this dance ... castagnettes and the *tambour de Basque* constitute essential accompaniments ... We must suppose that the two performers are supposed to be a satyr and a nymph, or rather a fawn and a Bacchant. It was certainly not of a nature to be performed except before a select company as the screams, starts and embraces with which it was intermingled gave it a peculiar character.[54]

A few hours after the guns had fallen silent off Copenhagen and he had reported his victory to Admiral Parker, Nelson sat at his writing-table in the great cabin of his flagship, the *St George* and wrote, '9 o'clock at night – very tired after a hard-fought battle'. He then wrote a verse that had been in his mind for some time. It was to Emma and began:

> From my best cable though I'm forced to part,
> I have my anchor in my angel's heart
> And, like a pilot, shall the pledge defend
> And for a prong his happiest quiver lend.[55]

Then he had returned to drafting his dispatch, giving details of the heavy losses on both sides, the overwhelming of the Danish defences and the capitulation of the city. The Baltic was now open to the British and the alliance constructed by the French was broken.

Four days after the Bacchanalia in Piccadilly, the victory at Copenhagen was celebrated at a strange little ceremony at the Foundling Hospital. Six children given into its care were to be baptized by the Reverend C. T. Heathcote, the chaplain, and three of the boys were given names commemorating the battle: Hyde Parker, after the commanding admiral; Baltic Nelson; and Moss Riou after two captains killed in the action. Another boy was named William Hamilton and a girl, Mary Thompson, Emma's *nom de plume* in her clandestine correspondence with Nelson, which only she would have known. Finally a girl was christened Emma Hamilton, a name surely chosen by the mother who had given her to the orphanage. Only Emma can have been the originator of those names; only she, who had invented the half-comical names of Marquis Nile, Earl Alexandria and Viscount Pyramid after the victory in Aboukir Bay, could have suggested Baltic Nelson. It is probable that Emma herself was present, for it was the custom for the chaplain to supply names if none were provided by those involved in the children's brief lives; it would have been natural for him to defer to her and equally likely that she herself took charge.

She had been thrilled by the arrival of Nelson's nautical love poem and replied to it:

> I think I have not lost my heart
> Since I with truth can swear
> At every moment of my life
> I feel my Nelson there.
>
> Where, where should Emma treasure up
> Her Nelson's smiles and sighs,
> Where mark with joy each secret look
> Of love from Nelson's eyes . . .[56]

This brought him to a new peak of excitement and young Captain Edward Parker, who had become a friend of the Nelson-Hamilton ménage ashore, wrote to Emma from the Baltic about her lover's eventual return: 'He says he will not let much grass grow under his feet after he lands until he sees you.'[57]

Fanny had heard of the victory at Copenhagen in a note from Lord Spencer while she was staying at Bath with her father-in-law and hurried to London, where she saw Sarah Nelson, but she soon returned as there was no immediate prospect of her husband's recall. She then received an unexpected letter from his sister Susannah, from whom she had heard little, asking, 'Could you for one moment, my dear Lady Nelson, attribute my silence to neglect?'

> Will you excuse what I am going to say? I wish you had continued in town a little longer as I have heard that my brother regretted he had not a house he could call his own when he returned. Do, whenever you hear he is likely to return, have a house ready to receive him. If you absent yourself entirely from him, there can never be a reconciliation. Such attention must please him and I am sure will do in the end. Your conduct as he *justly* says is *exemplary* in regard to him and he has not an unfeeling heart. I most sincerely love my brother and *did quite as much before he was Lord Nelson* and I hope my conduct was ever the same towards you as Mrs. Nelson as ever it was as Lady Nelson. I hope in God one day I shall have the pleasure of seeing you together as happy as ever, he certainly, as far as I hear, is not a happy man.

She then concluded with 'family chit-chat'.[58] Like her sister Kate, Susannah was confused by trying to remain on easy terms with both women.

In April, Fanny wrote to Nelson:

> I cannot be silent in the general joy throughout the Kingdom, I must express my thankfulness and happiness it has pleased God to spare your life. All greet you with every testimony of gratitude and praise. This victory is said to surpass Aboukir. What my feelings are your own good heart will tell you. Let me beg, nay, intreat you to believe no wife ever felt greater affection for her husband than I do. And, to the best of my knowledge, I have invariably done everything you desired. If I have omitted

> anything, I am sorry for it . . . What more can I do to convince you that I am truly your affectionate wife?[59]

He did not reply to her letter but, before it reached him, had written to Alexander Davison, 'You will, at a proper time and before my arrival in England, signify to Lady Nelson that I expect . . . to be left to myself without any enquiries from her: for sooner than live the unhappy life I did when I last came to England, I would stay abroad for ever. My mind is fixed as fate.'[60]

His father, to whom Fanny remained attentive, also sent congratulations to his 'good, great and affectionate son', praising the God that had 'bestowed on your great abilities and has granted you His grace to use them to His glory, the good of your fellow creatures and the salvation of your own soul', hoping for 'a return to domestic joys, the most durable and solid of all others'. But he added, 'Lady [Nelson] was heavily affected with her personal feelings at not receiving a line from your own hand.'[61]

Fanny could not know that the 'esteem' she had once inspired in him could never have competed with the neurotic infatuation that consumed him. In the Baltic, he had invited Admiral Parker and all the officers who had met Lady Hamilton to celebrate the 'Birthday of Santa Emma'. The invitation commanded 'you as well as all other Med. friends now in the fleet' to come on board his flagship to offer thanks to

> our guardian angel Santa Emma, whose prayers, I can answer, were offered to the throne of heaven . . . for our success and it is my firm belief that they had much more influence than any ever offered either to a heathen goddess, or any saint ever made by the best Pope, so it is our duty to express our gratitude.[62]

Meanwhile, he had received orders to succeed Hyde Parker in command of the fleet and, on 6 May, he sailed against the Russian fleet in the Gulf of Finland. But his capture of

Copenhagen had been enough; shortly after he began negotiating with the Russians, the pro-French Armed Neutrality of the North alliance was disbanded. In mid-June, he heard that he had been created a viscount, which, because he had hoped for an earldom, was as much a disappointment as his barony had been. Yet there was to be compensation, for a week later his own successor as commander-in-chief arrived and he sailed for England in a fast brig, arriving at Great Yarmouth on 1 July.

In London, he took rooms at Lothian's Hotel in Albemarle Street, around the corner from the Hamiltons in Piccadilly, but his happy reunion was shadowed by the news that his brother Maurice had died just as he was about to be promoted to be a Commissioner of the Customs and Excise. He had been living with his middle-aged mistress, Mrs Sarah Ford, whose poor eyesight had earned her the nickname Blindy, in the Thames-side village of Laleham in Middlesex. Nelson at once offered to support her, sending her £100 and writing to assure her that she must continue to live in Maurice's house and that he would provide her with 'horse, whisky . . . and every convenience to make your stay comfortable . . . Nothing, be assured, shall be wanting on my part to make your life as comfortable and cheerful as possible.'[63] He decided to visit her with the Hamiltons, combining this with a fishing expedition on the Thames for Sir William. They found at Laleham the antithesis of the Neapolitan and Sicilian exoticism in which their love affair had ripened; it was, in reality, his dream of simple, rural bliss. Weeks after their return to London, he was musing to Emma, 'Would to God I was with you at Laleham, I shall never forget our happiness at that place.'[64] It was there that he determined to create his own Laleham, conjuring up his pastoral fantasies and a shrine for the woman he saw as Santa Emma. The dream was not confined to England, for he had written from the Baltic to a friend that 'the moment Peace come, I shall go to Bronte and live under the shade of my great chestnut tree'.[65]

In July, Fanny wrote again, making the payment of her 'handsome quarterly allowance' the excuse to thank him for his 'generosity and tenderness' and asking him to accept 'my warmest, my most affectionate and grateful thanks', concluding, 'I could say more but my heart is too full.'[66] Soon afterwards, Davison wrote to her so kindly that he must have given her hope, telling her of Nelson's improving health and that he had gone to Surrey for a rest. Then he added, 'I need hardly repeat how happy I should have been to have seen him with you, the happiest. His heart is so pure and so extremely good that I flatter myself he never can be divorced from his affection.' But he continued in a less effusive style, 'I have the same opinion I ever had of his sincere respect for you.'[67] Respect was not, of course, all that she wanted from her husband.

His hope of Emma finding them an idyllic country cottage, or 'farm' quickened when she wrote about a house for sale between Turnham Green and Chiswick, only to be dashed by the threat of invasion. Called to the Admiralty, Nelson was told by Lord St Vincent that it was important for the enemy to know 'that *you* are constantly opposed to him'.[68] He was therefore given command of all naval forces between Orfordness and Beachy Head, including the part-time volunteers the Fencibles and a light squadron based on Deal in Kent. Characteristically, he chose to take the offensive, and the most promising target was the port of Boulogne, where the invasion forces were most heavily concentrated. On 15 August, he launched a night attack on the line of gunboats moored off the harbour mouth; but he did not accompany the boats himself and it was a disaster, much as Tenerife had been. Again Nelson's popularity carried him through a failure that would have collapsed the career of any other commander.

Yet even as he sailed down-Channel to launch his boarding-parties against the Boulogne flotilla, he was writing to Emma:

> From my heart I wish you could find me out a good comfortable house, I should hope to be able to purchase it. At this moment, I can command only £3,000; as to asking Sir William, I could not do it; I would sooner beg. Is the house at Chiswick furnished? If not, you may fairly calculate £2,000 for furniture . . . As you may believe, my dear

> Emma, my mind feels at which is going forward this night; it one thing to order an attack and another execute it . . .

He was longing for her company and asked, 'What place would you like to come to, Margate or Deal?'[69]

When he and the survivors of the attack returned to the Downs anchorage off Deal with the wounded (two of whom were Nelson's favourite young officers, Captain Edward Parker and Lieutenant Frederick Langford), he invited Emma to join him there:

> The Three Kings, I am told, is the best house (it stands on the beach) if the noise of constant surf does not disturb you . . . To come and see a poor forlorn sailor [would be] a charity to me and Parker and Langford and I hope you would benefit by the jaunt. You can bathe in the sea that will make you strong and well . . . I hate the Downs but if my friends come it will be a paradise.[70]

In the midst of his frustration at the failure off Boulogne and his worry about the wounded – particularly Parker – a letter arrived from Emma saying that she had found the ideal house. It was at Merton in Surrey, a village south-west of London near Wimbledon, an hour's ride from the Admiralty and near the Portsmouth road. The price was £9,000 and he at once replied, 'I approve of the house at Merton.'[71]

At the end of the month, Emma arranged a visit, accompanied by Sir William and Sarah Nelson, to whose husband she wrote:

> Could you not come to Deal with us? Lord, that would be nice, as the children say . . . Tom Tit has been in town, I heard, and Mrs. Nelson a few days ago saw, *met* the Cub, but he looked as if he was going to be hanged but did not speak to her. The precious couple are fit for each other.[72]

They had arrived, accompanied by their maids, and taken rooms opening on to a gallery in the Three Kings overlooking the sea.

Emma found Deal 'a dreary place'[73] but then Nelson came ashore, depressed, tired, seasick and with toothache; he even took up his wife's cruel nickname, denying that he had received another letter from 'Tom Tit'. So Emma set about cheering him with plans for the house at Merton.

As they settled into seaside life, Sarah Nelson recorded brightly, 'My lady call'd me this morning soon after six to go to bathe and a very fine dip we had; our maids do the same. I am now just come from making breakfast.'[74] They visited Parker and Langford in the house where they were lodged in the town, Emma ordering jelly and port wine for their meals and having a sofa moved into a ground-floor room for their convalescence. But it was too late for Edward Parker. Gangrene set in, the amputation of his leg close to the hip was an agonizing failure and, a week after Emma, Sarah and Sir William left for London on 20 August, he died.

Grieving for young Parker, Nelson sank back into depression. This was compounded by a surveyor's report on the structural state and probable cost of Merton, which would force him to live far beyond his means. Yet he remained determined, writing to Davison, 'I am after buying a little farm at Merton . . . If I cannot, after all my labour for the Country, get such a place as this, I am resolved to give it all up and retire for life.'[75] He began thinking of retirement – with Emma and Horatia, after Sir William's death – to Bronte; farming and gardening tools had already been sent there. Above all, he longed for the house at Merton he had never seen. 'You may rely on one thing, that I shall like Merton,' he wrote to Emma. 'I have that opinion of your taste and judgement that I do not believe it can fail in pleasing me . . . You will soon make it the prettiest place in the world.'[76]

The purchase of Merton Place was completed in his absence. Emma, her mother and husband moved in and the latter, who understood Nelson's fantasies, wrote to him at Deal:

> You are in luck for, in my conscience, I verily believe that a place so suitable to your views could not have been found

> . . . You have nothing but to come and enjoy immediately. You have a good mile of pleasant dry walk around your farm. It would make you laugh to see Emma and her mother fitting up pig-styles and hen-coops and already the canal is enlivened with ducks and the cock is strutting with his hens about the walks. Your Lordship's plan as to stocking the canal with fish is exactly mine. I will answer for it, that in a few months' time you may command a good dish of fish at a moment's warning.[77]

Nelson wrote to Emma insisting that, while the house must be entirely his property – 'I do earnestly request that all may be mine in the house, even to a pair of sheets, towels, etc.'[78] – that 'you are to be, recollect, Lady Paramount of all the territories and waters of Merton and we are all to be your guests and to obey all lawful commands'.[79] He saw himself both as gentleman-farmer – 'I admire the pigs and poultry. Sheep are certainly most beneficial to eat off the grass . . . I intend to have a farming book'[80] – and as a hospitable, church-going squire: 'Have we a nice church at Merton? We will set an example of goodness to the underparish . . . We will eat plain, but will have good wine, good fires and a hearty welcome for all our friends, but none of the great shall enter our peaceful abode. I hate them all.'[81]

Resentment of those who had snubbed Emma and withheld the highest honours from him still smouldered. His particular worry 'in these degenerate days' was of his Elysian Fields in Surrey being invaded by 'titled pimps', as he put it to Emma, preparing the way for the dreaded Prince of Wales. 'I am not surprised at that fellow wanting you for his mistress,' he wrote to her in early October. 'I suppose he will try to get to Merton as it lays in the road, I believe, to Brighton; but I am sure you will never let them into the premises.' The nightmare even undermined his longing for 'the farm' and, in moments of panic, he again began to look further afield, writing in the same letter, 'Do you think we shall soon get to Bronte? I should be very happy but I must first settle all my affairs in this country and Merton may become a dead weight on our hands. . .'[82]

Another worry was that sharing Merton with the Hamiltons, as he planned to do, would create such a scandal that it undermined his pretence, transparent as it was, that Emma and he were simply friends. So he pleaded with her to keep their intentions secret, for, he wrote, if they became public knowledge 'I believe it would kill me.'[83] He fussed, as Emma was negotiating for Merton Place on his behalf, that it might be thought that either he was supporting her financially or *she* was buying the house for *him*, and, he continued, 'For heaven's sake never do you talk of having spent any money for me. I am sure that you never have to my knowledge.'[84]

The war seemed to be coming to an end in the autumn of 1801. William Pitt had resigned and been succeeded as Prime Minister by Henry Addington, who appeared willing to allow generous terms for peace. This would, of course, end Nelson's exile at sea, and not only Fanny but her father-in-law and sisters-in-law hoped that it might lead to a reconciliation and an end to his enthralment with the notorious woman who was increasingly seen as both vulgar and grotesque. Caricaturists had been merciless throughout the year, drawing her as 'Dido in Despair' (a fat harridan wailing at the disappearance of her lover's ship over the horizon) and Sir William as a desiccated connoisseur mournfully examining broken phallic antiquities, with her telling a pipe-smoking Nelson, 'The old man's pipe is always out but yours burns with full vigour', to which he replies, 'Yes, yes, I'll give you such a smoke! I'll pour a whole broadside into you.'

Edmund Nelson had invited Fanny to stay with him at Burnham Thorpe. She had accepted and the news spread. The rector had told his son that, 'If Lady Nelson is in a hired house and by herself, gratitude requires that I should sometimes be with her.'[85] He had suggested to her that they might share a house in London, or Bath, but, lonely as she was, she declined the proposal as 'impracticable' because 'the deprivation of seeing your children is so cruel, even in thought',[86] as she could already see the coming divergence of loyalties. Characteristically, the old man replied, 'Be assured I still hold fast my integrity and am ready to join you. . . The opinion of others must rest with themselves and not make any alteration with us.'[87]

Edmund had already written to his son – at first, warmly but continuing ominously – beginning the letter:

> Upon the happy return of peace I may . . . address you in the words of the apostle and say, 'You have fought a good fight, you have finished your military career with glory and honour, henceforth there is laid up for you much happiness . . .' Now in a private station possibly you may tell me where it is likely your general place of residence may be so that sometimes we have had mutual happiness in each other notwithstanding the severe reproaches I feel from an anonymous letter for my conduct to you, which is such, it seems, as will totally separate us. This is unexpected indeed.[88]

He gave no hint that he might suspect Emma to be the anonymous letter-writer, if, in fact, he did.

In Bath, Kate Matcham chanced upon Fanny and affected not to recognize her banishment by her husband, and Fanny wrote to Edmund, 'I told Mrs. M. at Bath that Lord Nelson would not like your living with me. "Oh, my dear Lady Nelson. My brother will thank you in his heart for he knows no one can attend my father as you do." I had seen the wonderful change pass belief. She had not.'[89] Susannah Bolton did not admit to recognizing the extent of the change and, seeing Fanny as more acceptable than Emma, she tried to ensure friendly relations with both. Sending family gossip from Cranwich, she suggested that, if Fanny were visiting Lord Walpole at Wolterton – (an invitation that Emma could not hope to receive):

> I hope you will favour us with your company here. Do not say you will not suffer us to take too much notice of you for fear it should injure us with Lord Nelson. I assure you I have a pride, as well as himself, in doing what is right and that surely is to be attentive to those who have been *so*

> *to us* and I am sure my brother would *despise* us if we acted contrary.[90]

This delicate, simmering brew was now stirred by Emma through the medium of her new friend and ally Sarah Nelson, in whom she recognized a fellow-aspirant to social advancement. Flattery had won Emma the devotion of the stolid Dr and Mrs Nelson, who were otherwise far from the *beau monde* she usually courted, Sarah responding:

> You never, my dearest Lady Hamilton, said a truer thing when you said our hearts were congenial. I can with great truth say – from the moment I first had the pleasure of seeing you, I admired you and your kind attention since makes me love you . . . Your kind and affectionate letter, Mr. Nelson and I have read over many times, for reading your letters is next to being with you. I don't wonder my dear Lord Nelson receives so much pleasure from them.[91]

Writing to her from Merton in September 1801, Emma declared:

> I love Nelson's glory, his great and glorious deeds have made on my heart an impression *never, never* to be effaced. I love you. *You* and your husband are the only people worthy to be by *him beloved*. His poor father is unknowing and taken in by a very wicked, bad, artful woman, acting a *bad part by so glorious a son*. The sin be on their heads . . . Nelson's father protects this woman and gives a mortal blow to his son. The old man could never hear her till now and now he conspires *against the saviour of his country* and his darling, who has risen him to such a height of honour, *and for whom? A wicked, false, malicious* wretch, who rendered his days wretched and his nights miserable. And the father of Nelson says, 'I will *stab* my son to the heart', but indeed he says, 'My poor father is led now, he does not know what he does.' But oh! how cruel, shocking it is and I am afraid the Boltons are not without their share of guilt

> in this affair. *Jealous of you all,* they have, with the Matchams, pushed this poor, dear old gentleman to act this bad, horrible part, to support a false, proud, bad woman. . . Let her own wickedness be her punishment . . . 'Tis a bad bird befowls its own nest.[92]

In hysterical jealousy that matched Nelson's over the Prince of Wales, Emma was particularly suspicious of Susannah Bolton's correspondence with Fanny, telling Sarah, 'Pray what has old mother Bolton left the old gentleman for Tom Tit? . . . The Boltons are as close-tongued about her as they are close-fisted.'[93] Even that was not enough and she wrote later, 'Tom Tit is hated by even those that pretend to protect her.'[94]

Although still confined to his flagship at anchor in the Downs, Nelson's imagination was already in Merton and his letters brimmed with fantasies about the popular farming squire that he saw himself becoming. He had already decided to name the ornamental canal in the garden 'The Nile' and wrote to Emma, 'How I should laugh to see you, my dear, rowing in a boat: the beautiful Emma rowing a one-armed Admiral in a boat! It will certainly be caricatured. Well done, farmer's wife!'[95] He could not imagine Emma allowing any of their contented farm animals to be slaughtered, he told her.

On 1 October, the British and French governments signed an armistice to allow a full peace treaty to be negotiated. 'Although it is peace,' remarked Nelson, 'I wish all Frenchmen to the devil.'[96] Three weeks later, the Admiralty granted him indefinite leave and he was rowed ashore through the surf in a high-sided Deal galley to begin his journey to Merton Place. Emma Hamilton now awaited her hero's return with one small disappointment. 'You have not an idea what a sensation the peace has been,' she wrote to Sarah Nelson. 'If we could have had an idea, we might have made £30,000 by stock-jobbing.'[97]

9
Charlotte

Charlotte Nelson was aged fourteen in October 1801 and at school in Chelsea. Slightly built with dark, curly hair, eyes set wide in a heart-shaped face, unmarked, as yet, by any recognizable characteristics, her prettiness prompted an acquaintance, Lord William Gordon, to describe 'her cheeks of rose, her teeth of ivory – and eyes of sloes!'[1] The daughter of the ambitious cleric William and his wife, Sarah, she was a dutiful girl of whom her parents had high expectations. The Nelsons were grooming their two children, Charlotte and Horace, to ornament and even promote their own rise through the social strata. Horace was being educated at Eton College and his sister, after some initial schooling at Bath during her parents' stay there, had been sent to Whitelands School on the King's Road through Chelsea. Founded nearly thirty years earlier by a clergyman, who was the author of a work entitled *Female Education and Christian Fortitude under Afflication*, it was, Lady Hamilton noted, convenient for visits to Merton and she already had plans for Charlotte. Hers might not have been the sexually knowing eye that Mrs Kelly, the Arlington Street procuress, had once turned upon the young Emma but it was no more altruistic. Charlotte, as the great Lord Nelson's niece, could not fail to be received in society and even at court; she might catch the eye of some young magnifico and perhaps marry him. For her ascent into the social highlands of London she would need a chaperone – surely her mother, the simple clergyman's wife, would never do – and she would be made equally welcome, even if she were the socially and morally suspect Lady Hamilton.

Charlotte's education had, however, been arranged by Fanny Nelson, although Emma would never admit to this. As early as the spring of 1799, William had written to Fanny from Hilborough to say that he had been thinking of sending his daughter to a boarding-school in or near London and that a friend had recommended 'a school at Chelsea called White-Lands House', where, thanks to the staff of 'well-behaved, good-tempered, accomplished people . . . the attention paid to the health and morals of the young Ladies [is] unequalled by any other school'.[2] It was a small school, so the headmistress, Miss Veitch, could keep a sharp eye on her twenty boarders. Moreover, it was close to the Royal Hospital, where Dr Benjamin Moseley, Nelson's old friend from Jamaica, was now physician to the military pensioners, and his wife could be asked to watch Charlotte's progress. She had settled there happily and Miss Veitch was well aware of her pupil's connections: when the news arrived from Copenhagen, she asked Charlotte to invite her parents to a performance of music and dancing by the school in celebration of the victory.

In Emma's plan for welcoming Nelson to his 'farm', Charlotte – or, as she sometimes spoke of her from Neapolitan habit, 'Carlotta' – would have a part to play. She wanted him to find Merton Place the embodiment of his fantasies and this would, of course, include their daughter. However, as the presence of little Horatia would be difficult to explain at this stage, an older girl would take her place to complete what she hoped he would see as his new family circle, concentrated on herself, her husband and her mother. To this core could be added those members of the Nelson family who had rejected Fanny.

So the arrangements were made and, the day before Nelson was due to arrive from Deal, Emma wrote to Sarah Nelson, 'Sir William is gone to fetch Charlotte . . . She shall be early at school on Monday morning and as milord is to arrive on Friday for dinner, she shall be here to receive him and go back to school on Monday early . . . Sir William is quite charmed by her.'[3]

Charlotte was delighted by Merton Place. Built of rosy brick early in the century, with an elegant pediment, bow windows and verandahs, it was set among lawns and ornamental trees. Within, Emma had already transformed it into a shrine to Nelson and their love, with their portraits, paintings of his ships and battles, coats of arms and mirrors to catch their reflections, all lit by sunlight shining through glass doors and, by night, the soft glow of chandeliers. The evening before Nelson was due to arrive, Charlotte told her mother, 'I played at whist . . . with Sir William and Lady Hamilton and Mrs Cadogan. Lady Hamilton was quite surprised that I could play so well. I won the rubber.'[4] The girl was showing promise as an apt pupil and, potentially, was as useful a player on the social stage as at the card-table. To her, Lady Hamilton was a dazzling sophisticate and bountiful hostess and she did not see her through such eyes as those of a visiting artist, also named William Hamilton, who noted, 'she is bold and unguarded in her manner, is grown fat and drinks freely'.[5]

So eager was Nelson to reach the haven he had so long imagined that he drove through the night and reached Merton soon after sunrise on 23 October, before the household had risen, or the villagers and local militia were ready with the formal greetings of speeches and celebratory volleys of musketry. As Charlotte wrote to her mother later that day:

> My dear uncle arrived safe here this morning at eight o'clock. He looks very well and is much pleased with Merton. The Volunteers we expect every moment. We have had some people firing and they came in and saw my uncle; he spoke to them and they seemed so happy to see him. The horses were to have been taken out of his carriage and the people to have dragged him to Merton but they were all disappointed as my uncle came before they expected him . . .[6]

Before the letter was sealed and posted, Emma added a postscript to Sarah:

> It is now 2 o'clock and we have had such firing and all the people huzzaing. Now we are got quiet and comfortable . . . It was quite affecting to see the manner our Hero was received . . . Lord N. is delighted with Merton . . . He is better than I expected in looks . . . We are all so joyous today, we do not know what to do. Believe me, my heart is all convulsed, seeing him again *safe on shore*, safely *moor'd* with *we* – I must not say *me*. Charlotte behaves like an angel; her uncle is quite surprised at her improvement and delighted with her.[7]

Emma then looked to the future, pointedly remarking that Nelson 'had today a letter from his father saying how sorry he is for all that's past [*sic*] . . . and will come to Merton'. The old man had been in an agony of indecision. He was determined to maintain his friendship with Fanny, who had been staying with him in Norfolk at the end of September, but predicted in a letter to Kate, 'No prospect of better times for her, nay, I think worse.'[8] He sensed that his son was becoming increasingly defensive and even hostile, but did not, of course, know that Horatio had written to Emma about his father's continuing friendship with Fanny, 'If he ever mentions her name to me I shall stop that directly. I shall never go to see him; pray let him come to your care at Merton; your care will keep him alive for you have a kind soul. She has none.'[9] Three days before Nelson arrived at Merton, Edmund was writing to Kate, 'I hope the breach will not extend further; my part is very distressing. I am invited to Merton and have for the present engaged to be elsewhere.'[10] But he changed his mind and told Kate that, in November, he would visit Fanny in London and then his son at Merton while on his way from Burnham Thorpe to Bath.

Emma's other plan was that Nelson should become involved in politics once he had taken his seat in the House of Lords, when, she told Sarah, that 'Lord *Nosy* is to be one of his introducers',[11] this being a nickname of Lord Hood, his old commanding admiral. He had once hankered after a seat in the House of Commons and now Emma saw his right to sit in the

Upper House as a new career, one which would keep him at home and give her further opportunities for social ascent.

Nelson was transported with delight by Merton Place. He was shown his garden and the paddocks on the far side of the road and decided to build a tunnel to connect them; he ordered the ornamental canal – 'The Nile' – to be stocked with more fish, and as he looked at the charming house, embowered by trees and flowerbeds, and the view across his own land to Wimbledon Hill, he kept asking, 'Is this, too, mine?'[12] After dark, Charlotte recorded, 'there were some very fine fireworks, which falling into the canal, had a very beautiful effect'.[13] On Sunday morning, she helped her uncle into his overcoat before leaving for the morning service at the little Norman church of St Mary, where Nelson was received with the deference due to the squire, and she turned the pages of his prayer book for him. That afternoon she wrote to her mother, saying that she had already been fishing with Sir William and 'caught some carp', to which Nelson himself wrote a postscript, 'For carp, read pike. We caught three very fine fish.'[14] Early on Monday morning, Charlotte returned to school.

A week later, Nelson was in London to take his seat in the House of Lords and the next day spoke there for the first time. This was to second St Vincent's congratulations to Admiral Saumarez on a successful action off Gibraltar and he gracefully alluded to St Vincent and Hood as masters of the school where the admiral had been so well educated. His speech was warmly received and, eager to speak again, he was given an opportunity on 3 November. Politically, Nelson was unsophisticated and the Prime Minister, Henry Addington, had no difficulty in persuading him to speak in defence of the unpopular terms of the peace treaty then under negotiation. So he found himself belittling the strategic value of Malta, Minorca and the Cape of Good Hope, all of which Britain stood to lose. It was obvious that he did not believe what he had been asked to say and he wrote to a naval friend, 'You will see my maiden speech – bad enough but well meant – anything better than ingratitude. I may be a coward and good for nothing but never ungrateful for favours done to me.'[15]

Thereafter he was careful to stick to naval and military subjects, on which he could speak with authority, but the damage had been done and one senior politician wrote to Lord Dundas, the Minister for War, 'How can Ministers allow such a fool to speak in their defence?'[16] Even his staunch friend Captain Hardy remarked, 'I see by almost every paper that Lord Nelson has been speaking in the House. I am sorry for it and am fully convinced that *sailors* should not *talk* too much.'[17]

Although, as a woman, Emma was not allowed to attend debates, she was ecstatic, writing to Sarah Nelson:

> I am quite Nelson mad again for him as an orator . . . I think this is my Hero's second speech. I have been making him say it to me as he said it in the House. I could hear him talk for ever and am just as anxious that he should be admired in this his new career as I was when he went out to battle, but I fret and weep that I cannot go and hear him in the British Senate. How my heart would throb and beat high, how should I exult to see him standing up with his manly look and honest, dear, innocent, energetic-looking face, speaking truth to people who hardly speak it and then his glorious limbs and blood that he has lost for his Country . . . showing them perpetually that he has been their saviour and still is.[18]

As she wrote, Nelson entered the room and she scrawled, 'Nelson comes reading my letter. I tell him to read – 'tis all true.'[19]

Both were relieved when, at the end of the month, his father came to stay on his way to Bath. Emma played the thoughtful, generous hostess, but it was a performance, because she found her guest unsettling, writing to Sarah, '*Psha*! I am got out of bed the wrong side you will say but, no, I am in a good humour on the whole. The old gentleman is tolerably well content, contradicts *a little* every now and then. I find him *very feeble* and inclined to sleep.'[20] But when he left, she sent a present of a plaid rug to him at Bath. Edmund had seen that he could not hope to change the relationship, however much he disapproved of it, and in his letter of thanks to his son, confined himself to a pointed homily that would have found its mark: 'What you possess, my good son, take care of – what you may still want, consult your own good sense in what way it can be attained. Strive for honours and riches that will not fade but will profit in time of need.'[21] He concluded, 'From an old man you will accept at the approaching happy season, which is, I wish you a merry Christmas and a happy New Year. For multiplied favours, Lady Hamilton has my respectful thanks.' To Emma, he sent polite greetings, excusing his absence from the coming jollities by explaining, 'The severity of the season, which makes many a poor creature, such as myself, to shake, gives much pleasure to the skating parties, so that I hope all in their turns have their hours of enjoyment at a season when all the Christian world do celebrate with songs of praise the return of Christmas.'[22]

Emma's victory was almost complete. Then, just before the elaborate Christmas festivities began, Nelson received another letter from Fanny. On 18 December, she had written from Bath:

> My dear Husband, It is some time since I have written to you, the silence you have imposed is more than my affection will allow me and, in this instance, I hope you will forgive me in not obeying you. One thing I omitted in my letter of July, which I now have to offer for your accommodation, [is] a warm, comfortable house. Do, my dear husband, let us live together. I can never be happy till such an event takes place. I assure you again, I have but one wish in the world, to please you – let everything be buried in oblivion, it will pass away like a dream. I can now only entreat you to believe I am most sincerely and affectionately your wife, Frances Nelson.

The letter was returned to Fanny, opened and endorsed, 'Opened by mistake by Lord Nelson, but not read.'[23]

At Merton, Emma was busily rebuilding Nelson's family circle round herself. The Bolton and Matcham families were invited to stay, but the keystone of the new structure was to be Charlotte and her pliant mother. Not only did the girl become a regular visitor to Merton but Nelson combined a call on Dr Moseley at the Royal Hospital – to consult him about his eyesight – with a visit to her at school, much to the delight of the headmistress, and he asked her to give the girls a half-day holiday. As Charlotte told her mother:

> Miss Veitch gave us apple pies, also custards and then negus to drink my uncle's health. Miss Veitch gave us the toast, it was, 'Lord Nelson, may his future years be as happy as his past have been glorious . . .' How proud I am to have the approbation of my most glorious, victorious, virtuous uncle and my future life in every act and instance shall be to do honour to the near relationship, which I have the happiness to bear towards him. May God Almighty spare his precious life.'[24]

Sarah was kept informed by Emma and, sweetened with flattery and presents, wrote gratefully, 'I draped myself today in that pretty gown you gave me. How good you are to dear Charlotte, if she can give you spirits *pray send for her* when you like. . .'[25]

Between them, Nelson and Emma had turned her head. She was especially flattered by one particular present. 'My Uncle was so very good as to give me a diamond ring,' she told her mother. 'It is beautiful, indeed I am so proud of it I am always looking at it. Lady Hamilton was so kind as to choose it for me.'[26] Emma thought this might be misconstrued and so wrote to Sarah, 'You must not think Charlotte's diamond ring much but it is pretty and I told him it would please her and he likes to do anything to show your children he is attached to them and most sincerely. It is a little, single diamond and well set.'[27] Their beneficience included her brother at Eton. On hearing that Horace was being bullied because he had been christened with the name of Horatio Nelson and that he would inherit the dukedom of Bronte, his uncle wrote to the boy's father suggesting that he be moved from his boarding-house to lodgings and become a day boy; he too was included in family gatherings at Merton. As Christmas approached, these increased in size and intensity.

The festivities, which were planned to continue past Christmas, over New Year's Eve and as long as Emma and their guests felt inclined, were to concentrate on music, dancing and eating. Emma needed no urging to raise her loud voice but, as part of her scheme to infiltrate the grandest salons in the wake of Charlotte, she decided that they would sing duets. In this she was at one with the girl's mother, who had written, 'I wish you would get someone to teach Charlotte to sing at school, whoever you like, for I should like she should know something of it by Christmas.'[28] So, while she herself practised – 'Lady Hamilton is now singing', the girl noted in a letter home – Charlotte was to take lessons from Neapolitan singers. She practised singing hymns of praise to her uncle, such as those once composed by Cornelia Knight, one concluding with the lines:

> Old Neptune rise to save his Isle from harm
> And bid his sons, the Guardians of his reign,
> On to their posts to meet the foe again.
> The Tritons then produce the list of Fame,
> And first upon the hill is gallant Nelson's name![29]

Special dances were planned and rehearsed, including a formation dance for which the instructions began, 'Sprigs of Laurel for Adm. Nelson. Right hand across. Left hands back again. Lead down their middle and foot it . . .'[30] Hearing of this, Sarah Nelson wrote encouragingly to her daughter, 'Dancing well is certainly a great accomplishment and with a good figure always pleases . . . You are very much indebted to your good friend Lady Hamilton and with what pleasure will she hear your praises when you go to some elegant balls in Town.'[31] To encourage her daughter's mentor, she wrote to Emma:

> I expect Charlotte can't hold herself up well . . . I know [she] would wish to do everything to make her look the

Lady Hamilton: one of Emma's favourite portraits of herself by George Romney, which was to hang at Merton Place. (SOUTHSIDE HOUSE, WIMBLEDON)

(above) Powerful friends: King Ferdinand IV and Queen Maria Carolina of the Kingdom of the Two Sicilies.
(NATIONAL GALLERY OF SCOTLAND)

(right) Emma in Naples: a portrait by an unknown Neapolitan artist circa 1798.
(PRIVATE COLLECTION)

Nelson's Homes: (top) Merton Place in Surrey painted by Thomas Baxter.
(NATIONAL MARITIME MUSEUM)

(bottom) The Castello di Maniace: Nelson's house near Bronte in Sicily, which he was never to visit, as it is now.

(top) Seen fondly, as by her father: Horatia, daughter of Nelson and Emma Hamilton

(bottom) Seen cruelly by the caricaturist James Gillray: Emma Hamilton bewails the departure of her lover to sea.
(NATIONAL MARITIME MUSEUM)

(top) Seen in retrospect through the sentimental eye of an artist a century later: Nelson dances with Emma in Naples. (PRIVATE COLLECTION)

(bottom) Seen by an imaginative Edwardian artist: Nelson in church at Merton. (PRIVATE COLLECTION)

Charlotte Nelson, the admiral's niece, as she was when staying at Merton Place and before her marriage to Samuel Hood; painted by Isaac Pocock.
(PRIVATE COLLECTION/ NATIONAL PORTRAIT GALLERY)

Lady Hamilton and Charlotte caricatured by James Gillray in 'Attitudes Faithfully Copied from Nature and Humbly Dedicated to All Admirers of the Grand and Sublime'. (PRIVATE COLLECTION)

(top) Horatia mourns at the memorial to her father, painted by Isaac Pocock.
(PRIVATE COLLECTION)

(below left) as a young woman after returning to her father's family from Calais.
(NATIONAL PORTRAIT GALLERY)

(below right) Photographed as a widow following the death of the Rev Simon Ward in 1859.

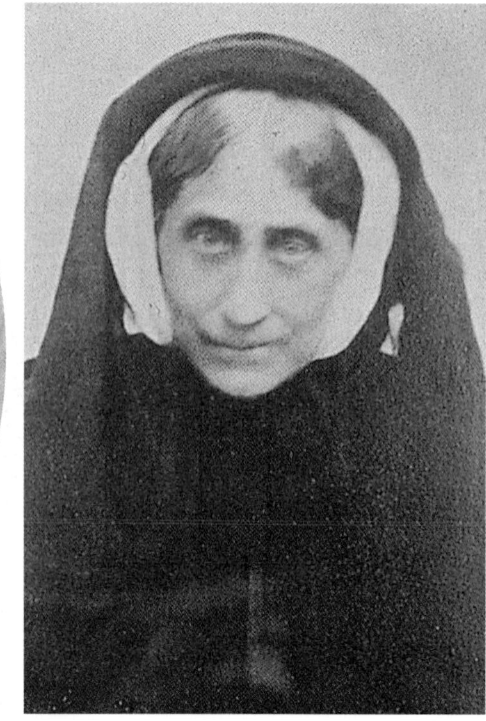

> Girl of Fashion, what pleasure she would have when she walk'd across the room to hear people say what an elegant young woman that is. [On a more practical note, she adds:] I *hope* you think with me that *her stays are much too tight*.[32]

Although Nelson was a frugal eater, he liked to be seen as a generous host and Emma was something of a glutton, writing to Sarah one Sunday, 'We have got for dinner today a turtle dress'd and a haunch of venison. Don't your mouth water?'[33]

Nelson was looking forward to Christmas as the final fulfilment of his shipboard fantasies of domestic bliss. 'I wish Christmas was come that we might all be jolly here,'[34] he wrote, but neither the Boltons nor the Matchams accepted Emma's invitation to stay, giving a variety of excuses, and an unspoken reason was probably their embarrassment at the treatment of Fanny and the absence of Edmund. But William and Sarah Nelson did accept, joining Charlotte and Horace, who were spending the school holidays at Merton. Christmas Day was, of course, marked by attendance at church but the dining and wining continued long afterwards. Once William and Sarah had departed, the party was joined by Lord Minto, young Sam Hood, the grandson of Lord Hood, and a schoolfriend of Charlotte's, a Miss Furse. After one night of heavy eating, drinking and cards, an unabashed Emma reported to Sarah, who was back in Norfolk, 'Miss Furse ate so much that in the evening she vomited before us all. Charlotte covered her *retraite* and got her out. She came in again and played at cards.' Lord Minto, who had also been at a card-table, had been 'charmed with Charlotte', but 'Mrs. Tyson was drunk and, when she talked nonsense her husband [Nelson's secretary] tipped her the wink and she held her tongue'.[35] But there was one triumph, Emma telling Sarah, 'Sam Hood is quite delighted with Charlotte. He seemed to devour her with his eyes. *That* would be *a good match*.'[36]

Lord Minto (formerly Sir Gilbert Elliot), who had great affection for Nelson, watched the proceedings and eyed his host and hostess and their house with a mordant eye, later writing to his wife:

> The whole establishment and way of life is such to make me angry as well as melancholy; but I cannot alter it and I do not think myself obliged, or at liberty, to quarrel with him for his weakness, though nothing shall ever induce me to give the smallest countenance to Lady Hamilton. She looks ultimately to the chance of marriage, as Sir W. will not be long in her way and she probably indulges a hope that she may survive Lady Nelson; in the meanwhile she and Sir William are living at his expense. She is in high looks but more immense than ever. She goes on cramming Nelson with trowelfuls of flattery, which he goes on taking quietly as a child does pap. The love she makes to him is not only ridiculous but disgusting: not only the rooms, but the whole house, staircase and all, are covered with nothing but pictures of her and him, of all sizes and sorts, and representations of his naval actions, coats of arms, pieces of plate in his honour, the flag staff of *l'Orient* [the French flagship at the Battle of the Nile], etc. – an excess of vanity which counteracts its purpose. If it was Lady H.'s house there might be a pretence for it; to make his own a mere looking-glass to view himself all day is bad taste.[37]

Flattered as she was by Emma's attentions to her daughter, Sarah was becoming apprehensive. As she had seen at Merton, the girl was being exposed to some fast company and, perhaps, given a taste for drinking and gambling and was certainly eating too much. She began carefully, under the guise of fussing about the health of all at Merton, writing, 'What very cold weather we have got again . . . I hope none of you have left off your flannels.' She then became slightly more specific:

> I am glad to hear of your being at those fine parties and I am likewise glad to hear you sometimes keep good hours, which is so very conducive to good health and without this we can enjoy nothing . . .[38]

After another report of excessive dining from Emma, Sarah wrote from Norfolk in early March:

> We read about you all yesterday and your turtle feast, I told the Doctor [her husband] I knew He would have liked to have some of the green fat, etc. He desires me to tell you and my Lord and all the party that he is not surprised at your frequent headaches and indigestions if you will glut and gourmandise and have turtle feasts, etc., you should mortify and fast during this season of Lent. He has had no qualms, nor bile, nor anything else since he came into Norfolk and been forced to return to his bread and cheese and small beer and such like homely fare added to a good rise every day for two or three hours on the Heath, which brings him home with a good appetite to his frugal meal.[39]

She also worried about Charlotte putting on too much weight and losing her looks, adding, 'Will you be so good when you are in Town to get dumb-bells for her and *make her use them* as much as you think it is right.'[40]

Emma's hospitality and her own enjoyment were shot through with bile. However triumphant she might seem, lurking jealousy and resentment of Fanny poisoned the feast, occasioning hysterical diatribes, particularly to Sarah, against 'that vile Tom Tit' and 'her squinting brat'.[41] She was haunted by her rival, asking Sarah, 'I wonder whither Tom Tit goes? I dare say I find in today's paper that she is arrived in Town. She must give five shillings to put in the papers such insipid stuff.'[42] She even attacked 'Poor Blindy', the widow of Maurice Nelson, for failing to show sufficient antipathy to Fanny. Sarah, eager to display equal venom, replied to this last letter:

> I am not surprised at anything you tell me about Mrs. Nelson, for I have always understood ever since I have been in the family that she was a woman by no means worthy of cultivating her acquaintance . . . The family all say she is deceitful and bad tempered but you and my

> good Lord will do the needful for her, with that she must be content. Her not seeing is worse than if she did for she now swallows things as her servants tell her.[43]

The balance of family relationships was further strained when old Edmund was taken ill in Bath. On 20 April, he wrote to Fanny with a shaking hand to tell her, 'rest assured that in all places I wish for your happiness'.[44] Shortly afterwards, George Matcham wrote to her and to Nelson, telling them that Edmund was not expected to live and Fanny at once travelled to Bath. Perhaps expecting that, Nelson replied:

> I have hopes that he can recover ... Had my father expressed a wish to see me, unwell as I am, I should have flown to Bath but I believe it would be too late. However, should it be otherwise and he wishes to see me, no consideration shall detain me a moment . . . I shall therefore only say that he is to be buried at Burnham.[45]

But on 26 April 1802, the day that he wrote this, Edmund died.

Fanny, her duty done, left Bath. Some days later, she received a letter from Susannah Bolton:

> Your going to Bath, my dear Lady Nelson, was all of a piece with your conduct to my beloved Father ... I am going to London in about a fortnight but, my dear Lady N., we cannot meet as I wished for everybody is known who visit you . . . but be assured I always have and always shall be your sincere friend.[46]

That was a blow, since Susannah had always seemed such a staunch friend, but there can have been no disappointment in missing a meeting with William Nelson. Piqued at having heard the news only second-hand from Horatio, he hurried to Bath, where George Matcham was already making arrangements for the funeral in Norfolk. Nelson wrote to George giving precise details of the construction of the coffin and the grave but pleaded ill-health as the reason for not being able to attend the funeral at Burnham Thorpe. Illness had seldom deterred him in the past, so the real reason was taken to be his fear of meeting Fanny, whom he expected to be there, although, in the event, sensing this, she did not attend. Yet he purported to be offended that Sarah had not come to Merton to join her husband and the mourning presided over by Emma, who was so well accustomed to assuming extravagant gestures of grief in her Attitudes. He, or she, persuaded Charlotte to reprimand her mother, writing:

> My uncle is very much hurt at your not being here this morning and he begs me to say it would be indecent for me to be at school and has ordered Lady Hamilton to write to Miss Veitch the reason for my not coming. We are all going into deep mourning as my uncle is very particular that all possible respect should be paid to my dear Grandpapa's memory . . . He would not let Horatio go a-fishing . . . this morning, nor do we see anybody. A written paper is shown at the gate to everyone that comes . . . My spirits are worn out seeing my good uncle's suffering.[47]

One close member of the family – albeit unrecognized publicly as such – was Horatia. She was yet to be baptized but she was known as Horatia Nelson Thompson, a child in whom Lord Nelson had a particular interest, variously known as his god-daughter, his ward and even his adopted daughter. Nelson longed for her to live with them at Merton, but Emma persuaded him that this would prompt speculation and gossip. So, from time to time, Emma would write to Mrs Gibson ordering her to hire a chaise for a day and bring the child for a brief visit to Merton as this would be unlikely to attract notice in the constant flow of guests through the house. These included their neighbours, notably the Goldsmid brothers (Abraham at Morden Hall and Benjamin at The Grove), rich and hospitable Jewish bullion-brokers in the City of London, and, at Wandle Bank House, James Perry, the editor of the *Morning Chronicle*, who soon proved useful in the handling of publicity. The Merton Place household was becoming the talk of the district, because of its attendant exotica as much as its celebrity: the Reverend Thomas Lancaster, the vicar of the parish church of St Mary the Virgin, had never officiated at a ceremony like the baptism of Lady Hamilton's Nubian maid Fatima, who – thanks to her mistress's obsession with suitable names – was christened as Fatima Emma Charlotte Nelson Hamilton.

Meanwhile, Sir William's dislike of the continual round of entertaining was becoming increasingly apparent, but Emma could not bear the thought of the quiet domestic routine for which her husband longed. The first sign of discord came when he, now seventy-one and exhausted by the continual entertaining of Christmas and New Year, complained to Charles Greville about 'the nonsense I am obliged to submit to here to avoid coming to an explosion, which would be attended with many disagreeable effects and would totally destroy the comfort of the best man and the best friend I have in the world [Nelson]'.[48] Perhaps expecting this, Emma agreed to an expedition which would please them all: a visit to the Pembrokeshire estates that Sir William had inherited from his first wife, combined with a triumphal tour of the provincial towns in southern England, Wales and the Midlands for Nelson. The war had finally and formally ended with the signing of the Treaty of Amiens on 25 March, and there seemed no risk of a sudden recall to duty, so Nelson could at last revel in the laurels that were his due. He had had a taste of this at the Lord Mayor's Show in London – the procession celebrating his election – just before Christmas, to which he had taken Charlotte. Nelson had been invited to ride in the Lord Mayor's coach, which had had it horses taken from the traces and been dragged by a cheering crowd. 'I wish you could have seen all the people jumping up to the carriage to see my uncle and thousands of people round him looking at him,' Charlotte told her mother. 'All the ladies had their handkerchiefs out of the windows when my uncle passed, they and the people calling out, "Nelson for ever!"'[49]

The girl followed a busy round, alternating school with days at

Merton, often in a family party. In May, for example, she was writing to her mother, 'I have been rowing Eliza and Anne [Bolton] in the boat and yesterday my aunt Matcham and Aunt Bolton were rowed by me . . . My aunts and Lady Hamilton are going in the sociable [a small carriage] to take a ride and me and my cousins will amuse ourselves at home . . . My cousins go with me to school on Monday.'[50] It was because of her return to Chelsea that she missed the excitement of the coming expedition.

The first event of the tour was on 22 July, when Nelson and Hamilton received honorary degrees in Civil Law from Oxford University and, out of courtesy, a Doctorate of Divinity was conferred on William Nelson; the *Morning Post* joked that Nelson should have been awarded the latter distinction 'because of his knowledge of cannon laws'.[51] The *Morning Herald* quipped that the records did not specify whether his brother's award was 'that of L.L.D. or A.S.S.' and the admiral remarked of William, 'He is as big as if he was a bishop.'[52] Horace Nelson had been given leave from Eton and the Matchams had come with their schoolboy son, George. From Oxford, the party visited Blenheim Palace, only to be snubbed by the Duke of Marlborough, who, although in residence, would not receive them and simply offered them some cold food while they admired the view of his park; they left, hurt and angry. 'I told Nelson,' said Emma afterwards, 'that if I had been a queen after the Battle of Aboukir, he should have a principality so that Blenheim Palace should have been only a kitchen garden to it.'[53]

At Gloucester, the Matchams left for Bath and the rest of the party continued into Wales. It was a cosy, domestic echo of their tour through Europe, with Nelson acclaimed as the conquering hero and Emma praising him in song whenever occasion arose. It was not all cheering, feasting and toasting: in the Forest of Dean, Nelson enquired into the state of timber production for ship-building; at Pembroke, he inspected the dockyard; at Milford Haven, he compared the harbour with that of Trincomalee in Ceylon. There, they were met by Charles Greville, who was ostensibly managing his uncle's estate, and they visited the country around Selbeck, where Catherine

Hamilton, William's first wife, was buried and where, he quietly decided, he would be too.

On their return journey they halted at Monmouth, where they had been warmly welcomed on their way west, and stayed for elaborate celebrations, including a banquet at the Beaufort Arms, when Emma sang her hymns to Nelson to the tunes of the national anthem and 'Rule, Britannia', ending with a patriotic song, which included the words:

> Come hither, all ye youths of Bath,
> Whose bosoms pant for glory . . .[54]

They continued through Ross-on-Wye to Hereford, where they were told about the cider industry and a local newspaper reported, 'The branch of an apple tree in full bearing being presented to Lord Nelson at Hereford, his Lordship, with all the gallantry of Paris, presented the *apple* to Lady Hamilton, thereby acknowledging her Ladyship a perfect Venus.'[55] They drove through Ludlow to Worcester, where Nelson ordered a large service of armorial porcelain, and on through the countryside, their progress being honoured by the naming of inns, flowers and even vegetables in the hero's honour. 'There is no man so busily employed in England as Lord Nelson,' joked the *Morning Post*. 'In one place we meet him as a *gooseberry*, in another as a *carnation* – sometimes we find him a *racehorse* and sometimes a prize *ram*.'[56]

At Birmingham, a performance of *The Merry Wives of Windsor* at the theatre was followed by a choral tribute to the hero, one song alluding to the current peace with the words:

> We'll shake hands; if they won't, why, what then?
> We'll send out brave Nelson to thrash 'em again!
> Derry down Derry, etc. . . .

At this, reported the son* of the theatre's manager, 'The crowded house was frantic in its applause at this sublime effusion.

*Charles Macready, the future actor-manager of the Covent Garden and Drury Lane theatres in London.

Lady Hamilton laughing loud and without stint, clapped with uplifted hands and kicked her heels against the foot board of the seat, while Nelson placidly and with his mournful look . . . bowed repeatedly to the oft-repeated cheers.'[57] They then travelled on to Warwick and then Althorp, to which Lord Spencer, the former First Lord of the Admiralty, had retired. Finally on 5 September, they returned to Merton.

But not for long. Nelson decided that both Emma and Horatia needed a holiday by the sea and bathing in salt water, so Emma took a reluctant Sir William to Ramsgate while Mrs Gibson and Horatia stayed nearby at Margate, where her mother could visit her in secret. Sir William did not know the real reason for their jaunt, nor why Emma became so distraught when she lost the address of Mrs Gibson's lodgings. When he complained that he wanted to return to Merton and his fishing-rods, Emma left a note for him: 'As I see it is a pain to you to remain here, let me beg of you to fix your time of going . . . I remember the time when you wished for tranquillity but now all visiting and bustle is your liking. However, do what you please.'[58] To this he replied:

> I neither love bustle, nor great company, but I like some employment and diversion. I have but a very short time to live and every moment is precious to me . . . The question, then, is what can we best do that all may be perfectly satisfied? Sea bathing is useful to your health . . . but I must confess that I regret, whilst the season is favourable, that I cannot enjoy my favourite amusement of quiet fishing. I care not a pin for the great world and am attached to no one so much as to you.'[59]

Soon afterwards, they returned to Merton.

It was time for a reassessment, both personal and professional. Nelson was worried about the cost of his peacetime way of life and he noted that other admirals had been more richly rewarded than he for their lesser victories. His capital, which was tied up in his property at Merton, amounted to £10,000 and his annual income was £3,418, his fixed expenditure was £2,650 ;so leaving him £768. Other than living and entertaining expenses, his principal outgoings were an annual allowance – now £1,800 – to Fanny, another £200 to Maurice's widow and £150 towards his nephews' education. He could not admit that, but for Emma's extravagance, he would be able to live comfortably within his means.

Nelson's forty-fourth birthday was celebrated soon after their return by another party at Merton, attended by their neighbours, the Goldsmids and the Perrys. After dinner, the Goldsmid daughters played the piano and Neapolitan opera singers performed as overtures to Emma singing yet another song of praise:

> Then live, ever live, to our gratitude dear,
> The hope of our Navy! May Fortune endeavour
> His days and his friends to increase ev'ry year,
> And Nelson and glory be coupled for ever![60]

This was described by James Perry in the *Morning Chronicle* with neighbourly generosity: 'There is no voice in England, which combines such uncommon volume and quality of tone with such richness and cultivation, and which receives from expression, gesture and articulation such force of truth and feeling . . . Lady Hamilton displayed the wonders of her talent . . .'[61]

It was clear that the social extravaganza that had been interrupted by the provincial tour would be resumed with unabated fervour. Soon afterwards, Sir William could stand it no longer and, shying away from a direct confrontation with Emma, delivered a written ultimatum:

> I have passed the last 40 years of my life in the hurry and bustle that must necessarily be attendant on a public character. I am arrived at the age when some repose is really necessary and I promised myself a quiet home and, although I was sensible and said so when I married, that I

should be superannuated when my wife would be in her full beauty and vigour of youth. That time is arrived and we must make the best of it for the comfort of both parties. Unfortunately, our tastes as to the manner of living are very different. I by no means wish to live in solitary retreat, but to have seldom less than 12 or 14 at table, and those varying continually, is coming back to what became so irksome to me in Italy during the latter years of my residence in that country . . . I have no complaint to make but I feel that the whole attention of my wife is given to Lord N. and his interest at Merton. I know well the purity of Lord N.'s friendship for Emma and me and I know how very uncomfortable it would make his Lordship, our best friend, if a separation should take place and am therefore determined to do all in my power to prevent such an extremity, which would be essentially detrimental to all parties but would be more sensibly felt by our dear friend than us.

Provided that our expenses in housekeeping do not increase beyond measure (of which I own I see some danger), I am willing to go on upon our present footing; but, as I cannot expect to live many years, every moment to me is precious and I hope I may be allowed sometimes to be my own master and pass my time according to my own inclination, either by going on my fishing parties on the Thames, or by going to London to attend the Museum, the R[oyal] Society, the Tuesday Club and auctions of pictures. I meant to have a light chariot, or post-chaise, by the month that I may make use of it in London and run backwards and forwards to Merton, or to Shepperton, etc. This is my plan and we might go on very well but I am fully determined not to have more of the silly altercations that happen but too often between us and embitter the present moment exceedingly. If really one cannot live comfortably together, a wise and concerted separation is preferable; but I think, considering the probability of my not troubling any party long in this world, the best for all of us would be to bear those ills we have rather than fly to those we know not of. I have fairly stated what I have on my mind. There is no time for nonsense, or trifling. I know and admire your talents and many excellent qualities, but I am not blind to your defects and confess to having many myself; therefore let us bear and forebear for God's sake.[62]

This seemed to have the desired effect. Sir William resumed his expeditions to the river bank and learned societies in London, taking Nelson to a meeting of the Literary Society. The latter had other appointments in London, notably with Addington, the Prime Minister, and St Vincent, the First Lord of the Admiralty. He was told that, in the event of renewed war, he would be appointed to command in the Mediterranean and his strategic advice was sought. He at once revoked his apologia for the terms of the peace in the House of Commons, urging that Malta should continue to be held. He was constantly in touch with, or visited by, naval friends, sometimes to discuss possible future commands and sometimes in the hope of promotion, Emma rising to these occasions. Among the latter was Midshipman Parsons, who had served under Nelson and, wanting him to sign his commission as lieutenant, dared to call at Merton. He was met by Tom Allen, the admiral's blunt-mannered servant from Norfolk, who warned him that his master would not welcome an unexpected visitor. Parsons recoded:

The voice of Lord Nelson, denoting vexation . . . declared most truly that he was pestered to death by young gentlemen, his former shipmates. Tom pushed me into the room and went in search of an able auxiliary, who entered the room in the most pleasing shape – that of a lovely and graceful woman; and, with her usual fascinating and playful manner, declared his Lordship must serve me. His countenance, which until now had been a thundercloud, brightened; and Lady Hamilton was the sun that lightened our hemisphere. She with that ready wit, possessed by the

> fair sex alone, set aside his scruples ... by dictating a strong certificate, which, under her direction, he wrote. 'Now, my young friend,' said her Ladyship with that irresistible smile. 'Obey my instructions minutely; send this to Lord St Vincent ...' My commission as an officer was dated the same as the aforesaid certificate.[63]

Nelson continued to call at the Royal Hospital in Chelsea to see Dr Benjamin Moseley about his eyesight, even though he knew that his old friend was not an eye specialist. It was there that another reminder of his past materialized for Mrs Matthews, the wife of Major Matthews, the staff officer in charge of the pensioners there, was the once haughty Mary Simpson, who had rejected him in Quebec.

He was spending more time in London because the new Parliamentary session was due to begin on 23 November 1802. France was becoming restive and belligerent and war might break out again soon. The threat was not only from across the Channel; within the country, subversion had been simmering below the surface and, a week before the opening of Parliament, it boiled over. A plot to kill the King, subvert the Guards in London and seize the reins of government had been discovered and its ringleaders arrested. The foremost of these bore a name that Nelson remembered from the dreadful campaign in Nicaragua: Edward Despard. They had been friends. Soon afterwards, Colonel Despard, of whom he had not heard for twenty years, wrote to him from prison, asking if Nelson would speak of his past services at his trial. With remarkable courage, at a time when those in power were terrified of anything that hinted at revolution or radical politics, Nelson agreed that he would do so when the case was heard in February.

Parliament reopened and Nelson was a frequent attender, prompting Emma to tell Kate Matcham, 'Don't you think he speaks like an angel in the House of Lords?'[64] although she had never heard him do so. Then Christmas was upon them and Emma exulted:

> Here we are as happy as kings and much more so. We have

> 3 Boltons, 2 Nelsons and only want 2 or 3 little Matchams to be quite *en famille*, happy and comfortable, for the greatest of all joys to our most excellent Nelson is when he has his sisters, or their children, with him; for sure no brother was ever so much attached as he is.[65]

On 3 January, Emma concluded the jollities with a children's party, Nelson writing to the absent George Matcham next day, 'Lady Hamilton gave a little ball last night to the children; they danced till 3 this morning and are not yet up . . .' and Emma added in a postscript, 'We have had a delightful ball. Charlotte outdid herself. Like an angel she was that night.'[66] The dance marked the arrival of Charlotte as a permanent member of the household at Merton, ostensibly to give her education a social polish, her instructress being Emma. Her mother reminded her, 'Although you are a fine girl, without accomplishments you would be nothing.'[67] There were two other motives. One was for Emma to accompany her to the grandest entertainments of the social season, to which she herself would not have been invited. The other was to widen the domestic scene at Merton, so that if Lord Nelson's niece was seen to be under Lady Hamilton's 'protection', it would also be easier to accept his 'adopted daughter' Horatia under his roof.

A month later, a macabre shadow fell across the household: the trial of Despard and his fellow conspirators opened at the Sessions House in Newington Lane. On 7 February, Nelson told the court that the Despard he had once known had been 'one of the brightest ornaments of the British Army'.[68] He also sent Despard's letter to the Prime Minister, who later said that it had moved him and his family to tears. But all Nelson was able to do for his old friend was to have his sentence of death commuted from one of hanging, drawing and quartering to hanging and decapitation after death. But he was able to recommend some financial help for Despard's black wife, who had accompanied him from the Caribbean. After Nelson spoke of the case to Lord Minto, the latter noted, 'Mrs. Despard, he says, was violently in love with her husband. Lord Nelson solicited a pension, or some provision for her, and the Government was well disposed to grant it.'[69]

When the Christmas celebrations ended at Merton, the household moved to 23 Piccadilly, which was warmer and more convenient for visiting the Admiralty and the House of Lords. Emma announced their return with a musical evening for a hundred guests at which, reported a newspaper, 'her Ladyship sang several bravura songs and played very difficult concertos on the pianoforte with such rapidity of execution as not only astonished but electrified her auditors'.[70] Sir William Hamilton had not been well but felt able to attend the Queen's birthday reception, although Nelson did not accompany him, perhaps because he feared he might see Fanny there. Exhausted by these efforts, Sir William slipped into a decline and Dr Moseley was called from Chelsea to pronounce, 'He can't, in my opinion, get over it.'[71]

He did not. He appeared tranquil, only asking not to be disturbed by well-meaning friends bent on comforting him. Alone with Nelson and Emma, he drifted away. Nelson sent a note to Alexander Davison, informing him, 'Wednesday, 11 o'clock, 6 April, 1803. Our dear Sir William died at 10 minutes past ten this morning in Lady Hamilton's and my arms without a sigh or a struggle. Poor Lady Hamilton is, as you might expect, desolate.'[72]

Sir William was buried next to his first wife at Selbeck in Pembrokeshire. In his will, he made Greville his heir, as promised, left Emma an annuity of £800 and settled her debts, leaving Nelson a small painting of his wife as a Bacchante. She and her lover were now alone. Because of Fanny, they could not marry, but at least they could now play at being man and wife.

10
Horatia

On 13 May 1803, Mrs Mary Gibson, the nurse, acting on Lady Hamilton's instructions, took the infant Horatia from Little Titchfield Street to the parish church of St Marylebone* for baptism. It seems that neither parent was present, presumably to avoid attracting public notice, and after the clergyman had named the child Horatia Nelson Thompson – without mentioning her parentage – he was given a double fee by Mrs Gibson on Emma's instructions. The child was then taken back to her playmate, her nurse's little hunchbacked daughter.

The ceremony had marked a stage in Horatia's acceptance as part of the family circle, if not as the child of Nelson and Emma. The latter had made a remarkable recovery from the shock of widowhood, although sharply aware of the attitudes expected from the grief-stricken. When she called on the portrait painter Marie-Louise-Elisabeth Vigée-Lebrun, she was dressed in black and her hair cut short in the new, severe Roman style, proclaiming that she was 'much to be pitied . . . and that she would never be consoled'. But, her hostess noted, 'I confess that her grief made little impression on me, since it seemed to me that she was playing a part. I was evidently not mistaken because, a few minutes later, having noticed some music lying on my piano, she took up a lively tune and began to sing it.'[1]

*Damaged by bombing in the Second World War and demolished in 1949; the large church beside it, completed in 1817, still stands.

On 18 May, five days after Horatia's christening, Emma gave a family party at 11 Clarges Street, a house she had rented off Piccadilly. This was to celebrate the engagement of Nelson's eldest niece, Kitty Bolton, to her first cousin, Captain William Bolton, Royal Navy, one of Nelson's protégés and son of the Reverend William Bolton, rector of Brancaster near Burnham Thorpe. All the Boltons were present, as were William and Sarah Nelson with Charlotte and Horace but not the Matchams, Kate having written to say that her eight children either had measles or would soon go down with it. Nelson was also absent, having left London for Portsmouth at four o'clock that morning.

War had that day been declared on France and the admiral, having been appointed to the Mediterranean command, was to hoist his flag in the first-rate ship of the line, *Victory*. He missed not only the engagement party but also his investiture as a Knight of the Bath in Westminster Abbey, which had been arranged for that day. Tom Bolton and Horace Nelson were to be his esquires and he asked William to accept the insignia on his behalf; as protocol required a knight for this role, the young man was hastily granted the accolade. Everybody was happy, particularly Emma to whom Susannah Bolton gave credit for the successful match-making. That was not the only reason for Emma's joy, for now she, and Nelson, knew that she was again pregnant.

Soon letters again began to arrive from the sea. Nelson had taken with him his favourite, and most flattering, portrait of Emma, which had been painted by Johann Schmidt in Vienna, and another of Horatia, but at first he could not bring himself to hang them on the bulkhead of his cabin as that would emphasize his separation from them. He again slipped back into the Thompson pseudonyms, writing:

> I look at your and my God Child's pictures but, till I am sure of remaining here, I cannot bring myself to hang them up. Be assured that my attachment and affectionate regard is unalterable . . . pray say so to Mrs. T. when you see her. Tell her that my love is unbounded to her and her dear,

> sweet child; and, if she should have more, it will extend to all of them.[2]

It was a week before he wrote again, as the ship heaved across the Bay of Biscay bound for the Mediterranean to blockade the strongest French fleet in Toulon. Between writing orders, reports and letters to friends, he told her that he had at last hung the portraits of her and his 'god-daughter' in his cabin, where they could be seen by all. He would sit at his writing-table, gazing at the pictures until, as he wrote, 'My heart is full to bursting!'[3] Sometimes, his mood would swing away from the euphoric to the fatalistic: 'I feel a thorough conviction that we shall ... remain together till a good old age ... God is good and His wisdom will unite us ... till Death and, if possible, longer.'[4]

Without the company of husband, or lover, and expecting a child, Emma's spirits sank, she took to drinking quantities of porter (dark, bitter beer) and even suggested taking Horatia and Charlotte to the Mediterranean to renew the Neapolitan idyll. This urge was strengthened when Nelson wrote in June, 'Close to Capri, the view of Vesuvius calls so many circumstances to my mind that it almost overpowers my feelings.'[5] His professionalism overcame the temptation and he rejected her suggestion as he had Fanny's: 'Imagine what a cruise off Toulon is. We have a hard gale every week and two days' heavy swell ... It would kill you; and myself to see you. And I, that have given orders to carry no women to sea in the *Victory*, to be the first to break them!'[6]

In the event, leaving her mother in charge of Merton Place, Emma went to Norfolk to stay with the Boltons at Cranwich, where she began to establish herself as the mentor of the Bolton girls, Eliza and Anne, much as she had 'brought forward' Charlotte. Their mother, Susannah, was a more robust, independent-minded woman than Sarah Nelson, yet she too was eager for her daughters to make a mark in society and marry well, so she welcomed Emma's attentions.

From Norfolk, Emma travelled to Canterbury. William Nelson, having been awarded a prebendary's (honorary canon's) stall in the cathedral in May, had moved his family to a house in the Close there. When he heard about the visit, Nelson fussed because of the danger of French invasion now that Bonaparte was at Boulogne with the *Grande Armée*. The most vulnerable English coast was, of course, that of Kent and his primary task was to prevent the most powerful French fleet escaping from the Mediterranean to cover such an attack. These worries did not dampen Emma's ebullience and she soon finished her host's small stock of expensive champagne; indeed her manners were such that invitations to the Nelsons from more senior clergy specified, 'But not Lady Hamilton'.[7] From there, she took the Nelsons for a seaside holiday and bathing at Southend. Yet Horatia was not summoned from London, nor, when Emma returned to Merton, was she installed there, much as her father wished it. Although he would sometimes write to Emma about 'our child', he also referred to her as his adopted child and called Emma her guardian, without taking any formal steps to implement this. He did, however, include a bequest of £4,000 to 'the dear little innocent',[8] and, while she still bore the surname of Thompson, he hatched a scheme to give her his own by urging that, when of age, she should marry his nephew, Horace Nelson. Meanwhile, he wanted to think of her living in his house and wrote in October, 'I am glad to find, my dear Emma, that you mean to take Horatia home. Aye! She is like her mother; will have her own way, or kick up a devil of a fuss. But you will cure her. I am afraid I should spoil her, for I am sure I would shoot anyone who would hurt her.'[9] Then, in thanking Emma for sending him one of the child's curls, remembered that he had promised a particular present for which Horatia had been asking and wrote:

> You have sent me, in that beautiful lock of hair, a far richer present than any monarch in Europe could . . . Your description of the dear angel makes me happy. I have sent to Mr. Falconet [a French émigré banker in Naples] to buy me a watch and told him if it does but tick and the chain full of trinkets, that is all which is wanted.[10]

He also wrote to Horatia herself, saying that he was sending her a lock of his hair to put in a locket 'and I give you leave to wear it when you are dressed and behave well'.[11] He continued, 'As I am sure that for the world you would not tell a story, it must have slipt my memory that I promised you a watch, therefore I have sent to Naples to get one and I would send it home as soon as it arrives.' Then, remembering that she had wanted another present, he added, 'The dog I never could have promised as we have no dogs on board ship.'[12]

As letters took at least a month to travel between London and the *Victory*, Nelson assumed that, in compliance with his wishes, Horatia had been taken to live at Merton; the idea of the two of them spending the winter of 1803 cosily together around his hearth was a comfort. Whenever clouds of naval and political thoughts parted, he imagined his house and garden and sent Emma detailed instructions about improvements, including:

> I also beg, as my dear Horatia is to be at Merton, that a strong netting, about three feet high, may be placed round the Nile, that the little thing may not tumble in; and then you may have ducks again in it. I forget at what place we saw the netting; and either Mr. Perry, or Mr. Goldsmid told us where it was to be bought. I shall be very anxious till I know this is done . . .[13]

The sight of Horatia's portrait on his bulkhead brought on sudden panics and he wrote again while off Toulon, 'Take care that my darling does not fall in and get drowned. I begged you to get the little netting along the edge and particularly along the bridges . . .'[14] Yet, despite Nelson's retreated entreaties, such as, 'How is my dear Horatia? I hope you have her under your guardian wing at Merton *fixed*',[15] Emma still refused to include her in her household.

She did, however, concede that she would be responsible for the child's education and began to make provision for a governess. Her maternal aunt, Mrs Sarah Connor, had three daughters, Sarah, Mary and Cecilia, and Emma had long wanted to give them the same advantages she had provided for Nelson's nieces. Sir William had not seemed to regard them as socially acceptable, although they had visited Merton as Nelson's guests, but now she was free to invite them. She saw them as suitable to act, in turn, as Horatia's governesses. Mary had accompanied Emma to Cranwich and now could be employed, as occasion demanded, in London. In any case, the presence, and acceptance, of her cousins could only strengthen her position in the event of any counter-offensive by Fanny. Although Emma still feared this, it was proving to be increasingly unlikely because the latter had withdrawn into a shell of formality, her visiting card printed, 'Viscountess Nelson, Duchess of Bronte'. She spent much of her time at Bath, where the Matchams were also living, and Kate dutifully reported to Emma:

> The Lady is, I believe, at Bath but too great a distance from us ever to see her. We have been at a ball, a concert and a play this week but she was not at either. My only desire is that we shall not be in the same room and circumstances are now so well understood by our friends that I don't think it is likely we shall ever meet her.[16]

For the time being, it was Charlotte and not Horatia who enjoyed the comforts of Merton and Clarges Street, mostly staying in London but enjoying visits to Surrey, where Mrs Cadogan remained as housekeeper. Charlotte continued her music and singing lessons, and her appearance was monitored by Lady Hamilton and her aunts. 'Mrs. Bolton thinks I am improved in my shape,' she told her mother. 'My Lady is so kind as to have some more short dresses made for me.'[17] But it was important that Charlotte should meet Horatia and accept the garbled explanations of her occasional presence at Merton. They were introduced and Emma instructed Charlotte to write to Nelson about the meeting. He was delighted and replied, 'I feel truly sensible of your kind regard for that dear little orphan, Horatia. Although her parents are lost, she is not without a fortune . . . I am glad to hear she is attached to you.'[18] He wrote to Emma, 'I am pleased with Charlotte's letter . . . As she loves my dear Horatia, I shall always like her.'[19] His vision of a cosy family circle, idealized beyond reality, had come even more sharply into focus.

Yet disaster could overwhelm at any time and, as the winter jollities began, Horatia was taken ill in Little Titchfield Street. Smallpox was pronounced. Nelson had long urged Emma to have the child vaccinated but this had not been done and now she was expected to die. However, she survived, and when Nelson heard of her illness and that she had recovered, he assumed the vaccination had saved her and wrote to Emma, 'I wish I had all the smallpox for her . . . I dreamt last night I heard her call "Papa" and point to her arm just as you described.'[20] His paternal longings were again unleashed and he wrote to Horatia, 'I send you twelve books of Spanish dresses, which you will let your Guardian Angel, Lady Hamilton, keep for you when you are tired of looking at them. I am very glad to hear that you are perfectly recovered and that you are a very good girl.'[21]

Emma was also indisposed, the ailment unspecified, Charlotte wrote home about her hostess being kept in bed for three weeks. The unannounced reason was, in fact, her advanced pregnancy, again concealed by her bulk and the voluminous style of current fashion. Nelson had insisted that if the baby was female she should be named after her mother, not realizing that this had already been done for the twin that had been sent to the Foundling Hospital. At the end of the year Emma gave birth to another daughter but she died almost immediately. When Nelson eventually learned of the loss, he was comforting and sentimental, writing of 'dear little Emma'.[22]

As cover for the secret birth, Emma kept her house full of children, who would give the impression of social activity and an additional excuse to refuse invitations. With the help of Nelson's agent, Alexander Davison, and the doctor, Benjamin Moseley, together with their families, the Christmas holidays in Clarges Street were as festive as at Merton. As they came to an end, Charlotte told her mother, 'Miss Connor, my cousins [the Boltons] and myself have been making ourselves a short dress trimmed with blue ribbons. The petticoats also trimmed with the same. We are to wear them on Tuesday to a dance at Dr Moseley's. Miss Connor and myself are learning a figure dance. . . Horatia went to the play on Friday with Mr, Mrs and Master Davison.'[23]

As soon as Emma was back on her feet, she resumed her social offensive with Charlotte as her trim little stalking-horse. The splendid parties given by the Goldsmids and other Surrey neighbours were taken for granted and each invitation to a grand London salon or ballroom was a triumph. Her plan to gain entry as the chaperone of Lord Nelson's niece had succeeded beyond her expectations, although she affected nonchalance. She wrote to Sarah:

> As to the grand routs, I hate them, but I thought it right to show myself in some respectable houses as Tom Tit said she would shut me out. I have been invited to every party about town, so has Charlotte; we went to the Ladies' Concert and to the most chosen places to show *we could do so* and your good sense will approve, I am sure. Charlotte is so much admired, and justly so, I think. The Duchess of Devonshire was so civil to Charlotte and told her she would invite her to all her balls. The Walpoles were there; everybody came up and spoke to me and made so much of us. The most fashionable ball next week is Mrs. Orby Hunter's; all the girls of fashion are to be there; also one on Friday at Mrs. Broadhead's and one at Mrs. Wolf's on Wednesday, where we are invited – also to Lady Louisa Manners.

Careful to cast herself as the attentive self-effacing chaperone, she continued, 'I never quit her for a moment. My whole time is given up with pleasure to this lovely girl . . . I took her to dine with Lady Stafford, who is in love with her . . . She will be the most accomplished girl of the age.' But occasionally the motivating steel gleamed through the effusion, as when she concluded, 'Tom Tit is in town, bursting with rage and envy.'[24]

Nelson's particular friends and their neighbours at Merton were attentive to Emma as occasion arose but she relied for advice on a friend of her own, a lively old roué, who still ogled young women even if he could no longer seduce them. This was a neighbour in London, the decrepit eighty-year-old Duke of Queensberry – nicknamed 'Old Q' – who lived around the corner from Clarges Street in Piccadilly. A relation and former crony of Sir William's, he had enjoyed an even more raffish career. As one friend put it, 'After exhausting all the gratifications of human life . . . he remained a spectator of the moving scene in which he could no longer take a very active part. His person had become a ruin but not so his mind.'[25]

The old man was enlisted to promote Charlotte, while Emma was particularly attentive to him, thinking that a handsome legacy might be forthcoming. 'The poor old Duke I think is going fast,' she noted. 'He admires Charlotte but is more like a father.'[26]

Despite the gloss that the girl was acquiring, she had, in Emma's view, yet to achieve the ultimate polish and poise; it was mainly a matter of elegant movement in entering or leaving a room, seating herself and dropping a curtsy to royalty. Although Charlotte, in 'a new dress of blue and white, spangled, look'd divine', she reported to Sarah, she did not think her 'fit to come out presentable at Court till next winter . . . she must practice every day for three months coming in and going out with a hoop [a wide, hooped skirt]', and this regime was begun. As it progressed, Emma proved a tireless instructor in 'setting down and getting up and all the elegancies that is necessary', stressing that 'beauty will not do without Grace and Elegance'.[27] Sarah Nelson was feeling distanced from her daughter. In a letter to Emma she wrote:

> I begin to long to see her and hear Charlotte again, how good you are to dress her so smart. I hope by the time my Lord arrives she will be able to accompany you in song.[28]

Early in 1804, Emma began the next stage of manipulation of the youngest member of her circle. Charlotte had met Horatia, now aged three, and this helped blur the actual state of relationships in a mist of sentiment. The girl had been told that Horatia was an orphan in whom her uncle took a benevolent interest for her parents' sake, and that Lady Hamilton was acting as a guardian in his absence. She was also told that Emma was taking a similar interest in another child, the daughter of the British consul at Palermo, who had just been sent to England and committed to his and Emma's care; so, Charlotte was given to understand, there was nothing unusual about either. But when, in April 1804, Nelson's two sisters came to stay in London and were generously entertained by Emma at her house in Clarges Street, which their children saw as 'a Fairy Palace',[29] neither met Horatia. The young people enjoyed lavish hospitality and a dance to celebrate Emma's birthday, Charlotte telling her mother, 'We sat down eighty to supper and danced till six in the morning.'[30]

Soon afterwards, Emma again visited William and Sarah at Canterbury and had returned home long before she received a letter from Nelson, wild with worry that she and, as he wrongly supposed, Horatia might again be in danger. 'Your trip to Canterbury I should suppose the worst you could take for on any alarm there you must stay, and in a town filled with soldiers,' he wrote. Then, as he paced the *Victory*'s quarterdeck, or stared at their portraits in his cabin, his imagination conjured up horrors and, supposing they might be bathing at Ramsgate, he continued, 'I am very uneasy at your and Horatia being on the coast for you cannot move if the French make the attempt . . . I shall rejoice to hear you and Horatia are safe at Merton.'[31] By then, Emma was, but Horatia was not, despite Nelson's instructions that she should live in his house as his ward with one of the Connor girls as her governess. He seemed confident that his elaborate and sometimes contradictory cover-stories would be believed, even writing a letter to Emma, but also for general circulation, which began, 'Before we left Italy, I told you of the extraordinary circumstances of a child being left to my care and protection. On your first coming to England, I presented you the child, dear Horatia . . .'[32]

For Emma, Horatia would prove an encumbrance, and possibly an embarrassment, as a permanent member of her household, hampering her successful ascent of the social heights during the busy autumn and winter season of 1804. Although as vulgar as ever and likened to 'one of the Bacchantes of Rubens'[33] by one acquaintance, but thought by another 'too large for the Bacchante',[34] she was hobnobbing with the aristocracy. She was entertained by, or seen chatting with, the Duchess of Roxburghe, Lady Abercorn and, above all, Lady Cholmondeley, at whose ball she danced till four in the morning. This was significant because the latter's was a Walpole title and her family owned Houghton Hall, the great mansion to which Captain and Mrs Nelson had never been invited during their years in Norfolk, despite his kinship. Yet presentation at court remained beyond her range and not only because of her reputation; the King was suffering recurrent bouts of insanity and fear of provoking Nelson's jealous rage deterred her from responding to the ogling of the Prince of Wales. But there were encouraging prospects in another area, for Davison had told her that, at Nelson's urging, Lord Melville, the First Lord of the Admiralty, had suggested to William Pitt, who had returned to power as Prime Minister, that her services in the Mediterranean warranted an official pension of £500. For Emma, the recognition would be as important as the money.

The ultimate prize of marriage to her lover still eluded her and could be delivered only by Fanny's death. Yet she had hopes which she could not help expressing, as in a letter to Alexander Davison, to whom she wrote of Nelson, 'What a sad thing it is to think of such a man as him should be entrapped with such an infamous woman as the apothecary's widow . . . Whilst I am free – with talents he likes, adoring him, that never a woman adored a man as I do my Nelson, loving him beyond this world, and yet we are both miserable . . . patience.'[35] Emma's long campaign of vilification had taken effect and both Nelson's sisters had joined in, Kate Matcham more enthusiastically than the usually open-hearted Susannah. Neither was fully at ease with the exuberant Emma but nor had they ever been wholly relaxed in the company of Fanny, who came from the other social extreme but with attitudes and more polished manners than those of the Nelsons. She was still in Bath at the beginning of 1805 and from there Kate wrote to Emma:

> We were in the same room with Lady N. a few nights since, for the first time since she came to Bath. She had then an opportunity of showing her insolence as far as looks could express, so I was told by some friends of mine who said she looked as I passed her in that scornful way, which could not but be noticed by all that saw her.[36]

Throughout 1804, Nelson had been expecting permission to return home on leave, but that was impossible once, on 14 December, Spain joined France in the war against Britain. Now the danger of enemy fleets escaping from their blockaded ports and combining to cover an invasion of the British Isles became critical. Nelson would still have to watch Toulon but there were also the Spanish Atlantic ports of Cartagena, Algeciras, Cadiz, Vigo, Ferrol and Corunna to cover. Then, on the first day of 1805, the French squadron at Rochefort escaped into the Atlantic. A fortnight later, risk became reality when, under cover of a stormy night, Admiral Villeneuve, commanding the fleet in Toulon, led his ships to sea and also escaped. Nelson had no way of knowing where they had gone. It might, as he feared, be towards the English Channel but it could equally be towards Naples or Sicily, still ruled by his friends King Ferdinand and Queen Maria Carolina. This was a repeat of the mystery and the long chase that had, seven years before, ended with the Battle of the Nile. The thought of a similar climax brought Nelson to a high pitch of tension and he ordered a chase without knowing where his quarry might be.

Again the strain sent his imagination racing with thoughts of victory and, perhaps, death and glory; but what would happen to Emma then? He began making plans for ensuring that she and Horatia would be 'independent of the world', but then, thinking that this would worry her, wrote rather clumsily, 'My Emma, your Nelson is not the nearer being lost to you for taking care of you in case of events which are only known when they are to happen to an All-Wise Providence and I hope for many, many years of comfort with you.'[37]

Only sketchy reports reached London of the desperate search for the French fleet. From 19 January, Nelson scoured the Mediterranean, following his old course to Aboukir Bay, and it was not until 18 April that, at last hearing that the enemy had passed Gibraltar, sailing west into the Atlantic, he decided, 'I am going out of the Mediterranean',[38] and the long search became a long chase. It was now realized that the French were bound for the West Indies, where the rich sugar islands would be at the mercy of such a force. Meanwhile, those waiting in England heard only rumours and the briefest of reports, and at Westminster and in Whitehall it could be deduced only that the Atlantic crossing was part of a more ambitious and dangerous strategy. This was to lure Nelson to the West Indies in pursuit, so leaving the western approaches to the British Isles sparsely defended; then to sweep back across the Atlantic, combine with other French squadrons and the Spanish fleet, and take control of the Channel for the invasion of England.

The French plan almost worked. Nelson followed to the Caribbean and Villeneuve headed back to Europe. Throughout the weeks of the chase, Nelson continued to write to Emma, although he must have realized that his letters would not begin their journey to England for weeks. He was beset by the loneliness of command, because, as he told her, 'Although I am good friends with all yet I am intimate with none beyond the cheerful hours of meals.'[39] At the beginning of June, he was sure that an action was imminent, telling her:

> My own dearest beloved Emma, your own Nelson's pride and delight, I find myself within six days of the enemy and I have every reason to hope that the 6th. of June will

> immortalize your own Nelson, your fond Nelson. May God send me Victory and us a happy and speedy meeting . . . Pray for my success and my laurels I shall lay with pleasure at your feet. A sweet kiss will be an ample reward for all your faithful Nelson's hard fag.'[40]

But allowing his own judgement to be overruled by what could later be seen as faulty intelligence, he failed to intercept them, having to tell her, 'Ah, my Emma, June 6th would have been a great day for me . . . My Genius carried me direct to the spot and all would have been well as the heart could wish . . . I have ever found that if I was left and acted as my poor noddle told me was right, I should seldom err.'[41]

Although a Spanish squadron had joined Villeneuve in the Atlantic, the French ships in Brest had been unable to break out and, after a brief action with a British squadron off Cape Finisterre, the combined force ran for the safety of Spanish ports. Nelson followed in their wake, but Villeneuve had escaped and all he could do was to return to the anchorage at Spithead. At once he wrote to Emma:

> I am, my dearest Emma, this moment anchored and as the post will not go out till eight o'clock and you not get the letter till eleven, or twelve o'clock tomorrow, I have ordered a Post Office express to tell you of my arrival. I hope we shall be out of quarantine tomorrow, when I shall fly to dear Merton . . . The boat is waiting, I must finish. This day two years and three months I left you. God send us a happy meeting as our parting was sorrowful.[42]

When Emma heard he would soon be home, she immediately spread the news and, by return, Susannah wrote from Cranwich, 'Thanks, my dear Lady, for your *scrap*. It was indeed short and *sweet*, for *sweet* was the intelligence that my dearest brother was arrived in England. What a paradise he must think Merton, to say nothing of the Eve it contains.'[43]

Landing at Portsmouth, he paid his respects to the admiral, then hired a post-chaise and took the road to Merton. He arrived there, as he had on his first visit, before the household was awake. It was an ecstatic homecoming. 'What a day of rejoicing was yesterday at Merton!' Emma wrote to Kate Matcham next day. 'How happy he is to see us all!'[44] Nelson had been changed by more than the passing of two years. Most of that time he had been on board his flagship and the social insecurity and signs of the lush life at Palermo and Merton had been replaced by confidence and health. 'His features are sharp and his skin is now very much burnt from his having been long at sea,' noted an American visitor who saw him in London, 'He has the balancing gait of a sailor. . .'[45] His nasal, high-toned voice still kept its Norfolk accent and, as a Danish visitor to Merton recorded, 'the penetration of his eye threw a light upon his countenance which tempered his severity and rendered his harsh features in some measure agreeable'.[46]

But this was to be no settling back into domesticity. The next day, the couple set out for London and a round of official visits; he lodging at an hotel near Clarges Street for propriety's sake because Mrs Cadogan, her daughter's nominal chaperone since the death of Sir William, remained in charge of Merton. There were calls at the Admiralty, on the Prime Minister, the Foreign Secretary and the Secretary for War, all of whom needed to hear his reports and his forecast; for the enemy fleets, trapped in their Atlantic ports, could still lend massive strength to any attempted invasion. There were naval friends with whom to discuss contingencies; there were Alexander Davison and William Haslewood with whom to make financial and legal arrangements; and there was royalty anxious to meet him. One day soon, he would most certainly return to his command at sea and what all expected to be the climactic battle. From the day of his return, his life and time marched to a drumbeat of inevitability.

On their return to Merton, Nelson and Emma began what were probably the happiest days of their lives. With them was Horatia, who had been hurriedly summoned from Little Titchfield Street. Now a lively, intelligent child of four and a half, wearing her fair hair cut short, she had begun to learn music from Emma and was able to speak a few words in French and Italian. Nelson's family were summoned from Canterbury, Cranwich and Bath, knowing that his stay would inevitably be brief. Susannah arrived before Kate, whose most recent child, a baby boy, had just died, and wrote to her from Merton, 'the sooner you leave such a melancholy scene the better . . . come immediately lest you should not be in time to see our dear brother . . . seeing him and hearing him will soothe your griefs'.[47] Kate and George Matcham obeyed, joining the Boltons and the William Nelsons with their children. The Matchams were followed by their son George, whose diary gave an impression of the crowded, excited household he joined late one night at the beginning of September and the subsequent mixture of amusement, boredom, irritation and excitement seen by a fifteen-year-old boy:

> On arriving at M., found them all in bed. Lady H. came out en chemise and directed me to my cousin T.'s [Thomas Bolton's] room, where I was to sleep. Had not seen him for ten years, soon made acquaintance.
>
> Wednesday, 4th. Paid respects to Lord N., the Dr. [William Nelson], Mrs. B. and N. Went out with my cousin Horace [Nelson] a'shooting. After a tedious morning, he shot a brace. Large company at dinner . . . Lost 11s. 6d. at cards. Lady H. presented me with £2. 2s. from Lord N.
>
> Friday, 6th. Fished in the pond. Caught nothing. Sauntered about the grounds. H.R.H. the Duke of C. [Clarence, the future King William IV] dined here. Like the King [George III, his father] . . . Introduced to the D. of C., talked much. His deference to Lord N.'s opinion. Violent against Mr. P—T [Pitt]; found out the reason. Seemed estranged from the K— [King]. Lord Errol with him. Heavy.

Presenting his three nephews – George Matcham, Horace Nelson and Tom Bolton – to the Duke, Nelson described them as 'My three props.' George continued:

Sunday, 8th. Went to Church. Sir Sidney S—th [Captain – later Admiral – Smith] came in. Handsome. Talked of Acre [where he had defeated Bonaparte on his retreat from Egypt].

Monday, 9th. Went with Horace, Charlotte and Anne to Mr. Goldsmid's . . . Fine house . . . After breakfast rowed in the boat. Horace showed his skill. Grounds poor. Very polite. Did not like their dinner; Jewish. The hall the height of the house, very gaudy, as are all the rooms but tasteless. H. [Horace] cut his jokes on me, let him go on . . .

Wednesday, 11th. This day, Mr. [William] Beckford [of Fonthill] dined here. Talkative. Praised his own composition. Played extempore on the harpsichord. Sung. I thought it a very horrible noise.[48]

Among the guests was Lord Minto, who had written such a sour account of Merton after his first visit; now he was more tolerant:

I went to Merton on Saturday and found Nelson just sitting down to dinner surrounded by a family party of his brother the Dean [Prebendary], Mrs. Nelson, their children and the children of a sister. Lady Hamilton was at the head of the table and Mrs. Cadogan at the bottom. I had a hearty welcome. He looks remarkably well and in spirits. His conversation is cordial in these low times . . . Lady Hamilton has improved and added to the house and the place extremely well without his knowing she was about it. He found it all ready done. She is a clever being, after all; the passion is as hot as ever.'[49]

Merton Place was, indeed, at its most charming in the late summer sunshine. Additional purchases of land had given it a total of seventy acres of gardens, kitchen gardens and paddocks, a brick tunnel beneath the road now connecting the grounds on either side of the road; in the lavishly planted gardens, vistas drew the eye to a new summerhouse and a raised walk that had been called the Poop. Indoors, the walls were hung with portraits of Nelson and Emma and paintings of his victories. His trophies and presentations were prominently displayed and new overmantel glasses had been emblazoned with his arms as a viscount. Upstairs were five large bedrooms with dressing-rooms and the newly designed water closets. The warlike aspects of the display were softened by flowers, copies of the latest periodicals – not only the *Naval Chronicle* but the *Critical Review* and the *European Magazine* – lying about and the presence of Horatia's rocking-horse and parrot.

While at home, Nelson wore plain clothes – usually black or brown coat and breeches – and seemed happy and at ease. The extravagance and vulgarity of Emma's hospitality were gone and young George Matcham was to remember that his uncle

> delighted in quiet conversation, through which occasionally ran an undercurrent of pleasantry not unmixed with caustic wit. At his table, he was the least heard among the company and, so far from being the hero of his own tale, I never heard him allude voluntarily to any of the great actions of his life. I have known him lauded by the great and wise; but he seemed to me to waive the homage with as little attention as was consistent with civility . . . In his plain suit of black . . . he always looked what he was – a gentleman.[50]

All his adult life, Nelson had been accustomed to having his portrait painted and the windows of print shops were full of engravings taken from the originals. Now he had two requests for sittings: one from the miniaturist Robert Bowyer, and the other from Catherine Andras, who modelled in wax and was hoping to mass-produce a medallion of him in profile. Time was pressing, so he agreed on condition that he sat for both of them together, although he 'laughingly remarked that he was not used to being attacked in that manner starboard and larboard at the same time'.[51]

In London, where he was recognized and cheered even when

in civilian dress, he was aware that the eyes of the nation were upon him and its hopes borne on his shoulders. The knowledge gave him a confidence and serenity he had not shown before. Occasionally the old insecurity came to the fore, as when, while waiting to see Lord Castlereagh at the Colonial Office, he fell into conversation with a young major-general he did not know and began to boast in 'a style so vain and so silly as to surprise and almost disgust me', as the soldier later said. Then, discovering from the office-keeper that he had been speaking with Sir Arthur Wellesley (the future Duke of Wellington), fresh from his triumphs in India, his 'charlatan style' was instantly replaced, and, said Wellesley, 'I don't know that I ever had a conversation that interested me more . . . he was really a very superior man.'[52]

It was now that Nelson decided to abandon any thought of a political future for himself, much as Emma desired it; his experiences in the House of Lords had revealed the scheming and duplicity of politics, for which an honourable and relatively unsophisticated naval officer was ill-suited. Visiting William Pitt, he announced, as he himself put it later, 'some specimen of a sailor's politics by frankly telling him that . . . I could not pretend to a nice discrimination between the use and abuse of parties and therefore must not be expected to range myself under the political banners of any man in, or out, of place. That England's welfare was the sole object of my pursuit. . .'[53] Indeed, England's welfare was about to demand his services again.

At Merton, the household was aware of his increasing preoccupation, as when he paced round his garden with his old friend Captain Keats, describing the strategy and tactics he planned to employ. Yet there was no elation about him and Kate, who happened to meet him in London, remarked that he looked tired, while her son, George, thought him 'more than usually pensive'.[54]

The expected call came at five o'clock on the morning of 2 September. The stamp and grind of horses' hoofs and iron-rimmed wheels on the gravel drive announced the arrival of Captain Henry Blackwood, on his way from Portsmouth to

London, carrying urgent dispatches from Nelson's second-in-command, Admiral Collingwood, to the Admiralty. He had decided to warn Nelson that enemy squadrons had left Ferrol and Corunna, combined forces at sea and sailed for Cadiz. There, more than thirty French and Spanish ships of the line now lay. If they manage to escape and join with the squadrons at Rochefort and Brest, they would present the overwhelming force of which Nelson had warned Pitt, and invasion of England might be possible. Nelson followed Blackwood to the Admiralty, where he was given the orders he expected: to leave and join his flagship, the *Victory*, as soon as all was ready. He then saw the Prime Minister and told him that if the enemy squadrons combined, 'they will have collected sixty or seventy sail of the line and there will be difficulty in overcoming them'.[55] Asked to take command of the fleet, he replied that Collingwood would be the best possible commander. 'No, that won't do,' said Pitt, 'you must take the command.' At this, he was said to have replied'* 'Sir, I wish it not. I have had enough of it and feel disposed to remain quiet the rest of my life.' The Prime Minister insisted and Nelson said simply, 'I am ready now.'[56]

On his return to Merton, the house party was beginning to break up. The children returned to school, the Boltons to Norfolk, the Matchams to Bath and the Nelsons to Canterbury. Maurice Nelson's widow, 'Poor Blindy', was leaving after her brief exposure to high drama, 'gone sad and alone to her nutshell',[57] as Emma put it. The latter tried to match her lover's stoicism but wrote to Susannah Bolton, 'I have had a fortnight's dream and am awoke to all the misery of this cruel separation. But what can I do?'[58] At last the household was pared down to Nelson, Emma, Horatia and Mrs Cadogan, and final preparations were made for his departure, which was scheduled for the night of 13 September.

First, there was to be a last visit to London, for he had been summoned to an audience with the once-feared and hated Prince of Wales. Emma accompanied him as far as Clarges Street,

*The validity of this quotation has been questioned.

so as to miss as little of his company as possible, but waited there while he continued to Carlton House for a formal meeting with the fat, cultivated libertine who had haunted his imagination for so long. At last they returned through the gates of Merton Place, two hours late for a final small dinner party at which their neighbour the editor James Perry and Lord Minto were to be guests. It was a subdued occasion, Minto remarking afterwards, 'Lady Hamilton was in tears all yesterday, could not eat, hardly drink and near swooning, all at table.'[59] Musing further on his long friendship with the extraordinary man upon whom the fate of the nation now seemed to rely, Minto mused, 'It is a strange picture. He is in many points a great man; in others, a baby.'[60]

As so often before battle, thoughts of death or glory came to his mind, although there was no risk in what might be to come that he had not faced before. He told Emma that, if he was killed, she should sing a Neapolitan song of mourning, a copy of which he had placed in the coffin made from the mast of *l'Orient* after the Battle of the Nile. 'But how could that be?' she asked. 'For, unless I sung it in madness, if I lost you, I should be unable to sing.' To which Nelson replied, 'Yes, I suppose you would.'[61]

With the clocks of Merton Place ticking away the final hours, Nelson felt the need for some climactic gesture towards Emma. Although they could not, of course, marry, he had for some time spoken of her as his wife in the eyes of God and he now followed his long sequence of rationalizing the relationship with a ceremony. This was to take Communion together and then, in the presence of Mr Lancaster, the rector, exchange gold rings. During this he continued the pious self-delusion by vowing, 'Emma, I have taken the Sacrament with you this day to prove to the world that our friendship is most pure and innocent and of this I call God to witness.'[62] Afterwards, he and Emma walked on the Poop in the garden and, as she later said, she had cheered and encouraged him, prompting him to exclaim, 'Good Emma! Brave Emma! If there were more Emmas there would be more Nelsons.'[63]

Nelson passed his last day supervising the packing of his

trunks and taking a final walk round his garden. After dinner, he was told that his carriage was ready and the time for farewells had come. Horatia was asleep in the night nursery and he knelt to pray beside her cot. As he rose and reached the door he turned and returned four times for a last look at his child. He bade farewell to Emma and walked across the gravel to the waiting coach, where a stable-boy held open the door. 'Be a good boy till I come back again,'[64] said Nelson and climbed aboard. The coachman cracked his whip, the carriage lurched forward and rumbled down the drive and on to the Portsmouth road. Later that night, halted at a coaching-inn for a change of horses, Nelson tried to put his thoughts together on paper and wrote with the facility of a parson's son:

> Friday night at half past ten, drove from dear, dear Merton, where I left all which I hold dear in this world, to go to serve my King and Country. May the great God, whom I adore, enable me to fulfil the expectations of my country; and if it is His good pleasure that I should return, my thanks will never cease being offered up to the throne of His mercy. If it is His good Providence to cut short my days upon earth, I bow with the greatest submission, relying that he will protect those dear to me that I may leave behind. His will be done. Amen, amen, amen.[65]

The small household at Merton had only forty-eight hours to wait before letters began to arrive. On reaching Portsmouth at dawn the day after leaving, Nelson had stopped at the George Inn and there met Mr Lancaster, the rector, with his fourteen-year-old son, who was to begin his training to be a naval officer on the *Victory*, and he offered to take a letter back to Emma:

> 6 o'clock, George Inn. My dearest and most beloved of women, Nelson's Emma, I arrived here this moment and Mr Lancaster takes it. His coach is at the door and only waits for my line. *Victory* is at St. Helen's and, if possible, I shall be at sea this day. God protect you and my dear

Horatia, prays ever your most faithful Nelson and Bronte.[66]

While awaiting the admiral's barge to take him out to St Helen's, Nelson called on Kate, who had come to Portsmouth to bid him farewell and was lodging at a house overlooking the parade ground. She found him in a fatalistic, sombre mood and he reminded her of a fortune-teller who had once told him that she could not foresee his life beyond the year 1805. 'Ah, Katty, Katty,' he said, 'that gipsy!'[67] Then he was gone, walking through the cheering crowds outside and to a narrow tunnel leading through the fortifications to the beach, where the bathing-machines* were parked and his barge was waiting.

Letters could be sent ashore from the anchorage and next day he wrote again to Emma. He himself received a letter from her on the following day but could not bring himself to read it at once, replying, 'I cannot even read your letter. We have a fair wind and, God will, I hope, soon grant us a happy meeting. The wind is quite fair and fresh . . . May Heaven bless you and Horatia . . .'[68] The *Victory* sailed on 15 September but mail could still be sent ashore and collected off Weymouth and Plymouth, so he continued to write. 'I love and adore you to the very excess of passion but with God's blessing we shall soon meet again,' he wrote from the former, 'Kiss Horatia a thousand times for me.'[69] On the 17 September, he was writing, 'I entreat, my dear Emma, that you will cheer up; and we will look forward to many, many happy years and be surrounded by our children's children . . . My heart and soul is with you and Horatia. I get this line ready in case a boat should get alongside.'[70] But gradually, he was slipping from the bonds of Merton and into those of the Navy and, in his letter of the 20th, written south-west of the Scilly Islands, he was suddenly worrying that he might be too late for the expected fleet action. 'A frigate is coming down . . . from the fleet off Cadiz. If the battle has been fought, I shall be

*Carts with hooded doors that were wheeled into the sea to ensure seclusion when bathing.

sadly vexed but I cannot help myself.' And instead of the usual outpouring of love, he simply wrote, 'May heavens bless you. Kiss Horatia for yours faithfully Nelson and Bronte.'[71]

Meanwhile, Emma, unable to stand the loneliness of Merton Place among all the portraits of her absent lover, decided to stay with the Nelsons at Canterbury. She left Horatia in the care of Mrs Cadogan, who, she told Nelson in a letter, 'doats on her, she says she could not live without her', but she was careful to give no hint of her parentage in case the letter went astray, adding, 'What a blessing for her parents to have such a child, so sweet, altho' so young, so amiable!'[72] She wrote to him:

> My heart is broke away from her. You will be ever fonder of her when you return. She says, 'I love my dear, dear god-papa but Mrs. Gibson told me he killed all the people and I was afraid,' Dearest angel that she is! Oh, Nelson, how I love her but how do I idolize you – the dearest husband of my heart, you are all in this world to your Emma . . . May God send you victory and home to your *Emma, Horatia* and *Paradise Merton*, for when you are there it will be paradise.[73]

The family was gathering together for mutual comfort: Tom and Eliza Bolton, home to Cranwich; then, because, as Emma reported to Nelson, 'Charlotte hates Canterbury, it is so *dull*; so it is',[74] Anne Bolton was sent to keep her company. Anne's mother joined the Matchams at Bath, from where she wrote to Emma accepting an invitation to stay at Merton in the third week of October. But even Susannah could not resist an unkind reference to her sister-in-law, who heard news of her husband only through the newspapers: 'I saw Tom Tit yesterday in her carriage . . . She looked then much as usual; had I seen only her hands spreading about, I should have known her.' Then, she reverted to her usual more generous self:

> I hope by the last Lisbon mails you have got letters from my dear brother and that, I am sure, will drive away all the

> blue devils in spite of screech owls, rooks, etc. You must keep up your spirits. What in the world will my Lord think if he comes back and finds you grown thin and looking ill?[75]

Emma found some distraction in the role of benefactress to her lover's nephews and nieces. Sixteen-year-old Eliza Bolton wrote her gossipy letters from Norfolk describing her niece, Lady Bolton's infant daughter Emma – named after Lady Hamilton – 'She does not talk much, but she tries'; adding that her sister Susannah will be sending Mrs Cadogan 'three or four bottles of ketchup' and, in a postscript, that one bottle of ketchup and one of pickled mushrooms had been sent; and saying of herself: 'I practice music, read and translate French every day.'[76] From Merton, the governess, Mary Connor, wrote about Horatia's progress:

> We read about twenty times a day . . . and she is now learning the names of the keys on the pianoforte. I am quite busy dressing her doll . . . She is uncommonly quick and I dare say will read tolerably by the time you see her again. I told her she was invited to see a ship launched . . . she wanted to know if there will be any *firing of guns*.[77]

That was what all the family awaited with such anticipation and apprehension.

In the Atlantic, over the horizon from Cadiz, the *Victory* joined the fleet on 28 September and, the next day, Nelson began to meet his captains to explain his strategy and tactics. His plan was to approach the enemy line in columns to cut the centre and rear from the van, so outnumbering and destroying them before the leading ships could turn and come to their aid. There were continual meetings as officers were rowed to and from the flagship over the slow oceanic swell and the admiral, when not in conference, was writing reports and letters, spending seven hours at his writing-table on the last day of September. On the first day of October, he wrote to Emma:

I believe my arrival was most welcome, not only to the commander of the Fleet [Collingwood] but also to every individual in it; and when I came to explain to them the '*Nelson touch*', it was like an electric shock. Some shed tears, all approved – 'It was new – it was singular – it was simple!' and from the Admiral down it was repeated, 'It must succeed, if ever they will allow us to get at them! You are, my Lord, surrounded by friends, whom you inspire with confidence.'[78]

Finally, on 19 October, Nelson, alone in the great cabin of his flagship, with the canting horizon and his own ships beyond its stern-windows, wrote to Emma again:

My dearest, beloved Emma, the dear friend of my bosom. The signal has been made that the enemy's combined fleet are coming out of port. We have very little wind, so that I have no hopes of seeing them before tomorrow. May the God of Battles crown my endeavours with success; at all events, I shall take care that my name shall ever be most dear to you and Horatia, both of whom I love as much as my own life. And, as my last writing before the Battle will be to you, so I hope in God that I shall live to finish my letter after the Battle.[79]

On the same day, he wrote to Horatia, boldly revealing himself as her parent:

I rejoice to hear that you are so very good a girl and love my dear Lady Hamilton, who most dearly loves you. Give her a kiss from me. The combined fleets of the enemy are now reported to be coming out of Cadiz . . . You are ever uppermost in my thoughts. I shall be sure of your prayers for my safety, conquest and speedy return to dear Merton . . . Be a good girl, mind what Miss Connor says to you. Receive, my dearest Horatia, the affectionate parental blessing of your Father.[80]

Then there was silence.

On 29 October, Sarah Nelson, having heard no news of her brother-in-law's actions at sea, wrote listlessly to Charlotte at Merton, urging her to persevere with her French lessons and saying that she awaited a reply from Lady Hamilton to her letter in which she had 'told her a deal about Tom Tit'. She concluded, 'Our weather is still wet and bad, we have nothing to make it cheerful, everybody is gloomy and out of spirits. I hope we shall have good news from your dear Uncle, or I know not what will become of us.'[81]

Ironically, it was Fanny, who had heard nothing from her husband, or her sisters-in-law, who was given the first news of him – and what had occurred on 21 October – on 6 November in a letter from Lord Barham, the First Lord of the Admiralty, that reached her in the stillness of Bath:

> Madam, it is with the utmost concern that, in the midst of victory, I have to inform your Ladyship of the death of your illustrious partner, Lord Viscount Nelson. After leading the British fleet into close action with the enemy and seeing their defeat, he fell by a musket ball entering his chest. It is the death he wished for and less to be regretted on his own account. But the public loss is irretrievable. I can only add that events of this kind do not happen by chance. I recommend therefore your Ladyship to His protection, who is alone able to save, or to destroy.[82]

11
Mrs Nelson Ward

One morning in March 1806, Lady Hamilton, accompanied by Horatia, now five, and another little girl, entered Westminster Abbey escorted by an Army officer as a guide to the monuments. It seemed an educational tour for the children but there had been another motive, which became apparent when a verger, not recognizing her, said, 'Perhaps, madam, the young folks would like to see the waxen image of the late Admiral Nelson? It has only been put up these two days.' At this, recalled the officer, 'Her Ladyship was much agitated, but bowed assent; the man led the way to a glass case in which stood the effigy of her idol and the nation's pride.'[1]

This was the figure commissioned by the Dean and Chapter from Catherine Andras, the wax-modeller, for whom Nelson had sat shortly before he had returned to sea for the last time. After his state funeral at St Paul's Cathedral, the Dean had wished to involve the Abbey in the national mourning, so the waxwork had been ordered and dressed in one of the subject's own uniforms.

Emma gazed at the brightly painted face and the familiar uniform, then remarked that a lock of hair would have hung in a different way and asked if she could adjust it. Still not recognizing her, the verger said that nobody was permitted to touch the waxwork. ' "I am sure", she said, with that bewitching grace with which she was pre-eminently gifted, "when I tell you that I am Lady Hamilton, you will not refuse me." "Oh, madam, who could refuse you?" '[2] replied the verger and unlocked the case. Emma moved the hank of artificial hair and then her control wavered. 'She would have kissed the lips but . . . the guide assured her the colour was not dry.'[3]

This was final proof that her lover was now a historical, almost mythological, figure; she and Horatia were on their own and part of his legend. That and their memories were all that remained to them of one described by a friend as being 'all manliness and mind'.[4] It was now four months since the terrible morning in November when Emma had heard distant gunfire. As she recalled:

> I had come to Merton, and, feeling rather unwell, I said I would stay in bed on account of a rash. Mrs. Bolton was sitting by my bedside when all of a sudden I said, 'I think I hear the Tower guns. Some victory perhaps in Germany . . .' 'Perhaps', said Mrs. Bolton, 'it may be news from my brother.' 'Impossible, surely. There is not time.'

Within a few minutes, or so it seemed, a carriage drove up to the house and Emma asked who had arrived. When a Captain Whitby of the Royal Navy was announced:

> 'Show him in directly', I said. He came in and, with a pale countenance and faint voice said, 'We have gained a great victory.' 'Never mind your victory,' I said. 'My letters – give me my letters.' Captain Whitby was unable to speak; tears in his eyes and a deathly paleness over his face made me comprehend him. I believe I gave a scream and fell back and for ten hours I could neither speak nor shed a tear.[5]

Before leaving, Captain Whitby left a short letter from the Comptroller of the Navy, giving her the news and ending, 'I can say no more. My heart is too full to attempt to give comfort to others.'[6]

Her shocked grief was being repeated across the country. The victory off Cape Trafalgar on 21 October – twenty-seven British sail of the line, using the essentials of Nelson's original tactics, defeating thirty-three French and Spanish and capturing twenty of them – should have prompted extravagant celebration. But it had been overcast by the death of Nelson, shot through the shoulder and chest by a sniper at the beginning of the battle. The news had brought more shocked sorrow than triumph. A week later, her friend Lady Elizabeth Foster called and reported:

> I found her in bed. She had the appearance of a person stunned and scarcely as yet able to comprehend the certainty of her loss. 'What shall I do?' and 'How can I exist?' were her first words . . . 'Days have passed on and I know not how they end or begin – nor how I am to bear my future existence.'[7]

The news was broken to William Nelson by the mayor of Canterbury, who sought him out in the Close rather than risk him seeing a newspaper in the public reading-room, where he went daily for news of the war, and he remembered, 'The Dr. seemed much affected and shed tears and turned back to his house, applying his white handkerchief to his eyes.'[8] Soon afterwards, he took his family to lodgings in London, already sensing the part he would be called upon to play. The Matchams hurried to Merton, from where Kate wrote to her son, George, 'Here we feel our loss more every day . . . Merton is very dull; quite the reverse of what you knew it.'[9]

Even before Nelson's body could be returned to England for the funeral, there was much to be done. William Nelson had been appointed his brother's joint executor with the solicitor, William Haslewood, and he at once wrote to Fanny about the will, saying that a copy would be sent to her as soon as possible. Significantly, his concluding words suggested a shift in the family's loyalties:

> If I could feel pleasure amidst so many mournful reflections as press upon my mind, it would be in the

> opportunity afforded me of renewing with your Ladyship that intercourse of kind offices, which I once hoped would have always marked our lives – which untoward circumstances have occasioned some interruption of, but which I trust will never again be suspended.[10]

Emma was already suspecting that she would lose the friendship of some, at least, of the Nelson family. Soon after the news of Nelson's death arrived, extracts from some of his letters to her were published in the *Morning Chronicle* and it was assumed that she had shown them to its editor, their neighbour James Perry in order to establish her position in Nelson's life. She angrily denied this, hinting that as she had shown them only to William Nelson, he might know more about their source than she. 'It is true he is leaky,' she said, 'but I believe would not willingly tell anything; but I have been told that something like some of my letters have been printed in some paper. I never now read a paper and my health and spirits are so bad I cannot enter a war with vile editors. . .'[11]

In his will, Nelson, as promised, had left Fanny comfortably provided for, with an annuity of more than £1,000, as well as the £4,000 she had already received, but this would be forfeit if she received a state pension of a similar amount; she was left no memento of any kind. Fanny accepted his decision without a murmur and set about ordering a full set of mourning dresses and hats. Yet an unfounded rumour began to spread that she planned to contest the will and Susannah Bolton wrote to Emma, 'The Viscountess is going to *law* . . . What a vindictive woman! Disputes even the last words of the man she once *pretended* to love. She has changed her mourning and is off for Cheltenham [the fashionable spa]. I hope it will purge away all her sins.'[12]

To Emma, he left Merton Place, its contents and seventy acres of land, and an annuity of £500 from the Bronte estate, so that, together with her inheritance from her husband, her annual income would amount to £2,000; to Horatia, he left a total of £4,000. It was known that he had added seven codicils and suspected that a final one might be on its way to England in the

Victory. Meanwhile, the first honours were being heaped upon the surviving members of the Nelson family, particularly William, who succeeded his brother as the second Baron Nelson and now became Earl Nelson in his own right. On hearing this, Emma Hamilton sneered, 'A man must have great courage to accept the honour of calling himself by *that* name.'[13]

When Captain Blackwood arrived at Clarges Street with a collection of Nelson's personal belongings from the *Victory*, Emma was able to employ her theatricality in displaying them to those who came to console her. When Benjamin Goldsmid arrived with his eight-year-old son Lionel, whose ambition it had been to go to sea with Nelson, she used the boy to help her performance. He recalled:

> I was a great favourite of Lady Hamilton's and bathed in tears as she was . . . exhibited the various gifts he had made her on different occasions. I was on the bed to aid in passing rings, shawls, bracelets, etc., shown to the company of about 15 people seated in a semi-circle at the foot of the bed . . . I came in for numerous kisses and her usual remark, 'Thank you, my funny boy', or 'Child, you must come every day.' The very coat in which the dear old admiral was dressed in the battle and received his death wound was on the outside of the bed; the hole, where the bullet passed through, stiffened with congealed blood.

However, Lionel Goldsmid was also to remember the occasion as 'serio-comic' and that, when his father had risen to leave and he himself scrambled off the bed, he had inadvertently pulled a shawl from around Lady Hamilton's shoulders and that 'she did not appear quite so wholesome in her freedom from stays.'[14]

Towards the end of November, George Matcham arrived to join his parents at Merton and await news of the return of his uncle's body and the great funeral that would certainly follow. Again he kept a diary: '17th. William now Earl Nelson. Horace by the title of Viscount Merton . . . Lord N. greatly lamented.' He noted the contents of the will:

Left Mrs. B[olton] the silver Turkey cup and to mama the sword given to him by the City of London . . . Thursday, Dec. 5 . . . This day appointed for a fast for the late glorious *victory.* A collection to be made at the churches for the Widows . . . Monday, Dec. 9th. *The Observer* of this day mentions the arrival of the *Victory* from Gibraltar with the body . . . It is to be laid in state at Greenwich Hospital and buried in St. Paul's.[15]

The change in loyalties that Emma had expected came at the beginning of January 1806, when the Earl found excuses for withdrawing Charlotte permanently from the household. One reason was his understandable aversion to Lady Hamilton as suitable company, whether for his brother or his daughter; another was that, while under Emma's wing, Charlotte had acquired a suitor and was planning to announce her engagement, but her father hoped that she could make a grander marriage. So word reached the Matchams that 'the match between a young gent. and Lady C[harlotte] was quite off and that the lady was to quit Lady H.'s and go home'.[16] As Horace was leaving Eton and going up to Cambridge University, which was much further away from Merton and London, she was deprived of his company too. Now the Earl and the new Countess, once so sycophantic and malleable, began to distance themselves – although they were to invite her to accompany them on a seaside holiday at Cromer – and so they joined Fanny in Emma's demonology and she redoubled her flattery of the Boltons and the Matchams.

That same month, Nelson's body was brought up the Thames to lie in state in the Painted Hall at Greenwich Hospital. From thence, again by river, it was taken to Whitehall, there waiting in a small room off the entrance hall for the funeral the next day, 9 January. It was an occasion that remained vividly in the memories of those present. George Matcham jotted down:

Thursday, Jan. 9th. Rose at 6. Put on our full dress and went to Clarges St. Took up the Boltons. Drove to the Earl's, where breakfast was laid out. Were not received at

> all by the Earl, nor introduced to anybody. Put on there the cloaks, etc. About half-past eight, the mourning coaches came. Lords Merton and Nelson went in the first, drawn by six horses. My father, Mr. Bolton, Tom and myself in the second . . . Went into St. James's Park. Found there a vast number of carriages, waited for some time . . . Saw all the captains and admirals much confused, not being able to find their carriages. From hence we moved by slow degrees and about one arrived at the Horse Guards, where the procession was joined by the Prince of Wales and the Duke of Clarence. The body was then put into the car, which represented the stern and [bows] of the *Victory* . . .'[17]

The great procession to St Paul's then began, the front reaching the cathedral before the rear had left Whitehall. The ceremonial within now began and at last Nelson's coffin was lowered into the crypt and its marble sarcophagus. Of the principal players in the life now ended, the two most obviously absent were Lady Nelson and Lady Hamilton.

The most pressing concern to the latter was the final codicil to the will; this had been made known to her by Captain Hardy, who had also sent her the letters to Horatia and herself that Nelson had been writing on the day he died. His final wish had been that the two of them should be left as a legacy to the nation, she because of 'her service to her King and Country while at Naples'. The codicil was shown to the new Lord Nelson, who at once referred it to the appropriate legal authorities and they declared that it was not valid as a will. It would therefore be a matter for the Prime Minister, who had liked Nelson, was thought to be sympathetic to Lady Hamilton and could arrange for a special grant. Emma was in no state to plead with William Pitt herself, but her mother took up her cause three days after hearing the news of Nelson's death, writing to his friend George Rose, Vice-President of the Board of Trade, pleading, 'Lady Hamilton's most wretched state of mind prevents her from imploring her dear, good Mr. Rose to solicit Mr. Pitt to consider the family of our great and glorious Nelson

. . . Lady Hamilton whose situation is beyond description, only prays that you, good sir, will do all you can for this worthy family.'[18] Yet Pitt was not well and, a fortnight after his friend's funeral, was dead at the age of forty-six. His successor, Lord Grenville, was unsympathetic, so it would have to be a question for the King; yet he had always been scandalized by Emma and, when the Earl was received by him and began to broach the subject, said only, 'He died the death he wished.'[19] However, in May, the King initiated a Parliamentary grant of an annuity of £5,000 in perpetuity for the Earl and his heirs, and £100,000 for him to purchase a suitable country seat, whereupon he tried and failed to buy Houghton Hall in Norfolk, the grandest Walpole mansion. There was £10,000 for both of Nelson's sisters but, for Emma, nothing.

Although the legacies of Nelson and Sir William should have been ample to support Emma, her mother and Horatia, the extravagant life at Merton continued and Emma wallowed deeper in debt. Tradesmen could be, and were, often ignored, but the more substantial demands had to be met and Emma sought to raise loans, first with the aid of the kindly Abraham Goldsmid.

Others from whom she sought help included her former lover Sir Harry Fetherstonhaugh of Uppark, now a sad and spoiled middle-aged bachelor. Although the Boltons and the Matchams were unaware of the extent of her financial trouble, they offered all other support and she and Horatia became regular visitors to them in Norfolk. From them she heard of the social ascension of the Earl and Countess Nelson, with whom her friendship was fast withering, and, of course, Lady Charlotte. As the favourite niece of the nation's lost hero and now a titled heiress, she was much in demand. As one admiring peer remarked, 'I wonder she is not married; she is a piece of goods that is worth anyone's while to look after.'[20] Emma no longer accompanied her to the grandest drawing-rooms and ballrooms, bitterly claiming that she herself had not only educated Charlotte but paid Horace's fees at Eton and had their parents to live with her over seven years when they were no more than relations to her hero.

After the Earl's first, tentative approach to Fanny, there had been no general reconciliation and she remained alone but for her son, Josiah. He had not proved a successful naval officer. Even though his stepfather had helped him gain command of a frigate, this had been an unhappy ship, the officers riven by feuding and beset by scandals over women. Despite the continuing war, he had not been given another command but had been retired on half-pay; however, he was beginning to prove a shrewd and enterprising businessman. Fanny continued to move between her house in Harley Street, close to the new Regent's Park, and lodgings in Bath until 1807. Then, looking for a home in surroundings that aroused happy memories, she thought of Exmouth on the Devonshire coast, where she and Horatio had spent a holiday soon after they married, and it was there that Josiah, now a bachelor of twenty-seven, had chosen to live. So she took the lease of a plain, red-brick house, 6 The Beacon, one of a row on a bluff overlooking the sea and the Exe estuary. Clear of the gossip of London and Bath, she could follow a quiet, ladylike routine against the backdrop of the sea that had shaped her life.

Horatia was proving a success and it was now generally accepted that she was indeed Nelson's daughter, although the identity of her mother remained wrapped in secrecy, Emma leaving many a false trail, one leading to Cornelia Knight and another to the Queen of Naples. Because she was his offspring, now legally known as Horatia Nelson, and also because she was an intelligent, lively child, both Susannah and Kate made much of her and she and Emma were frequent guests at their houses. But in the autumn of 1806, another daughter, also Emma's, made her unwelcome appearance. In 1782, a baby assumed to be the consequence of an affair with a naval captain named Willett-Payne had been born to her. Both Charles Greville and Sir William Hamilton had known about the child, but not Nelson, and she had been brought up with the Connor girls in Wales, described by Emma as their older sister. 'Ann Connor', as Emma called her, was also known as Emma Carew and now, at the age of twenty-three, she asked for her mother's recognition. Emma had no more difficulty in disowning her than she had had in sending the other Emma to the Foundlings' Hospital. In any case, her payment to the Connor girls for working as Horatia's governesses was so far overdue that she decided to break with all of them. Telling Susannah and Kate that Emma Carew was a scheming extortionist, she disowned her. The young woman, seeing that her attempt at reconciliation had failed, wrote an affectionate and dignified letter of farewell. Regretting that she had been unable to meet her mother again, she concluded, 'Such a meeting would have been one of the happiest moments of my life but for the reflection that it may also be the last as I leave England in a few days and may, perhaps, never return to it again.'[21]

Emma and Horatia remained frequent visitors both to the Boltons at Cranwich and to the Matchams, now living at a substantial house in Sussex, Ashfold Lodge, which they had bought with Kate's government grant. Emma had not wholly lost contact with Sarah Nelson and wrote to her flaunting her real, or imagined, social success, bandying about aristocratic names as 'all come to look at Nelson's angel . . . Princess Charlotte* is a charming girl and very kind and civil to Horatia'.[22] Listing the grandees whom she claimed to be visiting, she particularly mentioned the Cholmondeleys, as she doubtless knew of the Earl's failure to buy Houghton Hall from them. Indeed, Emma's social success reached new heights in the following year, when she gave a house party at Merton attended by three of the King's sons: the Prince of Wales and the Dukes of Sussex and Clarence, the latter having, of course, been a friend of Nelson when himself a captain in the Navy. She made the most of the social triumph, making sure that Nelson's brother and sisters knew of it and, in view of Nelson's neurotic jealousy six years before, sought to interest the Prince of Wales in Horatia: 'I beg his Royal Highness the Prince of Wales, as he dearly loved Nelson, that his Royal Highness will protect his child . . .'[23]

*Daughter of the Prince of Wales.

There was soon no need to score social points against Earl Nelson, because he was to suffer a devastating blow. As Horatio had adored Emma, so William's pride was his only son, Horace, now Viscount Trafalgar, who was up at Cambridge University and had, at nineteen, grown into a handsome, personable, if somewhat spoilt, young man and would eventually succeed to the earldom. Then, at the beginning of 1808, Horace fell ill. It was typhoid and he died on 17 January, breaking his father's heart, his mother crying, 'I am almost blinded by my tears.'[24] The boy was accorded the honour of being buried in St Paul's Cathedral, close to his uncle, but the earldom would now pass to Susannah's twenty-one-year-old son, Tom. Bitterly but fruitlessly, the Earl hoped for another heir to snatch the title back and, when both the Boltons and the Matchams suggested they legally change their own names to Nelson, he objected. Since Emma wrongly accused him of concealing the last codicil to Nelson's will, so depriving her of a grant, or pension, this led her to make further mischief between the families, prompting George Matcham to write to her:

> What you have written us in respect of the Earl has quite astonished me. I could never have conceived that he could have so betrayed Tom Bolton but it is evident that he is as great an enemy to us as our dear lost friend was our patron. The extinction of the whole family would be a matter of the greatest exultation to him, with the exception of his own dear self and Lady Charlotte.[25]

With almost poetic justice, catastrophe was now to overwhelm Emma herself. Her extravagance had been such that there was now no alternative but to sell Nelson's house and land at Merton. Her repeated appeals for a government grant in recognition of her services at Naples and Palermo had been shelved and then disregarded; financial help from the Goldsmid brothers and repeated borrowing against expected income had been squandered; Nelson's sisters never offered her a portion of their own government grants because, from what they knew of their brother's and Sir William's legacies to Emma and her opulent way of life, she could not be in need of such help. All of this meant that, by the spring of 1808, she owed more than £8,000. Again the Goldsmid brothers came to her aid and a trust was set up for her benefit – 'Goldsmid has been and is an angel to me,' declared Emma, 'and his bounty shall never be abused'[26] – and a third brother, Ascher Goldsmid, himself bought Merton Place a year later. This was some compensation because, as Susannah put it to Emma, 'I am glad to hear a *Goldsmid* has purchased Merton* rather than any stranger . . . Perhaps you and I may one day have the melancholy pleasure in tracing former times in those walks.'[27] Yet it was as if a curse touched all involved: in that same year Benjamin Goldsmid committed suicide, as did his brother, Abraham, two years later, because of financial disasters. The loss of Merton and of the house in Clarges Street marked the beginning of the end for Emma Hamilton and the end of the beginning for Horatia Nelson.

This put an end to Emma's hospitality and the family parties that had become the background to Horatia's childhood. But they were not homeless, because the raddled old rake the Duke of Queensberry, now eighty-four, had come to their rescue with the loan of a fine house at Richmond, Heron Court. Emma's chronic extravagance and poverty were such that she had taken to selling Nelson's letters to her and what had seemed to be other sacred relics. Debts prompted another move, this time back to furnished rooms in Albemarle Street, close to her old home in Piccadilly.

She still had the company and support of her mother, who had for so long provided some stability in their lives. Mrs Cadogan understood her daughter and knew her secrets, kept house for her and had been the principal organizer of the child-rens' parties that had once been so important. She was also aware of her daughter's deceptions and took part in them. When she squabbled with Emma over arrangements for Horatia, she reproved her in the child's presence, saying,

* Merton Place was again on the market in 1815 and was demolished in 1846.

'Really, Emma, you make so much fuss about the child as if she were your own daughter.' Forgetting herself for a moment, Emma snapped, 'Perhaps she is.' Mrs Cadogan at once resumed the deception, replying, 'Emma, that won't do with me – you know I know better.'[28] At the beginning of 1810, she lost that support. Mrs Cadogan had been suffering from bronchitis and, on 14 January, she suddenly died. Her loss was more devastating to Emma's stability than the death of either Sir William, or Nelson for she now lacked a confidante and practical adviser. The tough old lady was mourned not only by her daughter but also by the family of which she had become a part, Susannah Bolton writing of her, 'Dear Blessed Saint, was she not a mother to us all?'[29]

It was to be a fateful year, for at the end of it the Duke of Queensberry died and, despite her hopes, left her only £500, which never reached her after a creditor claimed it. Her former lover Charles Greville also died and, now that two of the Goldsmid brothers were also gone and her isolation from the Nelson family increased, she was alone with Horatia. Self-pity was sharpened when, in the summer of that year, her former protégée, Lady Charlotte Nelson, married the Honourable Samuel Hood, grandson of Admiral Lord Hood, who would inherit the title of Baron Bridport. He had been the boy, Sam, who had been so taken with Charlotte when they met at one of Emma's parties soon after the girl had arrived at Merton. This was a match Emma could justly claim to have promoted, if not arranged, but it was too late for any social reward.

It was also too late to use her charm in an attempt to clamber back up the social ladder. Now 'an elderly, vulgar-looking dame', wearing her hair 'tucked under a huge cap', she was said by Pryse Lockhart Gordon, who had known her in Palermo, to be 'still beautiful and that fascinating mouth from which sculptors had modelled yet retained its expression' but 'age and circumstances had made sad ravages in her formerly splendid countenance'.[30]

Next year came more changes, for the Boltons left the farmhouse at Cranwich, which had become second only to Merton in the happy memories of the families. Susannah was delighted to move to what was unmistakably a gentleman's country seat, Bradenham Hall, a square, pedimented country house east of Swaffham, where her son, Tom, would be able to live in appropriate style when he inherited the title of Earl Nelson. Emma and Horatia – now known as 'Cousin Horatia' by the Bolton children[31] – were to be guests there at Susannah's first house party and at the wedding of Eliza Bolton to her cousin Henry Girdlestone, a young country parson. After the hand-to-mouth living of recent months, this was a vision of bucolic bliss to the ten-year-old Horatia. It was also to be Emma's last visit to Norfolk and it gave the county a final echo of Nelson, when she told the boot-boy to take from her trunk the shot-holed coat he had been wearing at Trafalgar and spread it over the lavender bushes outside the back door to air in the sunshine.

From this point, Emma Hamilton's decline became fast and steep. Gradually she lost touch with Susannah and Kate, who were still unaware of the extent of her financial distress. Since she returned to lodgings at 150 New Bond Street, they assumed, as did Anne Bolton, writing to Horatia in November 1812, that all was well: 'Mama . . . hopes to see you both as soon as the gaieties of London will permit you.'[32] Jolly letters from Bradenham and Ashfold eventually went unanswered: Emma had been arrested for debt and January 1813 found her, with Horatia, committed to the King's Bench Prison in Southwark. Attempts by a few friends – James Perry, the editor, and Alderman Joshua Smith, a kindly magistrate who had admired Nelson, among them – to rescue her from debt and prison, together with her own pleadings to the government, succeeded only in her being allowed to live in lodgings within a prescribed distance of the prison. Other former friends were falling away: the Queen of Naples, who had once promised patronage in perpetuity, ignored her plight. Then, on 13 July 1813, the keystone of Nelson's surviving family, Susannah Bolton, died in Norfolk. Ever since the death of Catherine Nelson in 1767, Susannah's capable presence had been a centre of stability and reassurance.

Occasionally Emma's spirits rose, as when a few friends paid bills or she raised money by selling her own belongings. She even sold the coat which Nelson had worn at Trafalgar to Alderman Smith, although it legally belonged to Earl Nelson. Sometimes she entertained in the old style; even while living in the prescribed lodgings she gave a splendid dinner party at Christmas 1813, when the guests included the Duke of Sussex and an old naval friend, Admiral Dillon, who reported:

> I had to do the honours – carve, etc. The first course went off on complete order and I could not help thinking that rather too much luxury had been produced. H.R.H. did not expect such entertainment from the lady who received him. However, there was a sad falling off in the second course and a great deficiency . . . of knives and forks. I had to carve a good-sized bird but had not been supplied with the necessary implements . . . At last, Lady Hamilton said, 'Why don't you cut up that bird?' I told her I was in want of a knife and fork. 'Oh!', she said, 'you must not be particular here.' 'Very well, my lady,' I rejoined, 'I did not like to commit myself in the presence of H.R.H. but, since you desire it, I will soon divide the object before me. Besides, you are aware that, as a midshipman, I learnt how to use my fingers!' Soon the bird was in pieces. My reply produced some hearty laughter and the repast terminated very merrily.[33]

But there were more black moods brought on by depression and heavy drinking. These were evident in the scolding of Horatia, who was now twelve and trying to assert a degree of independence. 'Horatia,' Emma wrote, 'your conduct is so bad, your falsehoods so dreadful, your cruel treatment to me such that I cannot live under these afflicting circumstances; my poor heart is broken. If my poor mother was living to take my part, broken as I am with grief and ill-health, I should be happy to breathe my last in her arms.'[34] Then the cloud would pass and she would be affectionate again.

It was drink that broke her health with what she thought was jaundice but was probably cirrhosis of the liver, and this was compounded by a new scandal. A large collection of Nelson's letters to her were to be published as a book. Emma denied having sold them and indeed having any knowledge of how she had lost them, blaming James Harrison, one of the admiral's first biographers, who, she claimed, had stolen them. Not everybody believed her and Nelson's old patron, Lord St Vincent, declared, 'What a diabolical bitch!'[35]

Dark as her life had become, the clouds of international crisis rolled away in 1814 with what seemed to be the final defeat of Napoleon. In March, the allies entered Paris and a month later the Emperor abdicated and was exiled to the island of Elba. At last, after twenty years, the Continent was open to travellers and the sense of freedom was infectious. George Matcham even suggested in a letter to Emma that all the families bound together by Nelson's memory might settle abroad. She had once dreamed of life with her lover and their child in the shade of the chestnut tree at Bronte. Now that estate had passed to the Earl, who did pay her a little of the revenue from it, but she could no longer afford to travel far even if free to do so. However, travel she would, if furtively, as she needed to go abroad to avoid the debts she herself could never pay.

So, on 2 July, she absconded and, with Horatia, made her way to the Pool of London and there boarded a packet, the *Little Tom*, bound for Calais. The voyage lasted three days and, as their ship lurched across the choppy English Channel, drenched with salty spray, both were prostrate with seasickness. Ashore at last, they had their baggage taken to the best hotel as if by force of habit. Emma knew they could not stay there for long and began to look for lodgings, finding a house to rent just outside the town in the hamlet of St Pierre. But there was a dispute with the landlord over terms and they left after one night but found other rooms in a farmhouse nearby. It seemed ideal with the fresh sea air, which Emma had so valued at Deal, Southend and Ramsgate, and cheap, wholesome food, but, even here, her debts haunted her and her income dwindled further.

Brandy and wine were cheap and, as Horatia was to remember, fed 'the baneful habit she had of taking spirits and wine to a fearful degree'.[36]

Finally, that autumn, they took lodgings at 27 Rue Française in the town itself, sharing a bedroom, but, as Horatia put it, Emma 'took little interest in anything but the indulgence of her unfortunate habit'.[37] After a week, she retired to her bed, now attended only by the thirteen-year-old Horatia, who remembered, 'I never went out, no one could have called unknown to me and I hardly ever . . . left her room.'[38] Emma had by now pawned all her last little treasures – and Horatia's – and ran up more debts while awaiting the arrival of small allowances from what remained of her inheritance in London. Horatia herself wrote to Earl Nelson to beg a loan of £10 and to a friend – possibly Alderman Smith – who sent her a draft for £20. Any help would have been too late. Horatia was well aware that death approached and, knowing that Emma knew the secret of her birth and the identity of her mother, 'earnestly prayed her to tell me who my mother was but she would not, influenced then, I think, by the fear that I might leave her'.[39] Horatia, although remembering that Emma 'was not kind to me', added that 'she had much to try her'.[40]

In January 1815, as winter gales rattled the shutters and freezing fogs chilled the house in the Rue Française, Emma Hamilton was slipping away and on the 15th she died. Horatia was left to arrange the burial in a municipal cemetery,* with the help of the British Consul and the oak coffin was attended by a Roman Catholic priest and the skippers of British merchant ships lying at Calais. Her epitaph was to be in a letter from Horatia to the editor of her father's letters:† 'With all her faults and she had many – she had many fine qualities which, had she been placed early in better hands, would have made her a very superior woman.'[41]

* She was later reinterred and the site is now lost but a momument to her was erected near her original grave in what is now the Parc Richelieu in 1994.

† Sir Harris Nicolas.

Even in death, Emma Hamilton left a legacy of debt, so Horatia was not free to leave Calais. But the kindly British consul in the port and his wife took matters in hand, arranged for the bills to be settled and for the girl's return to England. The question of debts to tradesmen had not been finally concluded when Horatia, escorted by the consul, boarded the Dover packet on 28 January disguised as a boy. On landing, she was met by George Matcham, who took her straight to Ashfold Lodge, where she arrived just in time for her fourteenth birthday, young George writing in his diary, 'The Squire arrived with Horatia from Dover.'[42]

There could have been no more striking contrast to the misery of Calais than the welcoming household she joined. There, her charming aunt, Kate Matcham, awaited her with her children, Horatia's nine first cousins, five of whom were girls aged between eleven and twenty-three. She arrived, pale, drawn, shocked and jaded after her long ordeal, at a comfortable house in beautiful countryside. As the Matchams' neighbour William Haslewood, once Nelson's solicitor, put it, 'The kind of life she has passed during the past two years must have given a shock to her constitution. But, I trust, the invigorating breezes of Sussex will soon restore her bloom and increase her strength.'[43] A month after her return, Napoleon escaped from Elba, returned to France and the *Grande Armée*, and war broke out again. Had Emma Hamilton lived a few more weeks, both she and Horatia would have been interned in Calais, giving the French prizes of extraordinary piquancy.

While the crisis on the Continent mounted to its climax on the battlefield of Waterloo, culminating in the overthrow of Napoleon and his exile to the South Atlantic, Nelson's daughter blossomed in the peace and happiness of the Matcham household. Aged by experience, worldly yet tolerant, she was an intelligent girl, a natural linguist (versed in five languages, thanks to her mother), musical, an accomplished needlewoman and surprisingly well read. She took part in all the family's activities, including a visit to Lisbon in 1816, until the past – Little Titchfield Street, Merton, Clarges Street, the wandering and the imprisonment and, finally, Calais – receded in memory like strange dreams, some beautiful, some nightmares.

She was also in touch with the Boltons. After Susannah's death, her widower, Thomas Bolton, sold Bradenham Hall and moved to a charming, much smaller house in Burnham Market, a mile from Burnham Thorpe. He was soon sharing it with his daughter-in-law, Lady Bolton, and his daughter Anne with an older daughter, Susannah, as housekeeper. William Nelson had, in 1814, finally chosen a country mansion near Salisbury and renamed it Trafalgar House. In 1817, the Matchams also moved to Wiltshire, after young George's marriage to the heiress to Newhouse, an estate close to his uncle's. So the Ashfold household broke up and it was decided that Horatia should return to Norfolk to live with the Boltons.

There was, of course, another member of the Nelson family: Fanny. Following the Earl's guarded approach of 1805, he and she had finally met five years later in Bath when he and Sarah called at her house. 'They were much affected,' Fanny believed, 'and I think they have received some satisfaction from a shake of my hand.'[44] Josiah was her principal comforter and he married in 1819, finally cutting his links with the Royal Navy in 1825. He was by then a successful man of business, with a yacht and a house in Paris.

A few memories of the elderly Fanny were to survive. One was of a chance meeting in Lyons, when she was described as 'rather prosy'.[45] Once she showed a miniature of Nelson to her granddaughter, also named Fanny, and said, 'When you are older, little Fan, you may know what it is to have a broken heart.'[46] The same grandchild and her parents were staying at Geneva, accompanied by Fanny, and were being rowed on the lake by the poet Lord Byron. As 'little Fan' remembered, the boat lurched and she fell into the water and was rescued by Byron, who handed the dripping child to her mother, declaiming, 'Receive thy child! She hath been baptised in sorrow.'[47]

There was, however, a happy occasion in Paris, while Fanny was staying with Josiah at his house in the Champs-Elysées in 1824. The Matcham family – George, Kate and four of their children – were also in Paris, the two families met and one of the Matcham daughters wrote to Horatia that 'we see the old Viscountess Nelson almost every day, we have drunk tea with her once and are going again this evening'.[48] Finally, it seemed, Fanny had salvaged some happiness from the wreck of her life, but, on 9 July 1830, Josiah suddenly died of pleurisy in Paris at the age of fifty. It was the time of the revolution against the Bourbons, the streets of Paris were dangerous and Josiah's widow and three small daughters had to escape from the city in a farm-cart, dressed as peasants. His body was brought to England later and buried in the churchyard at Littleham, outside Exmouth. Fanny lived on for less than a year, dying at her London house on 6 May 1831, at the age of seventy-three. She was buried beside her son, who had once been the little boy with whom Captain Nelson had played and won his mother's heart.

Others were also about to leave the stage. George Matcham died in 1833 and, next year, old Tom Bolton, the father of young Tom, who, on the death of Earl Nelson, two years later, inherited the title and the reflected glory of his other uncle. Kate Matcham died in 1842, followed, a year later, by one who had charmed her brothers in the Caribbean six decades before, Mary Moutray, who had been living with her daughter in Ireland. Lady Charlotte, who inherited the title of Duchess of Bronte as well as Baroness Bridport, mothered nine children and died in 1873, the year that the typewriter and colour photography were invented. Horatia had settled happily with the Bolton family and lived in Burnham Market for seventeen years, growing into a charming young woman; an admirer in the neighbouring seaport, Wells, where her aunt Susannah had begun married life, wrote a hymn in her praise:

Welcome, admired Horatia, to our Wells –
Though pride of Burnham and thou Belle of Belles.
Great Nelson prostrate laid a world of foes –
Thy charms have prostrate laid a world of BEAUX![49]

But potential husbands were, in fact, scarce in rural Norfolk and were more likely to be curates than dashing men of the world, such as her aunt Kate had met in Bath. In 1817, she had become engaged to Robert Blake, the curate of the parish church, but broke it off two years later and had finally accepted another proposal of marriage from his successor, Philip Ward, who lodged in the house next door, a serious young man with pleasant looks and a wide, scholarly brow. She was aged twenty-one when she was married to the curate of twenty-six in the parish church across the road.

On 19 February 1822, Horatia and Philip Ward – or Nelson Ward, as she would be known – began a long and fruitful marriage. In the tradition of the Nelson family, there were Norfolk country livings at Stanhoe, a few miles from Burnham Thorpe, then, from 1825, Bircham Newton, for a further five years. In Norfolk, six of their ten children were born, the eldest named Horatio Nelson. Their next child, named Horatia, was born in Tenterden, the Kentish market town to which they moved in 1831. As the rector's wife, bringing up a large family in the reign of the young Queen Victoria, in which Horatia would see so many bewildering changes – steam trains, electric streetlighting and the telephone – the wild years at the beginning of the century would have seemed increasingly remote. Then, on Sunday 16 January 1859, as Philip was taking a cold bath before the morning service at Tenterden church, he suddenly died; he was fifty-seven. For Horatia, this was the beginning of a long widowhood, comforted by children and grandchildren. That same year, she moved to Pinner in Middlesex, to be near London, where her son Nelson was working.

Horatia Nelson Ward was to be remembered as a tall, intelligent, witty old lady with 'a deep smile'. Her grandson Hugh, taken to see her at the age of sixteen, wrote:

> I remember her as very thin and gaunt with great sunken eyes that looked right through me and curls all over her head with ringlets hanging down her cheeks. She placed me at the bottom of the sofa so that she might best see me and, after a time of gazing, she said, 'Yes, you are

exactly like him.' I felt too frightened to ask, 'Whom am I like?'[50]

On 6 March 1881, the life that was as old as the century, the embodiment of a lovestory that had, and would continue to fascinate, scandalize and touch generations, came to its end. Horatia died at the age of eighty, the cause simply given as old age. She had continued to insist that, while proud to be the daughter of Lord Nelson, she did not know the identify of her mother; yet she had sometimes seemed eager to prove that it was not Lady Hamilton. When *The Times* announced on 10 March, 'In Mrs. Horatia Nelson Ward, who died on Sunday at Beaufort Villas, Woodridings, Pinner, Middlesex . . . many of our readers will recognise Lady Hamilton's little daughter, Horatia', the family issued a fierce denial. More precise evidence that had come to the surface over the years had also been denied and it was not until Albert Morrison bought a collection of Nelson's letters soon after Horatia's death, and published them in 1894, that her parentage was confirmed in her father's own words. Then the lettering on her gravestone describing her as 'the Adopted Daughter of Vice-Admiral Lord Nelson' was changed to 'the Beloved Daughter'.

Horatia had survived into the lifetimes of Albert Einstein, Joseph Stalin, General Douglas MacArthur and Jacob Epstein, dying in the year of the births of Alexander Fleming and Pablo Picasso. Memories of the old lady who remembered Nelson were passed on by her descendants, some of them distinguished in their callings, to those living two centuries after her father's achievements. One told by a great-great-great-granddaughter, a magistrate living in Wales at the end of the twentieth century – herself with descendants named Horatio, Emma and Horatia – echoes across the years. It is that the daughter of Horatio Nelson – also Duke of Bronte, the Sicilian town named after the god of thunder, and himself nicknamed by his mistress 'My Lord Thunder' – and Emma Hamilton – once seen at her redoubtable best in that stormy passage to Palermo – enjoyed, when old, a particular pleasure that she liked to share with the children.

When thunder began to rumble and lightning flicker over Middlesex, she would take them to an upstairs window to watch the storm. As one of them would later say, 'She loved thunder and lightning.'[51]

Notes

Some of the references to quotations in the author's own earlier works cannot be otherwise identified because the original documents were seen and transcribed while changing ownership, sometimes through salerooms. The abbreviations BL and NMM refer to the British Library and the National Maritime Museum.

1: Catherine

1. Oman, Carola, Nelson, 1947, p.2.
2. *History of Woodton*, The Round Tower Churches Society.
3. Clowes, W.L., *The Royal Navy: A History* (Vol. 3), 1900, p.165.
4. Nelson, Edmund, *A Family Historical Register*, 1781.
5. Ibid.
6. Ibid.
7. Warner, Oliver, *A Portrait of Lord Nelson*, 1965, p.15.
8. Fiske, R.C, *Notices of Nelson*, p.7.
9. Oman, p.6.
10. *Gentleman's Magazine*, October 1767, Vol. 37, p.521.
11. Oman, p.5
12. Matcham, E. Eyre, *The Nelsons of Burnham Thorpe*, 1911, p.18
13. Pocock, Tom, *Horatio Nelson*, 1987, p.273. 'And all my mother came into mine eyes/And gave me up to tears.' *King Henry V*, Act 4, Scene 6.
14. Matcham, p.13.
15. Ibid., p.26.

16. Clarke, James and M'Arthur, John, *The Life and Services of Horatio Viscount Nelson*, 1809, Vol. 1, pp.13–14.
17. Ibid.
18. Ibid., p.24.
19. Nicolas, Sir Harris (ed.), *The Dispatches and Letters of Vice-Admiral Lord Viscount Nelson*, 1844–6, Vol. 1, p.67.
20. Ibid., p.34.
21. Pocock, *Horatio Nelson*, p.47.

2: Mary

1. Fiske Archive.
2. Ibid.
3. Pocock, *Horatio Nelson*, p.57.
4. Nicolas, Vol. 1, p.67.
5. Clarke and M'Arthur, Vol. 1, p.53.
6. Pocock, *Horatio Nelson*, p.57.
7. Fiske Archive.
8. Nicolas, Vol. 1, p.67.
9. Clarke and M'Arthur, Vol. 1, p.77.
10. Nicolas, Vol. 1, p.67.
11. Clarke and M'Arthur, Vol. 1, p.78.
12. Army and Navy Club Collection.
13. Clarke and M'Arthur, Vol. 1, p.53.
14. Nicolas, Vol. 1, p.70.
15. Ibid., pp.78–9.
16. Ibid., p.84.
17. Ibid., p.88.
18. Ibid., p.90.
19. Ibid., pp.89–90.
20. Ibid., pp.90–1.
21. Ibid., p.94.
22. Ibid., pp.93–4.
23. Ibid., p.96.
24. Ibid., pp.98–9.
25. Ibid., p.99.

26. Ibid.
27. Ibid., p.131.
28. Ibid., p.125.
29. Ibid., p.110.
30. Clarke and M'Arthur, p.96.
31. Ibid., p.97.
32. Hibbert, Christopher, *Nelson: A Personal History*, 1994
33. Nicolas, Vol 1, p.142.
34. Hughes, Edward (ed.) *The Private Correspondence of Admiral Lord Collingwood*, 1957, p.14.
35. Pocock, *Horatio Nelson*, p.69.
36. Nicolas, Vol. 1, pp.111–12
37. Ibid., p.110.
38. Ibid., p.122.
39. Ibid., p.128.
40. Ibid., p.119.
41. Hughes, p.258.
42. Ibid.
43. Nicolas, Vol. 1, p.124.
44. *Correspondence and Memoirs of Lord Collingwood*, p.13.
45. Nicolas, Vol. 1, p.131.
46. Ibid., p.144.
47. *Correspondence of Lord Collingwood*, p.257.
48. Naish, G.P.B. (ed.), *Nelson's Letters to his Wife*, 1958, p.24.

3: Fanny

1. Nicolas, Vol. 1, pp.124–5.
2. Clarke and M'Arthur, Vol. l, p.70.
3. Ibid., Vol. 1, p.468.
4. Nicolas, Vol. 1, p.145.
5. Ibid., p.162.
6. Ibid., p.77.
7. Ibid., p.78.
8. Ibid., p.151.
9. Naish, p.12.

10. Ibid., p.13.
11. Ibid., p.16.
12. Ibid., pp.16–18.
13. Nicolas, Vol. 1, p.145.
14. Ibid., p.144.
15. Ibid., pp.144–5.
16. Ibid.
17. Ibid., pp.160–61.
18. Ibid., p.34.
19. Ibid.
20. Naish, pp.32–3.
21. Ibid., p.37.
22. Ibid., p.38.
23. Ibid., pp.39–40.
24. Ibid., p.41.
25. Ibid., p.26.
26. Ibid.
27. Ibid., p.41.
28. Ibid., p.50.
29. Warner, Oliver, *A Portrait of Lord Nelson*, 1965, p.64.
30. Clarke and M'Arthur, Vol. 1, p.138.
31. Pocock, *Horatio Nelson*, p.81.
32. Nicolas, Vol. 1, p.258.
33. Matcham, p.45.

4: Mrs Nelson.

1. Pocock, *Horatio Nelson*, p.83.
2. Nicolas, Vol. 1, pp.275–6.
3. Matcham, pp.60–61.
4. Ibid., p.47.
5. Ibid., p.55.
6. Ibid., p.57.
7. Ibid., p.37.
8. Ibid., p.41.
9. Ibid., pp.38–9.

10. Pocock, *Horatio Nelson*, p.85.
11. Matcham, p.60.
12. Ibid., p.62.
13. Ibid.
14. Ibid., p.63.
15. Ibid., pp.26–7.
16. Ibid., p.63.
17. Ibid.
18. Ibid., p.64.
19. Ibid., p.65.
20. Ibid., p.71.
21. Ibid., p.39.
22. Ibid., p.74.
23. Ibid.
24. Nicolas, Vol. 1, p.287.
25. Clarke and M'Arthur, Vol. 1, p.161.
26. Matcham, p.76.
27. Clarke and M'Arthur, Vol. 1, p.161.
28. Matcham, p.38.
29. Naish, p.29.
30. Ibid.
31. Pocock, *Horatio Nelson*, p.85.
32. Matcham, p.76.
33. Pocock, *Horatio Nelson*, p.93.
34. Matcham, p.80.
35. NMM, *Matcham Papers*.
36. Nicolas, Vol. 1, pp.294–7.
37. Ibid., p.297.
38. Matcham, p.69.
39. Ibid.
40. Matcham, p.100.
41. Naish, p.73.
42. Ibid.
43. Naish, pp.74–5.
44. Ibid., p.75.
45. Ibid., p.76.
46. Ibid.

47. Ibid.
48. Naish, p.79.
49. Ibid., p.80.

5: Lady Nelson

1. Matcham, p.102.
2. Ibid., p.103.
3. Naish, p.84.
4. Ibid., p.86.
5. Ibid., p.91.
6. Nicolas, Vol. 1, p.328.
7. Naish, p.97.
8. Ibid., pp.87–8.
9. Monmouth Archive.
10. Naish, p.100.
11. Ibid.
12. Ibid., p.104.
13. Ibid., 13.
14. Nicolas, Vol. 1, p.480.
15. Ibid., p.484.
16. Naish, p.199.
17. Ibid.
18. Ibid., p.204.
19. Monmouth Archive.
20. Naish, p.262.
21. Ibid., p.253.
22. Monmouth Archive.
23. Ibid.
24. Matcham, p.127.
25. Ibid., p.109.
26. Ibid., p.119.
27. Naish, p.267.
28. Oman, p.134.
29. Ibid., p.135.
30. Hibbert, p.116.

31. Naish, p.304.
32. Warner, pp.92–3.
33. Hibbert, p.117.
34. Huntington Library.
35. Christie's, 21 June 1989.
36. Naish, pp.350–2.
37. Ibid., p.353.
38. Pocock, *Horatio Nelson*, p.132.
39. Naish, p.349.
40. Ibid., p.351.
41. Ibid., p.357.
42. Ibid., p.321.
43. Ibid., pp.324–5.
44. Ibid., pp.328–9.
45. Ibid., p.325.
46. Ibid., p.327.
47. Ibid., p.318.
48. Ibid., p.370.
49. Ibid., p.369.
50. Ibid., p.370.
51. Ibid., p.51.
52. Ibid., p.52.
53. Pettigrew, Thomas, *Memoirs of the Life of Vice-Admiral Lord Viscount Nelson*, Vol. 1, 1847, p.100.
54. Naish, p.331.
55. Fremantle, A., *The Wynne Diaries*, 1935–40.
56. Nicolas, Vol. 2, pp.420–1, fn.
57. Fremantle.
58. Clarke and M'Arthur, Vol. 2, p.53.
59. Naish, pp.332–3.
60. Warner, p.133.
61. Moorhouse, E. Hallam, *Nelson in England*, 1913, p.109.
62. Ibid.
63. Clarke and M'Arthur, Vol. 2, pp.67–8.
64. Pocock, *Horatio Nelson*, p.151.
65. Edgcumbe, Richard (ed.), *Diary of Frances, Lady Shelley*, Vol. 2, 1912, p.37.

66. Naish, pp.420–1.
67. Ibid., pp.388–9.
68. Ibid., p.390.
69. Ibid.
70. Ibid., p.391.
71. Ibid., p.423.
72. Ibid., p.392.
73. Ibid., p.424.
74. Ibid., p.421.
75. Ibid., p.428.
76. Corbett, Julian S., *The Private Papers of George, Second Earl Spencer*, Vol. 2, 1914, p.430.
77. Tucker, Jedediah, *Memoirs of the Rt. Hon. The Earl of St Vincent*, Vol. 1, 1862, p.438.
78. Naish, p.430.
79. Ibid., p.433.
80. Nicolas, Vol. 3, pp.11–12.
81. Harrison, Vol. 2, p.239.

6: Emma

1. Nicolas, Vol. 2, pp.17–18.
2. Morrison, Alfred (ed.), *The Hamilton and Nelson Papers*, Vol. 1, 1893–4, p.99.
3. Ibid., p.103.
4. Ibid., p.100.
5. Ibid., p.103.
6. Knight, Cornelia, *The Autobiography of Miss Cornelia Knight*, Vol. 1, 1861, edited by Roger Fulford, 1960, p.92.
7. Ibid., p.106.
8. Pocock, *Horatio Nelson*, p.156.
9. BL, Add. MS. 34,989 ff.1–3.
10. Sichel, Waller, *Emma Lady Hamilton*, 1963, p.211.
11. Naish, p.431.
12. Ibid., p.433.
13. Ibid., p.434.

14. Ibid., 428.
15. Ibid., p.439.
16. Ibid., p.440.
17. Nicolas, Vol. 3, p.125, fn.
18. Naish, p.448.
19. Knight, Vol. 1, pp.109–110.
20. Nicolas, Vol. 3, p.93.
21. Fraser, Flora, *Beloved Emma*, 1986, p.220.
22. Nicolas, Vol. 3, p.125.
23. Pocock, *Horatio Nelson*, p.171.
24. Goethe, J.W., *Travels in Italy*, translated by A.J.W. Morrison and C. Nisbet, 1892, p.315.
25. Pocock, *Horatio Nelson*, p.171.
26. Minto, Countess of (ed.), *The Life and Letters of Sir Gilbert Elliot, First Earl of Minto*, Vol. 2, 1874, pp.364–5.
27. Knight, Vol. 1, p.113.
28. Fraser, p.221.
29. Nicolas, Vol, 3, p.130.
30. Knight, ed. Fulford, p.64.
31. Naish, p.404.
32. Ibid., p.403.
33. Ibid., p.401.
34. Ibid., p.402.
35. Nicolas, Vol. 3, pp.143–4.
36. Pocock, *Horatio Nelson*, p.185.
37. Nicolas, Vol. 3, pp.144–5.
38. Ibid., p.74.
39. NMM, Hoste Papers.
40. BL, Add. MS 34,989, f. 16.
41. Ibid., f. 18.
42. Naish, p.462.
43. Ibid., p.479.
44. Nicolas, Vol. 3, p.138 fn.
45. Knight, Vol. 1, p.124.
46. Naish, p.479.
47. Pocock, *Horatio Nelson*, p.188.
48. Knight, Vol. 1, p.126.

49. Morrison, Vol. 2, p.35.
50. Sichel, p.252.
51. Morrison, Vol. 2, p.35.
52. Ibid.

7: Dearest Emma

1. Nicolas, Vol. 3, p.212.
2. Ibid., pp.212–3.
3. Morrison, Vol. 2, pp.35–6.
4. Naish, p.480.
5. Ibid.
6. Ibid., p.481.
7. Nicolas, Vol. 3, p.248.
8. Gordon, Pryse Lockhart, *Personal Memoirs*, Vol. 1, 1830, pp.205–8.
9. Naish, p.482.
10. Ibid., p.517.
11. Ibid., pp.482–3.
12. Ibid., p.519.
13. Harrison, Vol. 2, 136.
14. Nicolas, Vol. 3, p.354.
15. Gutteridge, H.C. (ed.), *Nelson and the Neapolitan Jacobins*, 1903, p.74.
16. Ibid., p.75.
17. Ibid., p.136.
18. Ibid., p.206.
19. Pettigrew, Vol. 1, p.235.
20. Giglioli, *Constance, Naples in 1799*, 1903, p.293.
21. Llangattock Papers, E71.
22. Pettigrew, Vol. 1, pp.234–5.
23. Parsons, G.S., *Nelsonian Reminiscences*, 1843, p.67.
24. Morrison, Vol. 2, p.68.
25. Fraser, p.244.
26. Pocock, *Horatio Nelson*, p.204.
27. Naish, p.487.

28. Sotheby's, 20 July 1989.
29. Pocock, *Horatio Nelson*, p.207.
30. Parsons, pp.16–17.
31. Gordon, Vol. 1, p.222.
32. Ibid.
33. Nicolas, Vol. 4, p.149.
34. *Apollo*, October 1972, p.303.
35. Naish, p.529.
36. Pocock, *Horatio Nelson*, p.209.
37. Morrison, Vol. 2, p.82.
38. Ibid.
39. Grant, N.H., *The Letters of the Countess of Elgin*, 1926, pp.22–4.
40. Ibid., p.21.
41. Phillips, 26 June 1980.
42. Warner, p.168.
43. Oman, p.333.
44. Christie's, New York, 19 December 1986.
45. Warner, p.107.
46. *Letters: Lord Nelson to Lady Hamilton*, Vol.1, pp.270–1.
47. Morrison, Vol. 2, p.86.
48. Parsons, p.11.
49. Knight, Vol. 1, p.142.
50. Ibid.
51. Ibid., p.147.
52. Parsons, p.47.
53. Ibid., p.51.
54. Ibid., p.53.
55. Ibid.
56. Mahan, Capt A.T., *The Life of Nelson*, Vol. 2, 1897, p.33.
57. Naish, p.547.
58. Pocock, *Horatio Nelson*, p.212.
59. Ibid.
60. Naish, p.551.
61. Ibid., p.533.
62. Ibid., p.555.
63. Fraser, p.261.

64. Minto, Vol. 3, pp.139–40.
65. Warner, p.168.
66. Knight, ed. Fulford, pp.120–1.
67. Naish, p.555.
68. Sichel, p.332.
69. Fraser, p267.
70. Trench, Richard Chenevix (ed.), *The Remains of the Late Mrs. Richard Trench*, 1862, pp.105–12.
71. Minto, Vol. 3, p.147.
72. Trench, pp.105–12.
73. Sichel, p.333.
74. Malmesbury, Third Earl of (ed.), *The Diaries and Correspondence of the First Earl of Malmesbury*, Vol. 2, 1844, p.222.
75. Knight, Vol. 1, p.153.
76. Warner p.209.
77. Ibid., p.210.
78. Fraser, p.273.
79. *Mariner's Mirror*, April 1935, Vol. 21, p.153.
80. Knight, Vol. 1, p.163.

8: Fanny Meets Emma

1. Naish, p.538.
2. Ibid., p.539.
3. Ibid.
4. Warner, p.182.
5. Broadley, A.M., *Three Dorset Captains of Trafalgar*, 1906, p.53.
6. *Morning Herald*, 11 November, 1800.
7. Fraser, p.276.
8. Hibbert, p.8.
9. Christie's, 8 May 1985.
10. Knight, Vol. 1 p.162.
11. Luttrell, Barbara, *The Prime Romantic: A Biography of Ellis Cornelia Knight*, 1965.
12. NMM/CRK/19/249.

13. Edgcumbe, Vol. 1, pp.78–9.
14. *Morning Herald*, 19 November 1800.
15. Oliver, J.W., *The Life of William Beckford*, 1932, p.240.
16. Fothergill, Brian, *Sir William Hamilton*, 1969, p.396.
17. *Morning Herald*, 13 November, 1800.
18. Keate, E., *Nelson's Wife*, pp.208–9.
19. Naish, p.573.
20. Ibid., p.619.
21. Pocock, *Horatio Nelson*, p.227.
22. Morrison, Vol.2, p.109.
23. Ibid.
24. Ibid.
25. Fraser, p.283.
26. Morrison, Vol. 2, p.110.
27. Ibid., pp.110–11.
28. Morrison, Vol. 2, p.211.
29. Sotheby's, 18 July 1991.
30. Morrison, Vol. 2, pp.111–12.
31. Gérin, Winifred, *Horatio Nelson*, 1970, p.10.
32. Morrison, Vol. 2, p.121.
33. Hibbert, p.247.
34. Pocock, *Horatio Nelson*, 1970, p.226.
35. Ibid.
36. Morrison, Vol. 2, p.123.
37. Pocock, *Horatio Nelson*, p.228.
38. Nicolas, Vol. 7, p.374.
39. Keate, p.212.
40. Sichel, p.366.
41. Naish, p.579.
42. Ibid., p.580.
43. BL. Add. MSS 28,333, ff. 3–4.
44. Morrison, Vol. 2, p.121.
45. Ibid.
46. Warner, p.232.
47. Morrison, Vol. 2, pp.127–8.
48. Ibid., p.126.
49. Ibid., p.127.

50. Ibid., p.128.
51. Ibid., p.132.
52. Phillips, 2 October 1980.
53. Morrison, Vol. 2, p.135.
54. Wraxall, Sir Nathaniel, *Historical Memoirs of My Own Time*, Vol. 1, pp.164–6.
55. Christie's, June 1983.
56. Bridport Papers.
57. Phillips, 16 June 1983.
58. Naish, pp.582–3.
59. Ibid., p.586.
60. Ibid., pp.586–7.
61. Naish, p.586.
62. Dyfed County Record Office, MUS 473.
63. Morrison, Vol. 1, p.156.
64. Naish, p.591.
65. Sotheby's, 24 July 1995.
66. Naish, p.588.
67. Ibid., pp.588–9.
68. Pocock, *Horatio Nelson*, p.245.
69. Ibid., p.249.
70. Ibid.
71. Ibid., p.252.
72. Ibid.
73. Ibid., p.254.
74. Ibid., p.254.
75. Ibid., p.257.
76. Naish, pp.590–91.
77. Morrison, Vol. 2, pp.175–6.
78. Ibid., p.170.
79. Ibid., p.172.
80. Hibbert, p.289.
81. Ibid.
82. Morrison, Vol. 2, pp.171–2.
83. Christie's, New York, 9 December 1998.
84. Ibid.
85. Morrison, Vol. 2, p.173.

86. Naish, p.594.
87. Ibid., p.595.
88. Ibid., p.594.
89. Ibid.
90. Ibid., p.587.
91. Sotheby's, 11 December 1997.
92. Naish, pp.592–3.
93. NMM/BRP/4.
94. Ibid.
95. Pocock, *Horatio Nelson*, p.259.
96. Ibid., p.258.
97. Ibid.

9: Charlotte

1. Pettigrew, Vol. 2, p.121.
2. Chelsea Society Report, 1985, p.45.
3. BRP/NMM/4.
4. Bonsor Papers.
5. Farington, James, *The Farington Diary*, Vol. 1, edited by James Grieg, 1922, p.307.
6. Ibid.
7. Ibid.
8. Matcham, p.191.
9. Christie's, 8 May 1985.
10. Ibid.
11. Bonsor Papers.
12. Pocock, *Horatio Nelson*, p.261.
13. Bonsor Papers.
14. Ibid.
15. Pocock, *Horatio Nelson*, p.267.
16. Ibid.
17. Sotheby's, 20 July 1988.
18. Bonsor Papers.
19. Ibid.
20. Christie's, 8 May 1985.
21. Pettigrew, Vol. 2, p.236.

22. Christie's, 8 May 1985.
23. Keate, pp.221–2.
24. Bonsor Papers.
25. Tribe Collection.
26. Ibid.
27. Ibid.
28. Ibid.
29. Bonsor Papers.
30. Author's collection.
31. Tribe Collection.
32. Sotheby's, 11 December 1997.
33. Pocock, *Horatio Nelson*, p.265.
34. Bonsor Papers.
35. Ibid.
36. Ibid.
37. Minto, Vol. 2, p.242.
38. Tribe Collection.
39. Ibid.
40. Ibid.
41. Christie's, 8 May 1998.
42. Ibid.
43. Tribe Collection.
44. Pocock, *Horatio Nelson*, p.271–2.
45. Ibid.
46. Ibid.
47. Ibid.
48. Morrison, Vol. 2, p.182.
49. Bonsor Papers.
50. John Wilson catalogue, 1990.
51. Harrison, Vol. 2, p.382.
52. BM, Add. MSS, 34,989.
53. Harrison, Vol. 2, p.382.
54. Pocock, *Horatio Nelson*, p.280.
55. Ibid., p.281.
56. Ibid.
57. Pollock, Sir Frederick (ed.), *Macready's Reminiscences*, 1875, pp.33–4.

58. Morrison, Vol. 2, p.195.
59. Ibid., p.196.
60. Pocock, *Horatio Nelson*, p.283.
61. Ibid., pp.283–4.
62. Morrison, Vol. 2, p.197.
63. Parsons, p.9.
64. Pocock, *Horatio Nelson*, p.288.
65. Matcham, p.204.
66. Ibid., p.206.
67. NMM/BRP/1.
68. Gurney, Joseph and William, *The Trial of Edward Despard*, 1803.
69. Pocock, *The Young Nelson in the Americas*, 1980, p.230.
70. Pocock, *Horatio Nelson*, p.290.
71. Ibid.
72. Ibid., p.291.

10: Horatia

1. Vigée Lebrun, M.L.E., *Souvenirs*, 1867.
2. Gérin, p.63.
3. Morrison, Vol. 2, p.211.
4. NMM/CRK/19/258.
5. Pettigrew, Vol. 2, p.310.
6. Pocock, *Horatio Nelson*, p.299.
7. Fraser, p.309.
8. Gérin, p.68.
9. Ibid.
10. Morrison, Vol. 2, p.220.
11. NMM/NWD/9594/16.
12. Ibid.
13. Gérin, p.69.
14. Hibbert, p.333.
15. Ibid.
16. Naish, p.604.
17. BRP/NMM/9292/4.

18. Ibid.
19. Pettigrew, Vol. 2, p.384.
20. Morrison, Vol. 2, p.239.
21. NMM/NWD/9594/16.
22. Gérin, p.70.
23. BRP/NMM/9292.
24. BRP/NMM/9292/4.
25. Warner, p.200.
26. BRP/NMM/9292/4.
27. Fraser, p.309.
28. Tribe Collection.
29. Gérin, p.81.
30. BRP/NMM/9292/4.
31. Pettigrew, Vol. 2, p.422.
32. Fraser, p.310.
33. Farington, Vol. 2, p.275.
34. Fraser, p.314.
35. Ibid., p.313.
36. Naish, p.604.
37. Monmouth Archive.
38. Oman, p.493.
39. Newhouse Archive.
40. Monmouth Archive.
41. Ibid.
42. Pettigrew, Vol. 2, p.486.
43. NMM/NWD/9594/7.
44. Matcham, p.226.
45. Silliman, Benjamin, *A Journal of Travels in England*, 1810, p.189.
46. Pocock, *Horatio Nelson*, p.307.
47. Matcham, p.227.
48. Ibid., pp.230–1.
49. Minto, Vol. 3, p.363.
50. Moorhouse, p.201.
51. Bowyer, Robert, *Memorials*, London, 1806, p.27.
52. Croker, J.W., *Correspondence of J.W. Croker*, edited by L.J. Jennings, 1885, pp.233–4.

53. Llangattock Papers.
54. Matcham, p.233.
55. Pocock, *Horatio Nelson*, p.312.
56. Matcham, p.234.
57. Pocock, *Horatio Nelson*, p.314.
58. Ibid.
59. Ibid.
60. Minto, Vol. 3, p.370.
61. Stuart, D.M., *Dearest Bess: The Life and Times of Lady Elizabeth Foster*, 1955, p.129.
62. Edgcumbe, Vol. 1, p.79.
63. Harrison, Vol. 2, p.456.
64. Pocock, *Horatio Nelson*, p.315.
65. Nicolas, Vol. 7, pp.33–5.
66. Pettigrew, Vol. 2, p.497.
67. Matcham, p.233.
68. Pettigrew, Vol. 2, p.498.
69. Monmouth Archive.
70. Rose, George, *The Diaries and Correspondence of the Rt. Hon. George Rose*, edited by L.V. Harcourt, 1860, Vol. 1, pp.264–5.
71. Morrison, Vol. 2, p.266.
72. Ibid., p.268.
73. NMM/NWD/9594.
74. Morrison, Vol. 2, p.268.
75. Naish, p.605.
76. Morrison, Vol. 2, p.266.
77. Ibid., p.267.
78. Nicolas, Vol. 7, p.60.
79. Ibid., p.132.
80, Ibid., pp.132–3.
81. Tribe Collection.
82. Naish, p.605–6.

11: Mrs Nelson Ward

1. Hill, B.E., *Recollections of an Artillery Officer*, 1836, p.173.

2. Ibid.
3. Ibid.
4. *Gentleman's Magazine*, Vol. 76, p.218.
5. Fraser, p.326.
6. NMM/GIR/1.
7. Stuart, pp.127–8.
8. Gérin, p.106.
9. Matcham, p.242.
10. Keate, p.277.
11. Rose, Vol. 1, p.245.
12. Morrison, Vol. 2, p.283.
13. Gérin, p.109.
14. *Transactions of the Jewish Historical Society*, Vol.14, pp.225–45.
15. Matcham, pp.242–3.
16. Ibid., p.250.
17. Ibid., pp.245–6.
18. Monmouth Archive.
19. Stuart, p.120.
20. Matcham, p.273.
21. Morrison, Vol. 2, p.342.
22. NMM/BRP/4.
23. Nicolas, Vol. 7, p.388.
24. NMM/BRP/9292.
25. NMM/NWD/9594/A.
26. Sichel, p.511.
27. NMM/NWD/9594/7/A.
28. NMM/NWD/9594/13–14.
29. Morrison, Vol. 2, p.336.
30. Gordon, Vol. 2, pp.388–90.
31. NMM/NWD/9594/13–14.
32. Ibid.
33. Tours, Hugh, *The Life and Letters of Emma Hamilton*, 1963, p.253.
34. Ibid., p.252.
35. Fraser, p.365.
36. NMM/NWD/9594/13–14.
37. NMM/NWD/9594/2.

38. Ibid.
39. NMM/NWD/9594/13–14.
40. Ibid.
41. Ibid.
42. Matcham, p.277.
43. Ibid., p.280.
44. Keate, p.276.
45. Ibid., p.286.
46. Hibbert, p.409.
47. Keate, p.284.
48. NMM/NWD/9594/34.
49. NMM/NWD/9594/1–5.
50. Tribe Collection.
51. Ibid.

Bibliography

Broadley, A.M., *Three Dorset Captains at Trafalgar*, 1906.

Clarke, James and M'Arthur, John, *The Life and Services of Horatio Viscount Nelson* (1809)

Clowes, W.L., *The Royal Navy: A History* (7 Vols.), 1900.

Collingwood, Cuthbert, Adm. Lord, *The Private Correspondence of Admiral Lord Collingwood*, edited by Edward Hughes, 1957.

——, *A Selection from the Public and Private Correspondence of Admiral Lord Collingwood*, edited by G.L. Newnham, 1828.

Croker, J.W., *Correspondence of J.W. Croker*, edited by L.J. Jennings, 1885.

Edgcumbe, Richard (ed.), *Diary of Frances, Lady Shelley*, 1912.

Farington, James, *The Farington Diary*, edited by James Grieg, 1922.

Fothergill, Brian, *Sir William Hamilton*, 1969.

Fraser, Flora, *Beloved Emma*, 1986.

Fremantle, A. (ed.), *The Wynne Diaries, 1935–40.*

Goethe, J.W., Travels in Italy, trans. by A.J.W. Morrison and C. Nisbet, 1892.

Gamlin, Hilda, *Nelson's Friendships*, 1899.

Gérin, Winfred, *Horatia Nelson*, 1970.

Giglioli, Constance, *Naples in 1799*, 1903.

Gordon, Pryse Lockhart, *Personal Memoirs*, 1830.

Gutteridge, H.C. (ed.), *Nelson and the Neapolitan Jacobins*, 1903.

Grant, N.H., *The Letters of the Countess of Elgin*, 1926.

Harrison, James, *The Life of the Rt. Hon. Horatio Viscount Nelson*, 1806.

Hibbert, Christopher, *Nelson: A Personal History*, 1994.

Hill, B.E., *Recollections of an Artillery Officer*, 1836.
Keate, E., *Nelson's Wife*, 1939.
Knight, Cornelia, *The Autobiography of Miss Cornelia Knight*, 1861, edited by Roger Fulford (1960)
Luttrell, Barbara, *The Prime Romantic: A Biography of Ellis Cornelia Knight*, 1965.
Mahan, Capt. A.T., *The Life of Nelson*, 1897.
Malmesbury, 3rd. Earl of (ed.), *The Diaries and Correspondence of the First Earl of Malmesbury*, 1844.
Matcham, E. Eyre, *The Nelsons of Burnham Thorpe*, 1911.
Minto, Countess of, (ed.), *The Life and Letters of Sir Gilbert Elliot, First Earl of Minto*, 1874.
Moorhouse, E. Hallam, *Nelson in England*, 1913.
Morrison, Alfred, (ed.), *The Hamilton and Nelson Papers*, 1893–4.
Naish, G.P.B. (ed.), *Nelson's Letters to His Wife*, 1958.
Nicolas, Sir Harris (ed.), *The Dispatches and Letters of Vice-Admiral Lord Viscount Nelson*, 1844–6.
Oliver, J.W., *The Life of William Beckford*, 1932.
Oman, Carola, *Nelson*, 1947.
Parsons, G.S., *Nelsonian Reminiscences*, 1843.
Pettigrew, Thomas, *Memoirs of the Life of Vice-Admiral Lord Viscount Nelson*, 1849.
Pocock, Tom, *Horatio Nelson*, 1987.
——, *The Young Nelson in the Americas*, 1980.
——, *Sailor King*, 1991.
Pollock, Sir Frederick, (ed.), *Macready's Reminiscences*, 1875.
Rathbone, Philip, *Paradise Merton*, 1973.
Rose, George, *The Diaries and Correspondence of the Rt. Hon. George Rose*, edited by L.V. Harcourt. 1860.
Sichel, Waller, *Emma, Lady Hamilton*, 1905.
Silliman, Benjamin, *A Journal of Travels in England*, 1810.
Stuart, D.M., *Dearest Bess: The Life and Times of Lady Elizabeth Foster*, 1955.
Tours, Hugh, *The Life and Letters of Emma Hamilton*, 1963.
Trench, Richard Chenevix (ed.), *The Remains of the Late Mrs. Richard Trench*, 1862.
Vigée-Lebrun, M.L.E., *Souvenirs*, 1867.

Walker, Richard, *The Nelson Portraits*, 1998.
Warner, Oliver, *A Portrait of Lord Nelson*, 1965.
Wraxall, Sir Nathaniel, *Historical Memoirs of My Own Time*, 1815.

Index

Abbott, Lemuel, 92, 107, 145
Aboukir Bay, 109–10, 113, 131, 136–7, 189, 210
Acton, Sir John, 79, 105
Addington, Henry, 170, 178, 194, 196
Allen, Tom, 73, 194
Andras, Catherine, 215, 225
Andrews, Elizabeth, 30–32, 34–5, 48, 53, 65, 88
Andrews, George, Capt., 30, 32, 35, 48, 83, 88
Andrews, The Rev. Robert, 30
Andrews, Sarah, 32
Antigua, 37, 46
Ashfold Lodge, 234, 238, 242–3
Aylsham, 69

Barbados, 36, 54
Barham, Lord, 224
Barsham, 8, 10, 12
Barton Hall, 63–6
Bastia, 80–82
Bath, 16, 21, 31, 34, 43–4, 60–62, 77, 80, 82–6, 93–4, 96, 106, 116, 125, 162, 170–71, 174, 177, 179, 186, 203, 209, 213, 217, 221, 224, 233, 243–4
Beccles, 10, 12
Beckford, William, 147, 150, 214
Berry, Capt. (Sir) Edward, 91, 137
Bircham Newton, 245
Blackwood, Capt. (Sir) Henry, 216–7, 229
The Rev. Robert Blake, 245
Bland, John, 11
Bolton, Anne, 189, 200, 214, 221, 238, 243
Bolton, Eliza, 189, 200, 221–2, 238
Bolton, Emma, 222
Bolton, Kate, 89, 106, 114, 199
Bolton, Lady, 222, 243
Bolton, Samuel, 20
Bolton, Susannah (neé Nelson), 12–13, 15–17, 19–21, 29, 31, 34, 63, 65, 73, 89, 106, 114, 125, 133, 163, 171, 173, 186, 189, 199–200, 203, 209, 211, 213, 217, 221, 226, 228, 230, 233–5, 237–9, 243–4
Bolton, Susannah, the younger, 243
Bolton, Thomas, the elder, 20, 29, 63, 65, 125, 133, 180, 183, 231, 243–4
Bolton, Thomas, 199, 213, 221, 231, 235, 238, 244
Bolton, Capt. Sir William, 73, 199
Bolton, the Rev. William, 199
Bonaparte. (Emperor) Napoleon, 80, 96, 106, 109, 125, 140, 201, 214, 240, 242
Boulogne, 166–7, 201

Bowyer, Robert, 215
Bradenham, 11, 238, 243
Brancaster, 199
Brighton, 152, 158
Bristol, 61
Bronte, 131–2, 165, 168–9, 181, 228, 240, 243–5
Burnham Market, 7, 12, 20, 70, 243, 244
Burnham Overy Staithe, 70
Burnham Thorpe, 7, 9, 12, 15, 21, 34, 61–6, 70, 74, 77, 87, 112, 124, 145, 170, 177, 186–7, 199, 243, 245
Burnham Ulph, 69, 74
Byron, Lord, 243

Calais, 29–30, 240–3
Calvi, 80–2
Canterbury, 200, 207, 213, 217, 221, 227
Capel, Capt. the Hon. Thomas, 108–9, 114
Carew, Emma, 233
Carraciolo, Commodore Francesco, Prince, 128
Castlereagh, Lord, 216
Charlotte, Princess, 234
Chatham, 16–17, 73–5
Chelsea, 90, 174–5, 189
Cirillo, Dr. Domenico, 130
Coke, Thomas, 66, 69
Collingwood, Cuthbert, Vice-Adm., Lord, 37–44, 51, 53, 153, 159, 217, 223
Copenhagen, 160–2, 165, 175
Connor, Mary, 202–5, 207, 222–3, 234
Connor, Mrs. Sarah, 202
Cornwallis, Couba, 21
Correglia, Adelaide, 84–5
Corsica, 80–1, 88
Cranwich, 125, 171, 200, 203, 211, 213, 221, 234, 238

Davison, Alexander, 27, 29, 34, 116, 147, 149, 153, 164, 166, 168, 197, 204–5, 208, 212
Deal, 166–8, 173, 175, 241
Denhall, 101
Dent, Lt. Digby, 58
Despard, Col. Edward, 195–6
Digby, Adm. the Hon. Robert, 28
Dillon, Adm. Sir William, 239
Duncan, Adm. Lord, 91
Dundas, Lord, 179

East India Company, 33
Elgin, Lord, 134
Elliot, Sir Gilbert (Lord Minto), 111, 183, 196, 214, 218
English Harbour, 37–9, 43–4, 51, 54, 56
Eton College, 10–11, 174, 181, 189, 230, 232
Exmouth, 61, 233, 244

Fagan, Robert, 133
Fakenham, 13, 20
Featherstonhaugh, Sir Harry, l02, 232
Ferdinand IV, King, 79, 104, 110, 116–18, 128, 130–1, 209
Fonthill Abbey, 150
Foote, Capt. Edward, 126, 128
Ford, Mrs, Sarah (Mrs Maurice Nelson) 165, 185, 217
Foundling Hospital, 156, 161–2, 204, 234
Fremantle, Betsey (née Wynne), 88–9
Fremantle, Vice-Adm. Sir Thomas, 84, 88

Füger, Friedrich, 142

Gahagan, Lawrence, 92
George III, King, 91, 139, 195, 208, 213, 234
Gibson, Mrs Mary, 156, 187, 191, 198, 221
Girdlestone, Henry, 238
Goldsmid, Abraham, 187, 205, 214, 232, 235–7
Goldsmid, Ascher, 236
Goldsmid, Benjamin, 187, 229, 235–7
Goldsmid, Lionel, 229
Gordon, Duke of, 160
Gordon, Pryse Lockhart, 122–3, 237
Great Yarmouth, 145–6, 158–9, 165
Grenville, Lord, 117, 232
Greville, the Hon. Charles, 127, 130, 134, 160, 188–9, 237

Hamilton, Catherine, 189–90
Hamilton, Emma, Lady, meets Nelson, 79; birth and early life, 101–3; greets and entertains Nelson, 111–13; bravery in storm, 119; vengefulness at Naples, 127–9; meets Fanny Nelson, 147; gives birth to twins, 154; buys Merton Place, 168; gives birth to short-lived daughter, 204; told of Nelson's death, 226; moves to Richmond, 236; committed to debtors' prison, 238; escapes to Calais, 240; death, 241
Hamilton, Emma, the second: born, 154; taken to Foundling Hospital, 156; baptised, 162
Hamilton, Emma, the third: birth and death, 204
Hamilton, Sir William: meets Nelson, 79; marriage to Emma, 103; greets victorious Nelson, 111; leaves Naples, 118; describes Merton Place, 168–9; visits Welsh estate, 189; rebukes Emma, 192–4; death, 197
Hardy, Capt.(Adm. Sir) Thomas, 131, 146, 179, 231
Harrison James, 240
Haslewood, William, 151, 212, 227, 242
Haydn, Joseph 142
Henley, Sarah, 13, 15
Hebert, John, 47, 49–53, 55, 57, 60–61, 73–4
Hilborough, 11–13, 63, 68, 74, 77, 175
Hood, Adm. Lord, 34, 50, 65, 73, 78, 177–8, 183, 237
Hood, the Hon. Samuel (Viscount Bridport), 183, 237
Hoste, Capt. Sir William, 73, 80, 108, 110, 114
Houghton Hall, 9, 208, 232, 234
Howe, Adm. Lord, 32, 61
Hughes, Adm. Sir Richard, 35, 37, 41–2, 52
Hughes, Lady, 35–7, 52
Hughes, Rosy, 35, 37

Ipswich, 93, 107

Jervis, Adm. Sir John (Lord St. Vincent), 78, 85, 87, 92, 97–8, 113–4, 119–20,126, 166, 178, 194–5, 240

Johnson, Dr. Samuel, 103, 136

Kauffman, Angelica, 104
Keats, Capt. Richard, 216
Keith, Adm. Lord, 120, 126, 133–40
Lady Keith, 136
King's Lynn, 17, 69
Knight, Cornelia, 103–4, 108, 111–12, 116–17, 120, 136–7, 140–2, 144, 147–8, 182, 233

Laleham, 165
Lancaster, the Rev. Thomas, 188, 218–19
Langford, Capt. Frederick, 167–8
Lansdowne, Marquis of, 93
Leghorn, 80, 84–5, 135, 140
Littleham, 244
Locker, Capt. William, 31, 41
Lockhart, James, 81
Lyon, Henry, 101
Lyon, Mary (Mrs Cadogan), 101–2, 122, 140, 147, 150, 176, 203, 212, 214, 217, 221, 236–7

Mack von Leiberich, Karl, Baron, Gen., 113, 116, 118
Margate, 167, 191
Maria Carolina, Queen, 103–5, 109–10, 118–20, 126–7, 129, 134, 140, 150, 209, 233, 238
Maria Theresa, Empress, 141
Matcham, George, 63–4, 66, 74, 76, 94, 125, 139, 180, 183, 186, 196, 213, 231, 235, 240, 242–4
Matcham, George, the younger, 66, 189, 213, 215–16, 227, 229–30, 242–3
Matcham, Kate (née Nelson), 14–15, 17, 21–2, 29, 31, 34, 43–4, 59, 61–3, 65–7, 69, 71, 73–4, 76–7, 90, 94, 125, 139, 163, 171, 177, 189, 195, 199, 203, 209, 212–13, 216, 220, 227, 233–4, 238, 242–4
Matthews, Major Robert, 25, 27, 28, 195
Melville, Lord, 208
Merton, from 167
Monmouth, 190
Moseley, Dr Benjamin, 90, 175, 181, 195, 197, 204–5
Moutray, Capt. John, 37–44
Moutray, Lt. James, 37, 82
Moutray, Kate, 37
Moutray, Mary, 37–45, 48, 51–2, 82, 153, 244

Nelson, Anne, 13–15, 17, 19, 21–2, 29–31
Nelson, Catherine (née Suckling), 7–10, 12–14, 239
Nelson, (Lady) Charlotte, (Baroness Bridport), 63, 174–8, 181–5, 187–8, 196, 199–200, 203, 214, 221, 224, 230, 232, 235, 237, 244
Nelson, the Rev. Edmund, 7–8, 10–12, 15, 17, 19, 59, 61–7, 70, 83–4, 86, 90, 115, 125, 146, 172, 177, 179–80, 183, 186
Nelson, Edmund, the younger, 14, 16, 64, 66
Nelson, Frances, Viscountess (née Woolward, later Nisbet): early life, 46–7; meets Nelson, 50; marries, 58; meets her father-in-law, 65; moves to Swaffham, 77; nurses Nelson, 90; buys

Roundwood, 93; meets the Hamiltons, 147; separates from Nelson, 152; final letter to Nelson, 180; told of Nelson's death, 224; financial settlement, 228; again meets Nelson's family, 243; death, 244
Nelson, Horace, 174, 181, 183, 189, 192, 199, 213–14, 229–32, 235
Nelson, Horatia (Mrs Nelson Ward), born, 154; first seen by Nelson, 157; baptised, 198; Nelson's farewell, 219; taken to Calais, 240; returns to England, 242; marriage, 245; death, 246
Nelson, Vice-Adm. (Viscount) Horatio: birth, 7; education, 15; joins the Royal Navy, 17; meets Mary Simpson, 26; meets Elizabeth Andrews, 30; meets Mary Moutray, 40; meets Fanny Nisbet, 50; marries, 58; returns to Norfolk, 65; recalled to sea, 72; meets Emma Hamilton, 79; meets Adelaide Correglia, 84; wins Battle of the Nile, 109; returns to Naples, 111; rescues Hamiltons from Naples, 118; created Duke of Bronte, 131; meets Fanny again, 147; leaves Fanny, 152; wins Battle of Copenhagen, 160; arrives at Merton, 176; death in Battle of Trafalgar, 224; funeral, 231
Nelson, Maurice, 8, 12–13, 15, 17, 21, 63, 65, 76, 125, 158, 165, 185, 192
Nelson, Sarah (née Yonge), 63, 157–9, 163, 167–8, 172–5, 179, 181–5, 188, 197, 200, 205–7, 214, 224, 230, 232, 234–5
Nelson, (the Rev.) Suckling, 16–17, 64, 77, 124, 130
Nelson, the Rev. William (Earl Nelson), 8, 12–13, 16–17, 29, 31, 35, 39–40, 43, 48, 51, 63, 65, 68, 77, 79, 125, 172, 174, 183, 186, 189, 199–201, 207, 213–14, 227–35, 239–40, 243–4
Nevis, 46–58, 67, 69, 74, 77fn., 99
Newhouse, 243
New York, 27–8, 40
Nicaragua, 20, 26, 32, 40, 195
Nisbet, Fanny, the younger, 243
Nisbet, Dr Josiah, 47
Nisbet, Capt. Josiah, 47, 50, 65, 73–6, 78–9, 81, 85, 88–9, 115, 121, 124, 157–8, 167, 233, 243–4
North Walsham, 15–16
Norwich, 15, 86

Parker, Capt. Edward, 162, 167–8
Parsons, Midshipman George, 129, 132, 136, 138, 194
Perry, James, 187, 192, 202, 218, 228, 238
Pinner, 245–6
Pitt, William, 49, 148, 170, 208, 212–13, 216–17, 231–2
Plymouth, 60, 77, 158, 220
Portsmouth, 21, 29, 75–7, 83, 87, 93–5, 152, 157, 159, 199, 212, 216, 219–20

Quebec, 23, 25–7, 195
Queensberry, Duke of, 160, 206, 236–7

Ramsgate, 191, 207, 240
Richmond, 236
Ringwood, 71, 76
Rose, George, 231
Roundwood, 93, 98, 106, 113, 139, 145–6, 152
Ruffo, Cardinal Fabrizio, 125–6, 128–9

St. Kitts, 49
Saint-Omer, 29–31, 34, 85
Schmidt, Johann, 199
Sedgeford, 73
Selbeck, 189, 197
Ships: *Agamemnon*, 73, 75–7, 80, 82, 104; *Albemarle*, 21, 26, 28–9; *Alexander*, 111; *Boreas* 35, 37, 40–1, 47–9, 51, 59–60; *Ça Ira*, 83; *Captain*, 85; *Colossus*, 122; *Culloden*, 111; *Dreadnought*, 9; *Foudroyant*, 126, 128, 136–7, 139fn.; *Généreux, Le*, 137; *Guillaume Tell*, 137; *Hinchinbroke*, 20; *Latona*, 41; *Little Tom*, 240; *Lowestoft*, 18; *Mediator*, 37; *Minerva*, 127; *Mutine*, 104, 108, 110; *l'Orient*, 184, 218; *Pegasus*, 55; *Raissonable*, 16; *Roehampton*, 59; *St. George*, 156, 161; *San Josef*, 153; *Seahorse*, 18, 126; *Thalia*, 121; *King George*, 144; *Theseus*, 89; *Unicorn*, 48; *Vanguard*, 95, 97, 100, 110–11, 117–19; *Victory*, 82, 139fn., 199–200, 202, 207, 217, 219–20, 222, 229–31
Simpson, Mary, 24, 26–8, 32, 195
Simpson, Col. Saunders, 24
Smith, Adm. Sir Sidney Smith, 214
Smith, Alderman Joshua, 238–9, 241
Spencer, Lady, 91–4, 148
Spencer, Lord, 91, 138, 148, 162, 191
Sporle, 11–12
Stanhoe, 245
Suckling, Capt. Maurice, 9, 14, 16–19, 32, 35, 91
Suckling, William, 9, 15, 17, 19, 21, 29, 33–4, 53–4, 73–5
Sussex, Duke of, 234, 239
Swaffham, 11, 13, 67, 74, 77, 79, 238

Tenerife, 88–9, 92, 166
Tenderden, 245
Tittleshall, 73
Toulon, 78, 80, 97–8, 100–1, 126, 202
Trafalgar, Cape, 227
Troubridge, Rear-Adm. Sir Thomas, 105, 125, 127, 135, 147, 159

Uppark, 102

Vienna, 140–41, 145
Vigee-Lebrun, M.L.E., 198
Villeneuve, Adm. Pierre, 209–11

Wales, George, Prince of, 148, 155, 160, 169, 173, 208, 217, 231, 234
Walpole of Wolteron, Lord, 9, 12, 16, 69, 80, 171
Walpole, Sir Robert, 9
Ward, Hugh Nelson, 245
Ward, the Rev. Philip, 245
Weatherhead, Lt. John, 73
Wellesley, Major–Gen. Sir Arthur (Duke of Wellington), 216

Wells-next-the-Sea, 12, 20–21, 34, 72, 244
West, Benjamin, 151
Whitelands School, 174–5, 181–2, 187
William Henry, Prince (Duke of Clarence; King Willian IV), 26, 28–9, 55–8, 60–61, 70–71, 81, 213, 231, 234
Woodton, 8–9, 12, 15
Woolward, William, 46
Woolwich, 21